Technical Management for the Performing Arts

Technical Management for the Performing Arts: Utilizing Time, Talent, and Money is a comprehensive guide to the tools and strategies of a successful technical manager. This book demonstrates how you can coordinate personnel, raw materials, and venues, all while keeping a production on a tight schedule and within budget. From concept to realization, through nightly performances, *Technical Management for the Performing Arts* focuses on the technical and organizational skills a technical manager must demonstrate and emphasizes the need for creativity and interpersonal management of a team.

- Covers a wide range of technical fields, from props and costuming to carpentry, scenic work, and shop supervision
- Gives you the tools necessary for cost-effective, creative, and thoughtful management
- Discusses the fundamentals and application of personnel management in a performing arts space

Mark Shanda is a professor at The Ohio State University and former resident technical director and Department of Theatre chair. He recently completed a five-year term as the dean of arts and humanities at Ohio State. He is now serving as president of USITT, where he is also Fellow of the Institute. He has authored numerous articles about theatre technology.

Now professor emeritus and former director of theatre at the University of Wisconsin-Madison, **Dennis Dorn** served as technical director and/or designer for more than 180 productions. An active member and Fellow of USITT, he remains active in various capacities within the performing arts community.

Technical Management for the Performing Arts

Utilizing Time, Talent, and Money

Mark Shanda
Dennis Dorn

Focal Press
Taylor & Francis Group

NEW YORK AND LONDON

First published 2016
by Focal Press
711 Third Avenue, New York, NY 10017

and by Focal Press
2 Park Square, Milton Park, Abingdon, Oxon OX14 4RN

Focal Press is an imprint of the Taylor & Francis Group, an informa business

© 2016 Taylor & Francis

Library of Congress Cataloging-in-Publication Data
Shanda, Mark.
   Technical management for the performing arts : utilizing time, talent, and money / Mark Shanda, Dennis Dorn.
      pages cm
   Includes bibliographical references and index.
   1. Performing arts—Management.   I. Dorn, Dennis.   II. Title.
   PN1584.S53 2015
   791.06′9—dc23
   2015030828

ISBN: 978-1-138-91076-8 (hbk)
ISBN: 978-1-138-91075-1 (pbk)
ISBN: 978-1-315-69324-8 (ebk)

Typeset in Perpetua and Bell Gothic
by Apex CoVantage, LLC

Cover:
The Rocky Horror Show, by Richard O'Brien, Southern Theatre,
Columbus, OH, November 17–22, 2005
Photo by Allison Walker
Produced by The Ohio State University Theatre
Directed by Mandy Fox
Scenic and Lighting Design by Daniel Matthews
Costume Design by Mary Elizabeth Yaw
Sound Design by James Knapp
Stage Manager Eric H. Mayer

Printed and bound by CPI UK on sustainably sourced paper

Contents

Figures

Acknowledgments

Oftentimes when an organization is looking to hire a new technical manager, the desire is expressed that the ideal candidate would be about 25 years old with something like 40 years of experience. Obviously this option is a mathematical impossibility, but that idea has served as part of the impetus for this book. Could we capture our years of experience in technical management in some practical ways to give early career managers some valuable assistance? We think we have done so and hope that you will agree.

None of this would have been possible without three significant groups with whom we have interacted.

To our colleagues in both commercial and academic venues, we say thank you for frequently challenging us, occasionally inspiring us, and always working hard to make the performing arts appropriately significant in our culture. Many of you have become dear friends through the years. We would like to extend a special thanks to David Stewart from The Guthrie Theater who served as our technical editor and whose observations and commentary helped make this work a better product.

To our students who have taught us daily with their enthusiasm, passion, and creativity freely applied to the production challenges they undertook. Our greatest satisfaction has come in watching you discover your own insights, succeed beyond your self-imposed limitations, and then go on to your own rich and fulfilling lives. You make us proud!

To our families, who have endured our long work hours and occasional bad moods and have accepted us despite our faults. Your support has meant the world to us and, despite an occasional lapse on our part, we have always tried to put family first. We celebrate the joys of family life each and every day.

We particularly thank our wives, Ginny and Kathy. We are indeed blessed by your patience and love that has allowed us to be effective partners in our writing endeavors, while occasionally being less effective partners with each of you. Our love to both of you and our enduring thanks!

Preface

This book is about technical management in the world of entertainment production—backstage work—and more specifically a resource for technical managers involved in the performing arts. This audience is both at once broad and to a certain extent specific. A few readers may need to interpolate what is discussed here in order to fit their own position, but since it is likely many actively employed in the entertainment industry got their start in live theatre, this bridge should not be insurmountable. Because of the authors' own experiences, much of the commentary and some examples will come from the theatrical technical direction field; however, the set of skills required to be an effective technical manager is rather universal and applicable regardless of the reader's particular discipline.

The term **"technical manager"** is common but might need some definition in order to best address the characteristics and responsibilities associated with the job. While **"technical"** implies a crafts-like aspect, we use the term to reference anyone who practices or directs a process to accomplish a task or to create a product. Of course, the world is full of people who fit this description, but our focus is on those associated with some aspect of the performing arts.

The term **"manager"** pertains to someone who has supervisory responsibilities over people, but it need not be so restrictive as to require a group of subordinates. Even individuals who work alone qualify as managers since they must be able to self-manage their own time, financial resources, and goals.

Juxtaposed, the terms "technical" and "manager" describe a person who deftly enables the creation of a thing or event through effective leadership and the combined efforts of self and others. Skills for success may be hand skills, calculating skills, or organizational skills, the latter sometimes referred to as "people skills" and "soft skills."

WHY WE WROTE THIS BOOK

Our goal in writing this book is to assist technical managers to develop a viable set of people skills and organizational skills to support performance-related activities. The environment in which many of the skills will be practiced is, as mentioned earlier, the field of theatrical technical direction, but our hope is that readers will see how the overarching principles and specific techniques can be broadly applied.

While there are a host of books that address design principles and construction considerations pertaining to entertainment enterprises, to our knowledge there are no books, or at least very few, that devote more than a brief chapter or two to the scope of production personnel management as it is practiced today. Sadly, we might rephrase that to say "as not practiced today." Inadequate consideration of this important topic in the training of future managers has been the pattern for many years. This is, or ought to be, very concerning, especially in light of discussions with both prominent and even low-level industry managers. When asked about the biggest challenges faced in their work, the majority nearly unanimously respond "people."

While there is no single-answer approach or solution as to how the talents of individuals can be successfully united to create a workplace filled with an enthusiastic, capable, and focused team of employees, there are practical tools and helpful approaches that can be studied and applied, in whole or in part, that help make us aware of the issues faced in attempting such a goal.

For many who are students, or interested observers, of organizations and their structures, much of what is said here should seem at least familiar. After all, we're talking about human nature, and we all qualify as members of the species. Several decades ago, a flurry of self-help books appeared that discussed many of these same issues, but they did not specifically target issues within a particular field such as the performing arts. Stephen Covey's *The Seven Habits of Highly Effective People/Restoring the Character Ethic* and a host of parable-style books such as Kenneth H. Blanchard's *One-Minute Manager* series made their way onto many bookshelves in offices across America.

When trying to apply business concepts to production efforts, production managers, technical directors, and production stage managers (to name a few) have probably bemoaned the absence of some of the tools these books brought to our attention. These devices included approaches such as product-goal presentations, fully inclusive meetings, and daily check-ins for personnel status and quality control. Regardless, based on our own experiences, and those of others who support this approach, the authors believe that a good number of fundamental personnel management principles can be applied successfully to our own studios and work environments. Awareness is growing; that is really the purpose of this book—to increase awareness of a long overlooked aspect of our industry.

GETTING INTO THE FIELD

Initially, what gets most technical managers interested in production work is their attraction to the technology and/or crafts to which they were introduced. That enthralls most of us for at least five to ten years. But over time, our success at such entry-level jobs gets us promoted into a leadership role. With that change, our responsibility expands beyond technology and hands-on work to the coordination of fellow workers. We end up tackling tasks such as budget projections, cost estimations, and workflow schedules; over time we become increasingly accountable for big-picture results.

In his 1969 book (an old book perhaps but still true today), Dr. Laurence Peter stated, "in a hierarchy, every employee tends to rise to his level of incompetence." Now known simply as *The Peter Principle*, the phenomenon of being promoted above our comfort level and training still remains far too common. Before we even realize it, we can find ourselves no longer doing what we most enjoyed but rather something for which we have received little, if any, training. Meanwhile, we find ourselves growing less proficient in our own technological expertise since both our time and our energy have, by necessity, been redirected.

WHAT CAN BE DONE ABOUT THE MILESTONE OF PROMOTION?

The above seems nearly inevitable; however, it is certainly addressable. We must prepare to become a technical manager at the same time we work in other capacities. This happens on many levels, as you learn about yourself: your own wants, needs, and ambitions. Learning what makes us satisfied participants in the range of activities needed to create your product, e.g., a smoothly run performance, informs you of your reactions to circumstances and personal interactions that will prove useful as your career progresses. Being an effective team member lays the foundation for effective leadership.

> The growth and development of people is the highest calling of leadership.
> Harvey S. Firestone

To be a good employee, you need to be provided with tools to do your job efficiently and effectively. As a technical manager, the responsibility of providing those tools sits on your shoulders. How do you succeed as a manager? In many ways it is as simple as creating an environment where people can perform their own best work, without delays, with a sense of direction and priority, and which is straightforward and uncomplicated. You become effective by being observant, thoughtful, gracious, flexible, and firm. You make decisions, take action, and communicate. You become a leader.

> Management is efficiency in climbing the ladder of success; leadership determines whether the ladder is leaning against the right wall.
> Steven Covey

HOW *TECHNICAL MANAGEMENT FOR THE PERFORMING ARTS* IS STRUCTURED

Our discussion begins with an introduction to the Time, Talent, Money Triangle, followed by a discussion of the characteristics of successful technical managers. After these introductory comments, we move on to identify specific tools to apply during various project phases.

All that we share can be expanded to apply more globally and can be further refined, but we hope that our suggestions will serve you well in growing into, or transforming yourself into, an effective technical manager.

Success is the sum of details.

Harvey S. Firestone

Part One

Introduction

Chapter 1

Meet the Manager & the Triangle

What and who are technical managers? What is a Time, Talent, & Money Triangle? How are these terms relevant to those of us engaged in aspects of live and recorded entertainment? And, if so, what's the relationship?

INTRODUCING THE TECHNICAL MANAGER

The principal purpose of the entertainment industry is to tell a story. The story may be fiction or nonfiction, live or recorded, sequential or pieced together, true or fantasy, simple or complex. Perhaps the story is complex yet simply conveyed. No matter how the project is categorized, any entertainment enterprise is an effort that can become very complicated as the number of participants expands.

In what is perhaps an extreme example, consider the setup, performance, and teardown of the NFL's annual Super Bowl Halftime Show (SBHS). While it is doubtful that the event was ever conceived to be small in scope, the entire concept of this halftime show might have started initially with the unpretentious idea of featuring an outstanding singing group to appear midfield and fill the space with aural delight while the football teams disappear into their respective locker rooms for a pep talk. To do justice to the performers, however, the huge cubic volume of the venue demanded technical support, i.e., microphones, speaker clusters, audio equipment board operators, and sufficient stage lighting luminaires and controllers to allow the large audience to focus its attention on the midfield activities. Technical support requires gear and crew, who in turn require the oversight and coordination of technical managers. Today, the SBHS has grown to include elaborate staging, extraordinary props, performers' flying gear . . . and the need for even more technical managers.

As a far less elaborate example, take the situation of a "stand-up" comedian who is doing a nightly one-man routine. The stage consists of two 4 × 8 platforms located in a corner of the room. Even in this small venue, the performer will likely request a mic, even if the audience will have no difficulty hearing without one, and at least two spotlights to ensure focus on the performer. Additionally, the mic will bolster the performer's confidence and give him or her a prop to occupy twitchy hands.

In many instances, within a short time, the production values associated even with this small setting will grow so that enhanced lighting and audio systems will be installed that require additionally sophisticated technicians and at least one technical manager. Grow the venue a bit more and the production values will become more complex, as will the coordination. Performance events require multiple disciplines and the involvement of many individuals to support the performance and enhance the audience experience. Guilty by association, all these technicians and their supervisors, as well as all performers, are part of the event and subsequently collaborators in its execution.

THE TEAM BEHIND THE SCENES

While the "talent," a.k.a. performers, are always the focus of any filmed or live-performance event, the success or failure of these events is commonly due in no small part to the genius and collaborative abilities of the teams of artisans, craftspersons, and managers who support the talent and story in ways that enhance the delivery of the performers' actions and the script. This supporting technical crew involves multiple teams of talented individuals and technical managers, all of whom contribute to the success of the overall venture.

The normal support team includes directors and choreographers; designers; dramaturges (sometimes); and key technical personnel in the fields of scenery, costumes, lighting, effects, props, and multiple similar disciplines. Together, along with supporting artists and craftspersons, these team leaders join their imaginations and creative skills to develop and enhance the story formation. Depending on the type and scale of the project, a team may be only a handful of people or, in the case of opera, industrials, arena concerts, and film, hundreds and even thousands.

Regardless of the importance of the lead creative team, the focus of this book is not about them. Our focus is on the contributions of the important midmanagement leaders who work alongside and coordinate the work done, most of them unseen by any audience.

The title of each manager in these collaborations varies from organization to organization, although chief lighting technician, costume supervisor, show rigger, prop supervisor, and SFX coordinator are some common titles. This person, in whole or in part, is vested with much or all of the overall management of backstage personnel, schedules, physical facilities, and equipment, as well as the coordination of various production elements. This is the person to whom this book is dedicated and to whom it will be most useful.

WHERE TECHNICAL MANAGERS ORIGINATED

Although history tells us of large-scale productions performed millennia ago, the management of such events has changed significantly since the mid-20th century. While this may only be simple conjecture, most likely technical managers derived from lead artisans, who oversaw the work of other craftspersons. Years ago, everyone learned their skills through apprenticeship and long periods of on-the-job experience. The Middle Ages in Europe saw the development of guilds whose craftsmen members were residents of their performance venue communities and familiar with their surroundings, their materials, and with each other. The pattern stayed much the same until the 20th century.

Beginning in the mid-1960s, rock-n-roll arena tours became more commonplace. They brought with them changes that have permeated the workings of even small local performance venues today. Production values became vastly more complex and certainly more corporate than in centuries past. With increased sophistication came a growth of disciplines, new and expanded technologies, and a recognition of the need for greater collaboration and efficiencies.

In professional circles, the lead craftsman's scope of responsibility widened to include tasks of an increasingly managerial nature. Over time there has become more knowledge to acquire, more skills to master, and more facets to coordinate. The result is that most craftspersons cannot function as independently as they had in the past. And the pace at which work needs to unfold requires that things be created at multiple locations, adding complications to the coordination and assembly of the numerous elements that have to come together and gel within tight schedules.

This change occurred first in professional circles, but quickly this pattern became part of academic and community organizations as well. For the latter, resistance to change and more limited resources meant a slower-paced recognition of the new trends. Today's fast-paced event timelines and the desire to train students to function ASAP after leaving formal training has resulted in more educational organizations incorporating more business-style management techniques to meet organizational expectations.

While a handful of performing arts professional programs within academic institutions have adopted more management-oriented training programs for students, there are currently few, and rather limited, published resources available. While most recently penned texts include a chapter on organizational structures, few provide any instruction in necessary management skills to function as a technical manager. In the past, these academic/professional programs have focused on the "nuts and bolts" of production work, and for the most part they still do. The emphasis remains on mastering technical/artistic skills rather than on development and awareness of people (soft) skills.

The paradigm shift to training the technical manager in requisite management skills is only beginning to emerge. As a result, many practicing technical managers feel ill equipped since they are strictly self-taught regarding skills needed to successfully manage. To emphasize the magnitude of the issue, research such as job satisfaction surveys has disclosed that most graduates of theatre technology programs indicate personnel management and group dynamics are among the most difficult aspects of their jobs and are singularly the one for which they feel least prepared.

Part of the confusion surrounding the need for effective management skills lies in the lack of a singular job description for a technical manager. Unfortunately, a single definition is not really possible, given that the exact duties of the individual holding such a title are very skill-and-organization specific. Rather than attempt to provide a definitive job description, this text looks at those essential qualities needed by anyone who serves in a technical management capacity within any of the performing arts and its wide-ranging related organizations and who must interact with not just *things* but people. Duties are examined and discussed with regard to the central theme of this book, *Technical Management for the Performing Arts: Utilizing Time, Talent, and Money.*

THE TIME, TALENT, MONEY TRIANGLE

To provide strong leadership, share specific technical knowledge, and establish high expectations, every technical manager must maintain focus on the actualities of each specific production event or project. Each effort has a limit of available resources, a model that we suggest may best be viewed in the context of the Time, Talent, Money triangle (TTMT) (figure 1.1).

The concept of TTMT is already familiar to most technical managers, even if it isn't known by this name. The three elements identify the primary aspects of a project that need management. Most performing arts projects have rigid deadlines that emanate backwards from an "Opening (Night)." By design, this finite schedule, in conjunction with a standard 40-hour work week, creates a somewhat unforgiving demand on the TTM Triangle, although variations are possible, which makes the concept a valuable tool. Technical managers must remain mindful of time constraints and subsequently utilize their management skills to begin and sustain a successful project or production schedule. While effective management of the **time portion** of the triangle is critical in making a production successful,

FIGURE 1.1 The Time, Talent, Money Triangle

in reality most technical managers are involved in jobs that are multiproject and multiyear in scope, adding significant complexity to this responsibility.

Like the time element, the **talent portion** of the triangle is inclusive of all participants involved in the production process. Whether artistic director or production intern, each and every individual has talents that impact a project. Although most technical managers have minimal control over the talent pool from which they may draw, all do have the power to recognize the talent available to them, hopefully using individual talents to their best end. This means identifying each individual's strengths and weaknesses and devising ways those talents can be best brought together.

The **money portion** of the triangle is identified by a lot of technical managers as their greatest challenge. Fabrication materials, skilled labor, production time, artistic talent, equipment, and facilities all cost money, so in many ways money is the most tangible of the three components. Script choices and design decisions are frequently focused on the "estimated dollar" cost of materials and performers, with little attention paid to the available pools of backstage time and talent. The truth of the matter, however, is that the money side of the triangle is probably the most easily worked. Additional money is often far easier to secure than additional talent or time.

> Capital isn't that important in business. Experience isn't that important. You can get both of these things. What is important is ideas.
>
> Harvey Firestone

What makes the Time, Talent, Money Triangle a uniquely useful management tool is that it is easy to foresee how any adjustment to one side impacts the other two. Conceptually depicted as an equilateral triangle, the TTM triangle closely resembles three points connected by a rubber band line. As illustrated in figure 1.2, alter the position of one vertex and there is a corresponding change in the length

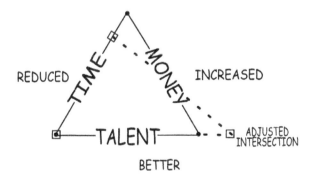

FIGURE 1.2 The Time, Talent, Money Triangle at work

FIGURE 1.3 Good, fast, or cheap

of two of the other sides. In order that the unaffected side remain constant, the other two sides are modified relative to the lengths of the original lengths of the sides. As an example, more highly skilled workers being compensated at above-standard wages can accomplish a similar goal in a shorter period of time.

While a given problem often has numerous solutions, when modeled on the TTM Triangle, the potential solutions can be carefully analyzed and a course of action determined. For example, additional money can make possible the purchase of better materials/products, which, in turn, may reduce fabrication/assembly time. If time is tightened, more money can help compensate. However, mistakes made when using these higher-quality materials will be costlier; subsequently, it would be wise to hire the most talented artists available, thus additional money is needed. The other side of the coin might be that less expensive materials can be utilized, with excellent results, if there is a longer timeline and sufficiently talented and experienced craftspersons and technicians on the jobsite.

The Time Talent Money Triangle impacts every decision in the production process. Cynics of this planning tool often joke about the relationship of these three components (fig. 1.3): "I can give you **quick**, I can give you **good**, or I can give you **cheap**: **PICK TWO!**" The sad truth, however, is that the joke is no joke at all.

Time, talent, and money are not the only parameters affecting a technical manager. The physical constraints of the workspaces and the quality and range of resources available to construct and assemble a project greatly impact a technical manager's role, as do organizational standards, community expectations, and production timetables. The technical manager can be most effective when production parameters are determined well in advance of the time that a project begins and the Time, Talent, Money Triangle is utilized to shape those decisions that must be made during the process.

Part Two

Foundations

Chapter 2

Roles

As a member of a production organization, a technical manager brings a diverse background of intellectual and acquired skills. This chapter focuses on how a technical manager interacts within a company or department during the development and life of a creative project. Much deals with personal interactions, the exchange of ideas, and "What if?" questions. In the instance of the technical manager, these often free-ranging conversations come with a caveat.

While initial concepts are brought to the table by designers, producers, and directors, those technical managers present are party to the introduction and exchange of bold conceptual ideas. At the same time, design team participants must also be mindful of the responsibility owed to the staff members who will work on executing the finalized plan. The technical manger's role extends beyond the ideas discussed at the meeting table to many others outside the room and for an extended period of time. We have identified five specific roles that we feel each technical manager must fill. These objectives are: **Artist**, **Creative Thinker**, **Colleague**, **Planner**, and **Positive Leader** (fig. 2.1). Effective technical managers certainly exhibit these characteristics all the time. Note how the roles parallel a project's development from inception to completion.

For the sake of simplicity, this discussion is focused on the role of one specific technical manager: the technical director. Although singular in name, the position

---

ROLES OF A TECHNICAL MANAGER

- Artist
- Creative Thinker
- Colleague
- Planner
- Positive Leader

FIGURE 2.1 Roles of a technical manager

is emblematic of nearly all who function in the technical manager role and, we trust, is useful in the establishment of the various capacities we wish to identify. The goal is to study the manner in which human dynamics unfold during the creative process. In real life, these dynamics are quite varied and may seem even irrelevant in some positions held by technical managers.

THE TECHNICAL MANAGER AS ARTIST

The technical director's role in the design process is one of a proactive and full collaborator within an artistic team. While there will arise in the process a need for breakout meetings between two or three lead team members, it is very helpful, actually essential, for the technical director to be part of the inaugural meetings where the project's overall goals and visions are put forward. Being aware of the full picture from the beginning helps a technical director shape questions and make decisions through the process.

The first phase of a production project is the design process and should entail an environment in which ideas and concepts can be freely exchanged with members of the production team while feeling safe to share preliminary ideas. These early meetings must be open and nonjudgmental, allowing focused time for exploration and creative input to trigger or enhance ideas with the design staff. These meetings, and the several that follow, are an unfolding process in which conversation is often wide ranging and may seem to lack direction.

Only as an informed member of the production staff can a technical director contribute suggestions that will be respected by colleagues. Every member of the artistic team earns respect by being fully prepared. For the technical director, this means a working knowledge of the script. To meet this goal, the script or project scenario must be studied several times before the first meeting. A comprehensive understanding of the storyline is imperative, but the technical director must be conversant with all referenced costume, scenic, property, lighting, and audio/special effects needs as well as stage directions, playwright notes, and actions required of performers during the event.

While the technical director needs to feel free to offer creative ideas to the designers, director, and/or choreographer, technical managers must recognize that some comments from technical managers are not always welcomed. Perhaps designers have had previous experiences with technical directors who were perceived as negative, which in turn was interpreted as door-slamming. Any technical director needs to allow issues such as scale, practicality, budget, schedule, and the like to enter the design process slowly, waiting until there is something of substance with general support before interjecting limitations.

To assure this doesn't become the case, a technical director must acquire artistic sensibilities as well as technical knowledge. The reality of the design process is that a technical director can be of great assistance to the designers and director by judiciously asking questions that attempt to distill from the ideas on the table those elements that are most poignant to achieving the desired goal. Distillation involves a concentration and refinement of those design ideas that are shared by all.

A technical director who has an artistic awareness can significantly contribute to the design process through a condensation and simplification of the language, i.e., cutting to the chase. In the role of the technical manager as artist, the technical manager is ideally articulate in both graphic and verbal communication. As just a simple example, given the wide range of interpretations within design terminology, it is quite possible for two members of a production team to use the same words to refer to two very distinct ideas. Using questions, perhaps accompanied by a picture, diagram, or sketch to further illustrate his or her points, a technical director can clarify and enhance concept precision.

The technical director should be sensitive to artistic desires when analyzing required time, talent, and money requirements and should strive to develop alternative solutions that best align goals with resources. That requires an artistic sensitivity as well as a diplomatic tongue, firm on the issue of resources (if possible) but a willingness to exhibit flexibility when priorities conflict.

The director's and designers' discussions are used to determine the visual appropriateness and aesthetic functionality of each design element. During this process, the technical director's aim should be to glean a sense of priority among the visual and working elements and verify these observations verbally. Once cost estimation and scheduling begins, this information bears a direct relationship to the Time, Talent, Money Triangle.

Frequently, an artistic team envisions a product that is simply not feasible given the resources of the technical support available. As ill-fitting as it often feels, technical directors, in fact all technical managers, face the responsibilities of negotiating compromises that can be achieved within parameters and providing an acceptable set of agreements that serve artistic as well as logistical needs. All technical managers must avoid being viewed as naysayers. A better approach is to express support for the ideas under discussion, while making suggestions that respond in positive ways to the challenges as they become obvious.

Avoiding a clash of interests is only possible when the technical director is involved from the beginning. The confidence held by some that a technical director can step in after all the artistic decisions are made and without repercussions implement the wishes of the director and designers must be deterred. Operating with a spirit of inclusion, the work of the team can avoid much of any perceived adversarial relationship between technical director and artistic staff.

Good design must balance many factors in order to produce effective results. Key to this success is the inclusion of the technical manager as a full partner in the conversations of the artistic team through the entire process from start to finish. Needs and demands are weighed against the considerations of production, emotion, morale, availability of materials, cost, use, etc. Adaptability and compromise are essential to finding success in this framework, i.e., realizing the best solutions to achieve the given production demands and artistic vision.

THE TECHNICAL MANAGER AS CREATIVE THINKER

The singular quality that characterizes the technical director is that of creative thinker. Nothing brings more joy to technical directors as a group than the opportunity to address problems as they arise and respond to them with creative solutions. Most often this phenomenon is referred to as playing "What if?"

Creative thinking, by definition, is what many of us know as brainstorming and should not be confused with critical thinking. The latter is associated with intensive scrutinizing of facts and things that are or as they should be. Creative thinking, on the other hand, involves a more relaxed, open, and playful approach that will require some degree of risk taking (figure 2.2).

The most common creative problem-solving process utilized is drawing things out on paper. (Computer use is certainly fine, but there is something about the more tangible elements of pencil sketches that produces more satisfactory results). Rough construction elevations and plans (shop drawings) can be developed, not only to communicate ideas with others but to provide a process by which decisions are made. Considerations include questions regarding how scenic units will fit together, their use during performance the design of any mechanical systems needed, and the selection of appropriate construction materials and techniques. Roughed-out, notated sketches or drawings allow decisions to be made at the drawing table (or monitor screen) rather than down the road and done on the more expensive studio floor. To make it even more playful, the same process can be done on graph paper, a scrap of wood,

---

CREATIVE THINKING TACTICS

- Look for many possible answers, not just one.
- Wild and crazy suggestions are as valuable as those that seem sensible.
- Don't judge ideas too early—some may contain a kernel of an answer.
- To doodle, daydream, or play with a theory or suggestion is a valuable activity.
- Be a risk taker and not afraid of making mistakes.

Be aware that these approaches involve making lots of suggestions that are unworkable and may even seem silly.

FIGURE 2.2 The pathway to creative thinking

or the back of an envelope. A detailed sketch conveys both information and confirms comprehension as a tangible manifestation of creative thinking.

As a creative thinker, the technical director must learn to isolate imagined problems from real problems, avoiding false limitations. The collaborative art form demands an understanding of fact verses perception, remembering that even the crazy ideas may well contain meritorious aspects. To truly allow free rein to their full creative capability, a technical manager needs to recognize that preconceptions alone are the cause of many problems.

In a bit of a mix of critical and creative thinking, most successful creative thinkers attentively try to comprehend and separate fact from perception, readily approached by applying the old axiom "A problem well stated is half solved." Regardless of the complexity of a challenge, once defined, a problem becomes easier to solve. This definition means the creative thinker can go to work and let imagination operate with abandon.

Institutional biases are present in all organizations. Organizational traditions and expectations often set up imaginary boundaries that limit production possibilities and that in turn stifle creative thought. A technical director should be constantly asking the questions which may have not been asked before. Questions that start with: "Would it be possible to . . . ?" or "Have you considered . . . ?" must be part and parcel of a technical director's vocabulary. Challenging conventions is what the performing arts are all about.

Creative thinking recognizes the power that expectations have on our performance and struggles to avoid stereotyping. The adage that there are only forty persons who work in the entertainment industry and they all know each other has some basis in how information about directors, designers, and actors is passed from one venue to another and eventually the truth is passed over by the fiction. People, whose reputations precede them, set up a chain of expectation that can cloud the production (creative) process. The creative thinker recognizes the destructive power of negative expectation and works to instill the spirit of open-mindedness in every individual engaged in the process.

Another example of how expectations can stifle creative thought is saturation. Saturation involves something, in this case a choice, becoming so routine that we no longer are conscious of other alternatives. If every false stage floor that a technical director has ever done has been covered in ⅛" Masonite®, then that technical director has become saturated with that method. The options of ground cloths, painting the actual stage floor, and the use of commercial flooring are not open due to the level of saturation present. If you don't believe that saturation is a major problem in the theatre, think of the number of times you have participated in a conversation that began: "Well, the way that I have always done it is . . . " Creative thinking prevents saturation from taking root.

Daydreaming, reflection, mental playfulness, and visualization have all been scientifically proven to be aids to creativity, conceptualization, problem solving,

15

and accomplishment. Wellness experts cite the need we all have for time to reflect and relax. The creative thinker utilizes these flights of fancy to recharge and to process complex problems. Creative solutions are often arrived at during those times when one is the most relaxed.

Despite the constraints of time and money and the frantic pace of most productions, intentional personal practices to enable such downtime are unapologetically essential.

THE TECHNICAL MANAGER AS COLLEAGUE

One of the joys of those who work in the performing arts is their interaction with other creative people. By definition, those who work with us are colleagues—although not necessarily buddies—pals, or partners. Regardless, to be effective in creative fields, participants must respect each other and be teammates and collaborators. In fact, the production process is absolutely one of collaboration; this requires accommodating the weaknesses of our colleagues as well as enjoying the benefits of their strengths.

Sensitivity to the human needs of self and others is requisite for success. The best technical managers find compromise during times of conflicting needs rather than assuming either extreme roles of tyrant or guardian angel. Such circumstances require a proactive spirit, shrugging off the posture of victim while assuming self-confidence (see figure 2.3).

Perhaps the adage of being a team player is overused, but the technical director must learn and remember how to function within an organization made up of a wide variety of people. While the technical director is positioned to serve as a bridge builder between the vision of the artistic team and the tangible realities facing the technical staff, such a role can be very challenging. Critical relationships must be sustained with the director, set designer, and producer as well as with

CHARACTERISTICS OF A GOOD
MENTOR AND COLLEAGUE
- Respects colleagues and employees in all levels of the organization and has their respect as well
- Exhibits enthusiasm for the field and work
- Values the opinions and initiatives of others
- Shares skills, knowledge, and expertise
- Provides guidance and constructive feedback
- Sets and meets ongoing personal and professional goals
- Values ongoing learning and growth in the field

FIGURE 2.3 Characteristics of a good mentor and colleague

16

the head carpenter, head electrician, and stage manager, to name a few. Technical managers must identify and empathize with the energies and needs of these individuals who guide the production vision as well as those individuals who work directly under their supervision to realize that vision.

As a rule, production-team members share dynamic communication, cutting across the layers of the perceived organizational hierarchy. While it is important that everyone understand the collation of decision makers, not all communication need follow a formal order. What actually works best is sharing production-related information between as many people as is reasonable. In this way, everyone knows the process and status at the same time, creating a truly transparent environment.

Organizational relationships often become even more complex when staff exchange roles (hats) from production to production, based on the particular assignment given to each individual. People do change roles and, during the various phases of production, even the perceived "chain of command" changes. In the role of colleague, the technical director must recognize this changing pattern of relationships and adapt based on the given circumstances. Being human and destined to make errors of judgment from time to time, unfortunate situations can arise. At that point, it is simply time to put the issue behind and move ahead, which is much easier said than done.

In the role of colleague, the technical director must also recognize one's own human nature. Creative individuals who enjoy working with others are the most successful in our field. Each must recognize his or her own needs and chart a career path that works towards satisfying those needs. The benefit from working with others in our demanding art form should not be underestimated, for through careful analysis we often find our personal involvement in theatre may have sprung from the basic principle of engaging and sharing with others.

THE TECHNICAL MANAGER AS PLANNER

A major function of technical managers is to think ahead, to anticipate, and to solve problems—or at the very least to arrange in advance for their proper handling. A well-developed plan is a means to an end that is forever in a state of metamorphosis. Hopefully, that plan is informed by the Time, Talent, Money Triangle and supports the efforts of the production team as it advances forward to meet the stated goals. That goal can be the successful execution of a single production, a season of shows, a festival, a business theatre event, or a building renovation or construction. The steps necessary to accomplish each of these goals is the same, regardless of their scale.

Through analysis and careful matching, the technical manager must be able to determine what needs to be accomplished, where it is to be done, what the process to get there might be, and what problems might be faced. As a planner, the

Seven Characteristics of Effective Planners

Modus Operandi	Gist
■ Break projects into realistic tasks with manageable deadlines	Write down tasks and cross off activities once they are finished; give everyone a sense of continual accomplishment
■ Operate in two time horizons	Use calendars and task lists for long-term and short-term goals
■ Begin projects early	Provide opportunity to gather information, ruminate, collaborate with others, and modify plans for as needed
■ Seek advice from others	Accept input from those who can assist or offer information
■ Delegate whenever possible	Delegate tasks to those you trust to get things done, and monitor without micromanagement; managers can't do everything
■ Have a plan "B"	Be persistent in the face of adversity by considering other avenues when encountering barriers. Never say "Die."
■ Realize that "No" is sometimes the appropriate response to a request	Say, "I will get back to you on that; let me think about it overnight" or "No, I cannot do that" if in doubt whether the request can be fulfilled

FIGURE 2.4 Characteristics of a good planner

Academic Success Center, Iowa State University, http://www.thepdfportal.com/characteristics_138332.pdf.

technical manager works with some basic ideas (fig. 2.4), all intimately associated with the Time, Talent, Money Triangle.

In theatre production, the one fixed point that drives all decisions is opening, therefore almost all scheduling is developed working backward from that point. Effective scheduling not only establishes completion dates and intermediate deadlines for projects, but it also allows opportunities for some things to remain undefined for a period of time before a decision is necessary. Good managers quickly develop the ability to discern between fixed decisions and those that are still under debate. The technical manager who refuses to recognize the fluid nature of production faces a difficult future.

Planning is not micromanagement, which suggests all decisions are made by the technical manager. The technical manager's function is to attain a solid comprehension of the project and use reliable planning tools and skills to assure that coworkers have both the tools and resources necessary to complete their tasks. Ideally, managers seek to engage staff in the process of executing the plans and providing guidance, while at the same time respecting each worker's own creativity and need to be treated as a valued collaborator. To this end, the plans developed by technical managers must be visible (not residing in someone's mind) and accessible to everyone involved through means such as published calendars, shared work schedules, and regular brief meetings with the staff. "Transparency" is the buzz word of the 21st century, and it applies in production just as much as in government.

Since work invariably expands to fill the time available, workers who do not have a full comprehension of a project's scope and sequencing frequently find themselves spending the last hours prior to opening facing unsatisfactory working conditions. Morale will quickly erode when factors such as extended workdays and the loss of personal satisfaction are felt when unable to do a job well and within the scheduled time frame. Concepts such as "big picture" and "transparency" are not just talking points but factors that make a big difference in creating and maintaining a satisfied and effective workforce.

What is addressed above pertains a bit more to objects than to people, but people are an even bigger factor when discussing project planning tools. In the role of planner, a technical manager must consciously create an environment free of internal conflict or at least make every effort to minimize conflicts as they arise. For example, it's important to link the right workers with the right task. Equally important is pairing workers since their joint ability to produce quality and timely work frequently rests upon successful partnering and is dependent on both complementary skills and compatible personalities.

The Time, Talent, Money Triangle is inherently connected to space issues, too. Limitations created by both the amount and the type of space available greatly impact the production process. Precious time can be gained or lost depending on the use and allocation of floor and ceiling space, the location of tools and resources relative to the designated work space(s), and a sensible sequencing of project elements and processes. Through careful planning, the technical manager can maximize the results of the labor pool and minimize the frustration level of the workers.

THE TECHNICAL MANAGER AS A POSITIVE LEADER

Last, but certainly not least, is the persona of positive leadership. In fact, this characteristic may well be the most important contribution of the technical manager and may be foreign to many. Positive leadership means that a capable technical manager does not simply agree with all ideas but rather assumes and projects that the task at hand can be completed, that any problems to be faced can be settled, and that any negative attitudes among staff or superiors can be addressed and resolved with satisfactory results.

Early in the planning process, the positive leader begins to develop a sense of the project's scope and ruminates on the steps and processes needed to accomplish

> A technical manager's vitality is directly related to staff output.
>
> **Keep in mind:**
> - If it's to be, it begins with me.
> - Back up your words with actions; seeing is believing.
> - If you can't quantify or describe it, you can't manage it.
> - Be aware of your artistic teams' values; what do they want/need to achieve their goals?
> - If you don't like the way things are, remain patient; everything will change tomorrow.
> - Don't sweat the small stuff (in the "big picture," isn't it all small stuff?).
> - What happens on the job is not personal, it's business.

FIGURE 2.5 Characteristics of positive leadership

the task or series of tasks. This process assumes an attitude that staff are similarly positive in their disposition toward their job, confidence in their skills, and willingness to problem solve challenges as they arise (fig. 2.5). The positive leader views staff as trustworthy and capable, but the positive leader is impatient with people who exhibit signs of negativity. The positive leader's personal commitment to success may well be interpreted as abrasive, but there is no place for negativity (spoiled-apple effect) in any collaborative enterprise.

In the truest sense of the phrase, every arts endeavor starts outs as a doubtful undertaking; there are no productions guaranteed to be successful, artistically or fiscally. But a positive attitude is the first step toward making a successful outcome out of a doubtful undertaking. By extension, the sheer fact that every production involves a team effort means that a technical manager can, and should, capitalize on the combined strengths and skills of the entire production staff. Surprisingly positive results are often achieved through the combined efforts of many talented individuals led by a positive leader.

To assist workers in understanding their role within the producing unit, the technical manager should strive to instill in all members a goal rather than task orientation. Workers should be informed of the relationship of their particular project to the whole production. By encouraging workers to see the relationship of each part to the whole, the technical manager strives toward a stronger level of personal investment in the entire project. With some good fortune, perhaps a worker, having completed a task, recognizes that there is more to be done and becomes more likely to ask, "What's next?" By assuming the role of positive leader and by challenging workers with high personal expectations, the technical manager can help the production staff achieve more than the sum of their individual efforts.

Chapter 3

Authority

Regardless of the employing organization, in order to function within that organization and have influence on the Time, Talent, Money Triangle, a technical manager must establish and sustain a level of "authority" in his or her work. Authority is defined here as a capacity recognized by others that supports an individual's successful management and completion of a given task. More succinctly, and in personal terms, authority rests in the level of confidence that an individual exhibits and that others grant in recognition of that person's ability to complete a job. There is recognition that the manager possesses the skills, training, and personality to effect mundane and even seemingly insurmountable odds in working to achieve a goal.

THE ORIGIN OF AUTHORITY

A common euphemism for authority is "power." Although power has gotten a bad reputation in recent years, each individual within any functioning organization must possess power in order to move forward. Power is the energy that drives the engine of progress and is not equally distributed throughout any group. Rather, various types of power are granted to, or developed by, each individual; the degree of power is dependent on three principal factors, shown in figure 3.1.

The **position** a person holds within an organization is defined by a job description that lists duties, responsibilities, and lines of accountability (Chapter 6 has specifics on job descriptions). Just knowing the title someone holds within an organization often gives observers a good idea as to that person's degree of authority.

The **personality** traits that an individual brings to an organization bear a great influence on how others perceive the person. These characteristics instinctively establish the measure of our authority within a group. Demeanor and work history help to define each person's corresponding power within an organization.

The **role** a person holds within an organization may differ vastly from a rather narrowly defined position description. Actually, role power is assimilated over time as the skills we bear, combined with our personality, convince others of our potential to make unique and valuable contributions within the organization.

SOURCES OF PERSONAL POWER

- ■ *Position*
- ■ *Personality*
- ■ *Role*

FIGURE 3.1 Sources of personal power

POSITION POWER

Position power is probably the easiest of the three power sources to recognize. Through the development and distribution of detailed written job descriptions, organizations delineate each employee's specific tasks, rightful expectations, and performance standards. These documents clarify the needs of an organization and inform each person of his or her responsibilities within the producing organization.

Often informed by an organizational chart, job descriptions convey desired communication lines, i.e., the chain of command, that employees are expected to follow. The higher an individual ascends up the organizational pyramid, the more position power the individual holds. For example, within a regional theatre company there is a vast difference between the power affixed to the position of artistic director and that of light board operator. While in actuality, the board operator may, at the moment, have far more direct influence upon a performance, the artistic director is recognized as the person having final authority, i.e., influence over the organization's production work.

Among the group of individuals who fit the description of technical manager, there is a significant range of associated position power. In fact, the position of "technical manager" can span from an individual who sits in an office overseeing a large staff and an extensive facility to a custodian who occasionally constructs scenery for the in-house drama club but primarily is responsible for building maintenance.

To be able to make the most of position power, a technical manager must occupy a well-defined job with ease and confidence. Each manager must put into practice appropriate training and skills to assure that specified tasks are, or are being, completed in order that both personal and organizational expectations will be met. As standard practice a savvy technical manager will continually seek opportunities to increase personal knowledge. By taking this route, a manager continuously gains additional tools with which to expand personal Position Power. So vital is Position Power that it forms the foundation that supports the other two cited powers and is the quintessential element of the talent portion of the Time, Talent, Money Triangle.

PERSONALITY POWER

Every individual has an unique personality. Numerous books already exist detailing, or at least theorizing, on how human personality develops from infancy all the way through adulthood. While many technical managers perform similar duties to one another, there is such diversity among the group that, try as we might, no one can absolutely identify the personality traits that make someone a successful technical manager. However, the authority that each technical manager reaps through personality does draw from the common characteristics noted in figure 3.2.

Sense of purpose implies that the technical manager acknowledges his or her primary function is to get the job done, typically achieved through collaborative actions. An accomplished technical manager recognizes the unique contributions each staff member brings to the production process and is satisfied with, and appreciative of, staff performing to the best of their ability. The technical manager must identify, evaluate, and methodically resolve the challenges of production that are presented to the team, recognizing that each associate is a key contributor to the success or failure of each endeavor undertaken. An understanding of the Time, Talent, Money Triangle and the technical manager's ability to affect its components is crucial to maintaining a sense of purpose.

Enthusiasm is infectious. As a leader, the technical manager's actions and words must impart personal enthusiasm to collaborators. Although everyone has a personal style, a technical manager needs to personify a "can do" attitude. By emanating a positive attitude, the technical manager will be seen within an organization as a person who has confidence in the ability of a team to work together effectively. When excited by and committed to a project, most people stay upbeat and perform to the best of their capacity. The effect of our attitude on our work is profound. By approaching each day as an opportunity for success, our chances for success are greatly enhanced.

Personal reputation is the most valuable asset a technical manager has to convince others to perform to their own ability level. If a technical manager

---

PERSONALITY TRAITS OF SUCCESSFUL TECHNICAL MANAGERS

- Sense of purpose
- Enthusiasm for the job
- Commitment to a set of specific values
- Self-confidence
- Balanced lifestyle
- Sense of humor

FIGURE 3.2 Characteristics of a successful technical manager

possesses a positive reputation, the individual usually can successfully influence others to be willing to assume greater responsibility. A good reputation commonly comes by committing to simple values: honesty and integrity. (Integrity is about conduct; honesty is about adherence to the facts.) These values form a bond of trust that must exist between you and your colleagues if you are to work together in harmony. When little or no trust exists, no amount of "authority" really matters.

Self-confidence doesn't seem like it needs much explanation, but it is certainly worthy of mention. Simply stated, self-confidence implies that a person approaches each experience, even challenges, with the expectation that he or she will not only persevere but will likely be better for the experience. Like enthusiasm, confidence is also infectious, achieved largely through habit and self-evaluation. Self-confidence comes with practice. Whether making a presentation to a group, creating a project estimate, or making work assignments based on a project's budget estimate, by analyzing our personal efforts, a technical manager becomes better and better at the job . . . and confidence increases. Lack of confidence and trust in others is extremely limiting, to the extent of being self-defeating. Sustaining self-confidence is a daily exercise to which every technical manager must pay attention.

A **sense of balance** within our day-to-day life is essential, so essential that it's going to receive two paragraphs worth of attention. Working in an entertainment field is for most people totally consuming. Our behaviors are influenced accordingly without our even being fully aware how we are affected. The combination of long hours and hard work take a toll very early in many a career. This phenomenon is particularly true for technical managers, many who experience career burnout even before the ages of 30 to 35, not even close to the expected midcareer crisis. What often is missing in many of these regrettable situations is balance—finding separation in daily life that segments work, social, exercise, and mental relaxation activities. Intellectually, many managers recognize the value of lessons borrowed from Eastern religions but allow themselves to be too busy to observe them. Balance implies an understood ebb and flow of energy and activity, which accommodates both the consuming needs of our industry *and* our individual need for growth and personal development.

Achieving balance requires development of solid time-management skills and recognition of the principles discussed by Steven Covey in his two books: *The 7 Habits of Highly Effective People* and *First Things First*. Figure 3.3 is taken from the latter book and illustrates the quagmire in which many of us find ourselves—typically self-created. Entertainment world technical managers need to maintain a healthy perspective about projects and comprehend the life needs of people, personnel, and colleagues. To be an effective technical manager means being able to see both the trees and the forest. Understanding the needs of others and working toward meeting those needs serves to create a positive work environment, allowing the group's collective talents to be productive and efficient. Without absorption of balanced-life principles, the technical manager's ability to manage two-thirds of the Time, Talent, Money Triangle is crippled and personal wellness endangered.

FIGURE 3.3 Stephen Covey's *Fire Within*

Covey Leadership Center, Inc. Covey, Stephen; Merrill, A. Roger; Merrill, Rebecca R.; *First Things First*, 1994, Fireside Publishing, New York, NY, p. 47.

Possession of a strong **sense of humor** is the greatest armor in protecting one's self against a lack of balance. Humor relives tension, heals little hurts, and promotes collegiality among members of a group. One of the highest compliments often given a person who is being recognized for effective leadership is that they have a good sense of humor. The ability to laugh at one's self is of immense value. We are all prone to make mistakes; the sooner each of us realizes our personal fallibilities, the better. The ability to laugh at yourself and your own errors engenders you to your fellow workers while simultaneously creating an environment in which others are comfortable taking risks. The most effective technical managers strive to create an environment in which colleagues are not afraid to dare, care, and laugh out loud.

While noting that there are numerous other factors that shape our personality and influence our individual source of power, the above six factors form the foundation. Personality characteristics that make us likable as a person are not always sufficient to make us effective technical managers. When exercising a leadership role, the technical manager must move beyond being charming and easygoing and must move toward being seen as someone who is fair, consistent, understanding, and worthy of respect. Associates need to see the technical manager as a leader who is worthy of following. And although much of what is defined as being our personality is established through some sort of developmental mystery, an awareness of our relative strengths and weaknesses aids each of us in our growth as a technical manager and as an individual.

ROLE POWER

Of the three sources of authority discussed in this chapter, for many of us, **role** is the most difficult to grasp, which is natural in that it is completely intangible. Only when a person leaves a job and the resultant void is discovered do we really perceive that person's impact within the organization. Suffice it to say that the specific role of an individual within an organization is delineated over time through the combination of job description (Position) and persona (Personality).

Without fail, a technical manager who is recognized as a thoughtful and compassionate problem solver becomes a trusted advisor and mentor to many, regardless of people's position on the organizational pyramid. Frequently, by virtue of the specific set of skills possessed, a technical manager becomes the resident computer guru or group facilitator, volleyball captain or even a brownie baker and seller. Effective technical managers are active listeners, constantly seeking out information to assist in their efforts and often supporting their perceived role as confident and counselor. Role characterizes how an individual fits within an organization, i.e., the unique contributions a person makes by his or her input, time, and talent.

Interestingly enough, this spirit of giving is often potentially dangerous to the individual technical manager. Every manager, technical or not, needs to have an awareness of what responsibility is uniquely his or hers, that which is not, and that which could be but only if you choose it to be yours. Arts managers, for a variety of reasons, are notorious for assuming additional workplace responsibilities. While actions like this often satisfy some need within the individual technical manager, unregulated helpfulness can easily eat away at a balanced life. Every manager must be careful and fully aware.

At times, technical managers are asked to take on additional responsibilities, making the fault not one of their own making. Role awareness aids us to say "No" when an inappropriate request has been made. Being talked into assuming a responsibility that is really of no interest can result in both unneeded stress and lousy job performance. Each technical manager needs to be careful to do "first things first" and contribute, in light of both temperament and job description, without extending commitments beyond his or her capabilities and interests.

To better understand your own personal role power within an organization, employ the techniques of visualization to evaluate your value to that organization. Consider fully the contributions you make to your employer, the impact you have on day-to-day operations, and the potential loss the company would suffer should you decide to move on. By determining one's self-worth, an individual can better lay out a course for your future both within and possibly outside the organization. By carefully examining day-to-day activities, you will find that many of the additional tasks you take on as part of your role are among the most satisfying things done each day, but note equally that the opposite can and may be true in some circumstances.

Careful application of the three sources of power will result in the development of an authority by which a technical manager can truly manage the resources encompassed by the principle of the Time, Talent, Money Triangle. Without such an authority base, the technical manager will be ineffectual in providing leadership within a producing organization.

Chapter 4

Personnel

The successful management of a project's most precious resource—the people involved—is far more complex than overseeing materials and equipment. In spite of this, personnel management is one of the least emphasized areas of study in performing arts education. This is similarly the case in manufacturing and other industries, where personnel management training takes a back seat. So called "hard skills" like welding, construction, and assembly are emphasized over "soft skills" such as communication, task assignment, mentoring, evaluation, and performance review. Successful personnel motivation and supervision are the hallmarks of the effective technical manager and are practical soft skills that *can be learned* through practice and application.

Technical managers contribute to project efforts through the leadership they provide. Their mission is to capitalize on the skills and talents of the various gifted individuals who make up the production team. To achieve production and project goals, the performing arts rely on the collective efforts of diverse individuals who need to work together in an organized, harmonious, and team-oriented approach. Every technical manager is often challenged to select and place team members into the most effective and efficient positions, trust their collective strengths, and occasionally correct their errors to see a project through to success (quality control).

THE IMPORTANCE OF GESTALT

Technical managers start with a "big picture" mentality, understanding the overall goals of any work effort while having an awareness of the multiple details involved and their critical sequencing. This is the reason for full partnership in planning activities. Armed with comprehensive knowledge, the technical manager starts things off by assuming the responsibility of positive leadership. The positive leader believes that problems can be solved; goals can be achieved; and, when working together, the sum of all will greatly exceed the individual contributions of those involved.

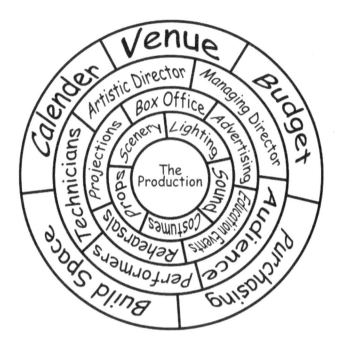

FIGURE 4.1 Production elements

INDIVIDUAL NEEDS

While the technical manager maintains responsibility for the overall endeavor, every effective leader must recognize that most projects cannot be completed without the efforts of many (fig. 4.1). The technical manager is called to create an environment where individuals will be self-motivated, acting not just because they are directed or due to pressure by peers, but rather because they recognize that their actions are a critical part of an artistic whole. The inherent collaborative nature of production makes this approach all the stronger.

Progress and performance are directly related to the technical manager's expectations and treatment of personnel. As a rule, when high performance goals are set, they can and will be achieved. Self-aware technical managers recognize this quality of great expectations in themselves and apply it to the individuals they are leading. When more is asked, people try harder and generally produce better results. The challenges, therefore, are to find practical ways to address individual needs and to have all involved focus on the effort.

A foundational motivational tool is responding to the needs of those being led. Individual needs start with the essentials like rest, shelter, and food and progress all the way up to an expectations of understood value, self-esteem, and fulfillment.

FIGURE 4.2 Maslow's Hierarchy of Needs

Maslow's Hierarchy of Needs (fig. 4.2) is a long-recognized illustration of human need rankings. Unless the lowest tier needs are met, it is pretty much impossible to reach the top levels of achievement.

The successful technical manager is aware of these baseline human needs and takes practical actions to address them. Workdays are scheduled with meal breaks and appropriate rest periods. Individual contributions are placed in context with the overall project. Informing a staff member of how his or her specific effort is contributing to the whole greatly helps to keep each person motivated. Credit is given where credit is due, and accountability is held high so that all can understand the impact of their work. The occasional purchase of donuts in the morning or a spur-of-the-moment after-work happy hour are also deeply appreciated. These seemingly small gestures can go a long way to building up the strength of a production team.

RECRUITING & SUPPORTING

Connected with meeting individual needs is the establishment of an atmosphere of fair and equitable accountability by the technical manager. Staff accountability must be carefully spelled out. Detailing expectations is one function of a well-written staff handbook. A handbook can have everything from corporate philosophy statements to detailed information about wage and hour laws. Such a document articulates both formal policies and anticipated procedures, resulting in a basic yardstick to measure performance against, to inform all involved of expectations, and to assign accountability.

One way to establish personal accountability is for the technical manager to distinguish those decisions that can be made by workers without report, those that can be made and followed up only by a report to the supervisor, and finally those decisions that must be brought back for consultation to the technical manager prior to any action being taken. Establishing this understanding sets ground rules to address future problems and helps leverage the overall talent who have been assembled.

In order to make accountability valid, the actions of staff must be followed up. Follow-up may be the single most important factor in the success or failure of working with staff. A technical manager needs to develop an inherent understanding of when best to check in, when best to delegate to the stronger skill set of another, and when best to insert his or her own ideas into a work effort. Having the humility to understand one's own limitations and the courage to ask for help when needed adds to both credibility and success. Follow-up with specific feedback also provides a learning opportunity and sparks growth in the individual, further benefiting the organization.

DEFINING THE POSITION AND FUNCTION

As part of the job description, a technical manager has the responsibility to define the tasks that need to be done and then connect with staff for the purpose of successfully addressing those tasks. Lacking definition or specific assignments, people simply put in their time and don't bring their best, so a fundamental challenge is to define the goals and directions of any project. In working toward the clarity level for success, a technical manager needs an inherent unwillingness to accept half-truths, foggy interpretations, and unclear goals. A baseline expectation of honesty and integrity in all exchanges and a clearly articulated vision is a must. The better defined the problem, challenge, or opportunity, the more likely the success.

By establishing both clarity of thought and high standards of performance, a technical manager can rightfully expect others to align with these values, putting away self-interest and placing the project and the advancement of the organization at the forefront. There must be a sense of mission instilled in each staff member, and there must be appropriate recognition given for productivity. A shared attitude with clarity of purpose is a significant advantage for any arts organization and truly serves to harness the talents of the assembled team.

AFFIRMATION

In order to recognize the value of others' work, one must recognize and relate to each individual's strengths. Technical managers, as well as all others involved in a project, have a unique set of skills and abilities that they bring to the work effort. Through recognition of self, you can see in others how they contribute and respond accordingly with positive affirmation. Positive affirmation includes specific reinforcement, immediacy, and an understanding of context. A sincere thank you, a direct compliment, and even a brief public acknowledgment can go a long way in keeping staff motivated and happy. Take note that these intangible rewards should be offered in the context of appropriate financial compensation and workplace policies.

Being an advocate for the staff is also a critical role for an effective technical manager. As a frontline supervisor of both projects and people, the technical manager is in a unique position to fully understand the breadth of operation and the depth of talent in an organization. Whether speaking to improved working conditions or just informing upper management of successes, the technical manager can be an effective conduit to others to keep them informed and to help to advance the overall success of any operation.

> If anything goes bad, I did it.
> If anything goes semi-good, then we did it.
> If anything goes real good, then you did it.
>
> Bear Bryant, Univ. of Alabama Head Football Coach

People do their best work and are more content when they can complete within a specified time a definite job for which they have an aptitude. Fortunately,

SERVANT STRIKE ASSIGNMENTS

	Debra	Jim	George	David	Toni
Capacities	Head carpenter— Direct load-in	Outstanding metal working skills	Strong and well organized	Responsible for all soft goods	Responsible for all properties
Task #1	Photograph for restoration guidance	Reweld center railing of the house	Strike practical lanterns	Strike S.R. Legs	Strike all props to storage
Task #2	Label lower flooring panels	Remove all remaining railings	Strike masking flats to studio North wall	Remove door shutters Stretch goal	Pack props for storage
Task #3	Strike awning and drop rigging lines	Strike pipes and return to stock	Strike upper level walls	Strike step units	Sort hardware back into stock

FIGURE 4.3 Task assignment chart

nearly all the performing arts rely on this basic concept. Fostering an environment appropriate for the maximum performance of personnel is a significant element of any technical manager's job. While mechanical efficiency of machinery can be measured, the capacity of a single, motivated individual, when properly cared for and appropriately tied into the work effort, is beyond measure.

In assigning tasks, the technical manager contributes his or her own experience and insights to each effort. The technical manager does not do the job for someone but rather shares best practices and suggests approaches, allowing the staff member to take ownership of the given task. Once parameters are understood and the project is launched, staff members are responsible to furnish solutions, not problems. The technical manager approaches the task at hand with the effective delegation, empowerment of individuals, and regular monitoring of performance and progress (fig. 4.3).

CHALLENGING & AFFIRMING

Aligning skill sets with opportunities is a fundamental task of the technical manager. Often this effort goes for the path of least resistance. "I know that Sally has done this task successfully in the past; therefore, let's give this one to Sally." This can be a most effective management approach, but from time to time the technical manager should be aware of his or her obligation to the staff to enable them to develop additional skills and achieve personal growth. Sometimes a challenging assignment is just what is called for to increase satisfaction and expand the potential and talent of the workforce. This approach of taking the occasional risk with a staff member also develops an inherent depth chart of talent and is greatly beneficial to the organization in the long run.

Within the producing organization, the technical manager must help to establish an environment where feedback is standard and evaluation is constant. Feedback is useful in that it allows the technical manager to evaluate the present and aids in charting the course for the future. Feedback conversations or timely check-ins throughout a project should focus on results, specifically productivity and achievement. In addition, a pattern of standard job reviews conducted at least annually give the chance for both the technical manager and the staff member to look objectively at the performance of the individual as well as the performance of the organization, recognizing both strengths and challenges. Honest evaluation takes real courage and great trust but is essential for success.

The brief check-in or progress review conversation typically includes these questions:

1. How is it going?

2. What challenges are you facing?
3. What additional support would make the task easier to more likely create an opportunity for success?

In such a progress review, the project under discussion is assessed through the lens of the original objectives, making comparison as to what has been accomplished to date to that which was projected. Once answered, the suggested, basic questions can lead to rapid adjustment in provided resources, schedule modifications, and expectation changes. Goals can be raised and demands increased or additional resources may be brought to bear to assure greater success informed by the knowledge of the current status of the project. Depending on the phase of the project at hand, these brief check-ins can be scheduled daily, weekly, or even monthly. What is critical is to develop a pattern where such contact and feedback is standard operating procedure within the organization. Every project or work effort review is a chance for improvement in productivity, performance, and completion schedule.

EVALUATION/PERFORMANCE REVIEW

Individual work evaluation reviews should take on a more formal approach that begins with a known record of job performance measured against clearly articulated expectations. The bedrock of these expectations is the previously discussed job description. A well-written job description provides a framework from which performance can be measured and expectations can be understood. The formal performance review provides concrete feedback of job performance that acknowledges both excellence and areas for improvement. Many companies that employ technical managers will have required systems in place to evaluate employee performance, but regardless of the process the technical manager embraces such effort as a vital tool.

An evaluation conversation is a two-way street, a shared journey with the goal of empowering an employee to do his or her very best, while at the same time advancing the organization toward goals of effectiveness and achievement. Due to the personal nature of this type of exchange, this review should always be conducted face to face and should be scheduled so as not be a surprise. The process is an ongoing cycle of performance planning, including feedback between supervisor and employee, that can focus on coaching for advancement (continuing education), performance evaluation (goals achieved), reward (salary increase) or modification (job change) or correction (reassignment), and a return to the planning stage (what's next?). Nothing in the review should come as a surprise to the employee. Any written

	Performance Period: 7/1/2015–6/30/2016
Employee Name:_____	

CURRENT APPRAISAL

1. List significant contributions and achievements during performance period.

2. Cite the results achieved for performance objectives for the position.

3. Identify any new tasks or additional duties taken on outside of your regular duties.

4. Note any professional development activities taken.

PLANNING AHEAD

5. Project at least three mission critical goals to accomplish in the next 12-month period.

6. Provide any other comments to inform this review.

EXCHANGE

We have discussed the above and confirm its accuracy.

Employee:_____   Supervisor:_____
Date:_____   Date:_____

FIGURE 4.4 Sample evaluation form

documentation should reinforce conversations/objectives/issues raised throughout the year (fig. 4.4).

Effective evaluation is far more than a reward-and-punishment system; rather, it is one of the most powerful planning tools available to the technical manager for maximizing performance, development, and job satisfaction among employees. Additionally, the exchange should be documented with some basic notes regarding what was discussed and articulating a refined new set of goals and objectives for the next review. A good practice is to have both parties sign off on the notes taken to verify their accuracy and acknowledge their importance for ongoing improvement of both the individual and the organization.

One of the best ways to approach evaluation with an employee is to develop shared **SMART** expectations for their role within the producing organization.

- **S**pecific—detailed and clearly identified results
- **M**easurable—metrics such as time, standards, quality levels
- **A**ttainable—challenging but realistic within the available Time, Talent, and Money
- **R**elevant (results oriented)—of value to the organization
- **T**ime bound—clear due dates (often openings and closings)

Establishing **SMART** objectives in concert with an employee often results in both greater personal and professional satisfaction. Even when not meeting previously identified goals, value can emerge, for at least two things can be learned from such failures. The first is the discovery of what doesn't work, and the second is the opportunity to try something new, often resulting in an even better solution. People who claim to never have failed have not been trying hard enough or possess an appropriate willingness to take risks. Long-term failure of any kind cannot be sustained, but short-term failures often lead to the greatest advances for any organization.

Another effective tool for performance evaluation is to break an individual's job down into broad, banded categories of expected areas of competency and then rank them with a numeric score supported by narrative comments. Categories could include:

- Customer service
- Collaboration
- Teamwork
- Change
- Innovation
- Skills
- Leadership

35

The numeric score enables easy cross-personnel comparison and can be used as a simple indicator of progress toward goals, while the narrative documentation forms a record of the conversation and identifies expectations for future evaluation. Performance objectives articulate a goal as well as provide a specific completion timeline. Open-ended expectations are difficult to enforce, whereas those with greater specificity are more easily evaluated. (I want to lose weight is too open; I want to lose 10 pounds over the next two months is measurable.)

Occasionally during the evaluation process, it may become necessary to be critical of a staff member's performance or to address an error that has been made. When handled correctly, such criticism can be a positive experience. The goal of a corrective conversation is to focus on the act and not the person. Keep in mind that your reprimand is for poor performance. Separate, as much as possible, what the person did from how you are feeling about it. State that an error has been committed, that others have made similar mistakes in the past, that those in the past learned from their errors, and that you have confidence that the staff member in question will as well. Then go on to elaborate how you feel the current error can be addressed and how future errors could be prevented. Remind the staff that, despite the error, everyone remains a valuable and worthwhile part of the production team.

When making such a correction, be specific about the error and the proposed remedy. The more specific the conversation, the less likely the critical comments will be seen as a personal attack. Avoid generalities and utilize reflective listening skills to make the conversation as clear as possible. Be sensitive to the time and place of such a conversation, and under no circumstances should correction be conducted in front of others. Criticism is difficult enough to handle without the knowledge that your peers may be overhearing every word that is being said. Correct in private, praise in public.

Often, your sense of humor may be a useful tool in lessening the tension in a critical conversation. However, be mindful of its use; inappropriate humor can often be misconstrued and increase rather than decrease the challenge of the conversation at hand. Gauge your use of humor based on past experiences with the person being critiqued. If the situation becomes edgy, be willing to set the joking aside for the time being.

All review and evaluation conversations, whether progress or performance, should provide time for a true exchange between the parties involved, i.e., a conversation rather than a monologue. To facilitate the conversation, a draft of any written evaluation should be provided in advance to the person under review. This prevents the person reading the materials in front of the supervisor and gives him or her the chance to prepare a response, partially leveling the playing field of knowledge. As suggested, face-to-face feedback requires a commitment to honesty and a willingness to take risks. In the role of a leader, a technical manager models a level of openness in such exchanges that can set a tone throughout an organization. The personnel that the technical manager is charged with leading are an almost limitless resources of energy, creativity, and productivity when led effectively. Effective leadership requires both candor and diplomacy.

CONFLICT MANAGEMENT/RESOLUTION

From time to time, a conflict will undoubtedly arise between a technical manager and a staff member, or between two staff members, and some intervention will be required. Conflict management and resolution are learned skills, and there are literally volumes written on the subject that can be consulted. Nearly all references, however, follow the basic guidelines for addressing a conflicted situation shown in figure 4.5 and detailed in the paragraphs following.

1. **Commit to treating those involved with respect to build the trust necessary to work through the problem.** All too often, the commitment among staff gets broken when lack of respect for the efforts of others is given and an assumption is made that not all are working toward the same goal. While this loss of focus of the group may occasionally be true, most of the time a gentle reminder that all are indeed working toward the same outcome can help to reset the boundaries of respect.

CONFLICT MANAGEMENT GUIDELINES

1. Treat those involved with respect to build the essential trust.
2. Learn about the various positions on the topic of the disagreement.
3. Use reflective listening to affirm what is being heard and seek clarification.
4. Be direct with the person involved in the dispute.
5. Focus on the matter at hand and not on the underlying motives.
6. Take ownership of your own feelings and concerns within the conversation.
7. Whenever possible, identify points of agreement early on.
8. Recognize your authority to resolve conflict, but use your power sparingly.
9. Take the time necessary to resolve the conflict, within limits.

FIGURE 4.5 Conflict management guidelines

2. **Be vigilant in learning about the various positions that are present on the topic of the disagreement.** An effective technical manager understands that every issue involves multiple perspectives and strives to at least develop a basic understanding of the views of others. While there are often multiple views on how to effectively address a challenge, the greater the depth of knowledge that the technical manager has about the whole issue, the more likely a successful resolution will be found.

3. **Make use of reflective listening to affirm what is being heard and to seek clarification.** Reflective listening requires listeners to state what they think they heard before adding additional information into the conversation. "I think I hear you saying that the lack of light in this corner of the studio is one of the reasons for your decreased productivity. If I am correct, what would be the challenges of relocating your project to a better illuminated space?" Once what has been said has been confirmed, progress can be made on the next point in the conversation.

4. **Be direct with the person involved in the dispute.** All too often, we are reticent to work directly with the person by whom we are challenged. Rehearsing a conversation with a knowledgeable but disinterested colleague may be of benefit, but discussing a conflict behind the back of those involved does nothing good to advance the discourse. The anxiety of facing a problem is quickly displaced by the relief when a dispute has been resolved. The technical manager should be vigilant in addressing disputes directly and as soon as possible.

5. **Focus on the matter at hand and not on the underlying motives.** Here, too, assumptions about the motivation of the other can create additional challenges for us. Rarely, if ever, is it possible for the technical manager to fully put themselves in the shoes of the other, so while it is valuable to try to understand the perspective of the other person involved in the dispute, seeking out motivational answers is often a folly. Further, assuming that you fully understand the other person's position can undermine your ability to be open to a creative solution that you may not have already thought about.

6. **Take ownership of your own feelings and concerns within the conversation**. Simply put, there should be more "I" sentences than "you" sentences. "I am concerned about your progress on this project" is better than "Why are you falling behind?" Allow your personal experience with the situation to inform your approach, but avoid preconceived notions that may get in the way of your clarity of thought.

7. **Whenever possible, identify points of agreement early on.** Establishing common ground often helps to diffuse the situation and adds to the development of the trust necessary to work through

the problem. At a minimum, we need to define the conflict under consideration with similar terms. Just arriving at a common definition is a significant step toward conflict resolution.

8. **Recognize your authority to bring a conflict to resolution, but use your power sparingly.** Taking the stand of "my way or the highway" may provide temporary relief and get things moving forward, but that approach more than likely won't address the underlying issues of the disagreement. More often than not, when this approach is taken, the conflict is reduced for a period of time but quickly flares up again with even greater intensity. Giving individuals a chance to be heard and potentially impact change can be a highly effective way to reduce conflict.

9. **Take the time necessary to resolve the conflict, *within limits*.** Conflict resolution takes time, and sometimes the window of opportunity is just too narrow to seize or is made even more complex by other circumstances. Generally speaking, the sooner resolution occurs, the better for all involved. This may also be a good time to seek out additional helpful resources to assist in bringing a conflict to a close, including other trusted staff, human resources managers, or consultants. At a minimum, it may be possible to get conflicted parties to agree to temporarily set aside their differences to advance the group's effort, with the promise that, once certain achievements have occurred, the technical manager promises to revisit the situation. By essentially tabling the conflict, cooler heads may be present when the group returns to the resolution process.

The last paragraph uses the word "within limits." Sometimes it is necessary to simple move on and hope for the very best due to other scheduling challenges. This is quite different from simply ignoring a situation, but it is rather "putting it on the shelf" or "in the parking lot" until it can be addressed. Informing the conflicted parties at this stage that this is the plan for now and promising a specific revisit time may allow the larger effort to make progress and may dissipate the conflict so that it is easier to address in the future. However, returning to the matter and fully addressing it remains an obligation that must be met.

Once in a great while, the only effective solution to a personnel matter is to end the working relationship. This can involve either reassignment to a different role or termination and separation from the organization. Here, too, effectively managing those involved is complex but necessary. Assuming other means have failed, the time may arrive to let someone go. Dismissal conversations are never easy, but the more direct and businesslike the technical manager can make them, the better. The technical manager must delicately balance the need to make the organization's wishes clear and treat the individual being dismissed in such a way for him or her to maintain self-respect.

Assuming that adequate and accurate feedback has been provided throughout the work effort, rarely do the actions of dismissal come as a complete surprise. Still, the finality of the event combined with what has often been a complex history, and often other failures of communication, makes for such a moment to be emotion filled. Here, too, the dismissal conversation should be held in private, but a third-part observer is highly recommended to witness the exchange and verify the event that occurs. The technical manager should get right to the point, cite specific reasons for determining dismissal, and provide written documentation outlining the result. By showing respect for the individual involved, despite the inherent differences creating the challenge, the technical manager supports the dignity of the person. Many a fine individual has had to part ways with an organization, only to go on most rapidly to bigger and better things.

While managing personnel is challenging, the effective relationships that can develop within an arts organization are often most rewarding. The collaborative nature of the work that is done breeds lasting relationships and creates a common bond among those involved. The technical manager has much to celebrate when the collective efforts of the group achieve the goals as outlined, on time, on budget, and with minimal strife.

Chapter 5

Communication

Communication forms the connections between the three aspects of the Time, Talent, Money Triangle, making it similar to the connective tissue of the human body. An effective technical manager makes use of various methods and modes of communication and, with practice, becomes expert at selecting the appropriate method to achieve specific project goals. Communication is about the transmittal of information that needs to be shared by many in order to create a whole. The associated skills are key to everything that occurs in all sectors of the entertainment world. President Thomas Jefferson tells us why it is so important to communicate.

> When you don't keep people informed you get one of three things: rumor, apathy or revolution.
>
> Thomas Jefferson

Clearly, none of these three outcomes is desirable. To ensure such outcomes do not occur, technical managers ideally have proficient communication skills and further hone their abilities to rapidly determine what needs to be communicated and how best to get that message across. Given the common refrains regarding miscommunication as the root of confusion, lost time, and misdirected energy, keep in mind that if something can be misunderstood, it probably will be. This is not meant to signal inevitable despair but to alert us to be mindful in all we attempt through our communications. While we will discuss the K.I.S.S. principle later on as well, the message it contains is to keep communication simple and direct. The more direct the means used to deliver information, the more likely the information will be correctly heard.

From an analytic viewpoint, all forms of communication involve two parties: one, a transmitter or source (a technical manager), and two, one or more receivers, e.g., staff members. The rationale behind the need to communicate

Communication Mode	Action	Means
Verbal	Words	■ Face to face ■ Telephone ■ Voice mail
Physical	Kinesthetic actions	■ Body language ■ Gesture
Graphic	Visual image	■ Drawings ■ Sketches ■ Charts
Written	Visual text	■ Memos ■ Letters ■ Books

FIGURE 5.1 Four modes of communication

is to share essential information. If, after transmitting the information, staff does not correctly understand the manager's intentions, the technical manager has failed as a communicator and the project at hand is in jeopardy. Regardless, the onus to rectify the situation remains the technical manager's responsibility. Hopefully the technical manager realizes that the communication was not successful and makes another attempt to clarify the task before work commences.

There are four principal modes of communication, as shown in figure 5.1. Three serve as the basis of the ideas discussed in both chapters 5 and 6, as we examine both commonplace and specific uses of verbal, graphic, and written communication skills necessary to the many who fit the description of technical manager. The fourth mode, physical communication (primarily understood as gesture and body language), will not be discussed in detail because its scope is large and merits an entire other book. While admittedly it is awkward to separate these behaviors, we've done so in order to provide an appropriate overview of the proficiencies a technical manager must have to perform to a level of mutual satisfaction.

Although most of us assume that communication skills come naturally, sadly this is not so. There is much to be learned in order to be an effective communicator. The term "effective communicator" describes a person able to share knowledge, transmit decisions, and make others aware of his or her plans for the project before the group. Figure 5.2 notes three factors that should be considered when disseminating information.

FACTORS WHEN DISSEMINATING INFORMATION

- Know what you want to communicate.
- Make your delivery clear and understandable.
- Present your information with authority.

FIGURE 5.2 Three factors when disseminating information

VERBAL COMMUNICATION

Listening and speaking consume over two-thirds of the time we spend communicating with each other. To be successful, a technical manager must be engaged, an active listener, and a skilled speaker. Comprehending what others say and responding clearly, either one on one or in a group situation, are two of the most valuable skills a technical manager can develop. Communication informs Time, Talent, Money Triangle connections, with listening and speaking skills the elemental building blocks of those connections.

Verbal communication has one strong advantage over the other modes of communication being discussed—immediate feedback. Being sensitive to listener reaction helps a speaker identify the extent to which information is truly being transmitted and received and allows the speaker to modify what is being said in order to improve the conveyance of the information. While most human beings have the ability to comprehend spoken communication, surprisingly few are actually skilled active listeners. This condition makes speaker awareness even more critical.

After a conversation or presentation has begun, participants hopefully continuously switch roles. Besides being the speaker, the technical manager must also assume the role of **active listener**. As an active listener, a technical manager must focus on the individual speaking, striving to be fully engaged with the speaker—often called being "in the moment." Active listeners typically demonstrate engagement by maintaining good eye contact with the speaker, leaning forward to signal through body language a connection with what the speaker is stating, occasionally nodding their head as an indication of understanding, and asking clarifying questions.

While few of us are born active listeners, having some appreciation of good listening skills is the first step to turn into an active listener. Focusing on the information being exchanged, keeping an open mind to the ideas being presented, avoiding interruptions, and taking both mental and/or written notes to help recall the information being shared are all key steps. Additionally, active listening skills

---

USEFUL QUESTIONS WILL . . .

- Be open ended
- Avoid predetermined favorable answers
- Better the discussion
- Ask for one answer at a time
- Be followed up by another question
- Inquire, not interrogate
- Be asked, even if unclear in the asker's mind

FIGURE 5.3 Crafting questions

OPEN QUESTION		CLOSED QUESTION
What's today's progress on the staircase construction?		Is the staircase done?
Where are the texture samples for us to consider?	vs.	Is that the texture we are using?
How can we make the best use of stage time Tuesday?		Can we use the stage at 2:00?

FIGURE 5.4 Open vs. closed questions

are enhanced by having an ability to summarize the ideas presented by the other person and an aptitude to ask articulate questions to further the exchange of information. The clearest exchanges of information usually occur when a carefully fashioned question is asked and answered. Some aspects to keep in mind when crafting questions are enumerated in figure 5.3 and discussed further in the following text.

Good questions should:

- **Be open ended.** Open-ended questions require the responder to supply something beyond a simple "yes" or "no" answer (fig. 5.4). An open-ended question invites the responder to share their insights about the topic and shows respect for the thoughts and opinions of others. Our closed-end-question habit is difficult to change, but when we ask open-ended questions, we learn more in-depth information about each other's thoughts and feelings. While democratic in principle, the process requires more time but is usually well worth the investment.
- **Do not seek predetermined answers.** All of us have been in situations where someone asks questions hoping to receive a reply that aligns with what the questioner wants to hear. Sensing this

uncomfortable situation, we struggle to ascertain the person's desired response rather than allow ourselves to focus on the issue under discussion.

- **Better the discussion.** Each question should serve as the foundation for a follow-up point so that progress is made toward achieving a solution or, barring resolution, further a better exchange of information.
- **Solicit one answer at a time.** People can only process and respond to one question at a time. Although the information you need may have many facets, asking question one at a time and then waiting for a response will allow you to more efficiently and effectively achieve your goal.
- **Follow up previous remarks.** Follow-up questions lead to further exploration of the subject and the opportunity to gain greater depth of knowledge. Follow-up questions also offer a degree of reinforcement and feedback to the responder by acknowledging the other person's responses.
- **Encourage queries and avoid interrogation.** Inquiry affirms interest in what the responder has to say. Interrogation places a person on the defensive, consequently preventing a healthy exchange. Inquiry breaks down barriers while interrogation builds them up.
- **Be asked, even if the asker feels uncomfortable.** Although a rather trite expression, it is nevertheless very true: "The only dumb question is the one that remains unasked." None of us should ever be afraid of being judged foolish by merely asking a question. While we universally recognize that only fools remain silent, do not participate, and make assumptions, we also know this is hard for many of us to do.

There are a few other matters that may hinder full participation. These are:

- When responding to questions, **avoid being an echo.** There are only two reasons for repeating an answer: one, to reinforce the fact that you are in agreement with the response; and two, to ensure that others have heard what was said who might have missed the remark the first time.
- **Receive the response graciously.** When someone answers your question, he or she is taking a risk by sharing a small part of him/herself. Recognize the effort even though you may not agree with the answer given.
- **Do not underestimate the strength of silence.** Many individuals find the silence that occurs during a conversation to be uncomfortable. Recognize that by being silent you allow communication to unfold naturally, and you buy yourself some mental processing time. Processing time can also be found by capitalizing on the difference between the

usual rate of thinking (250 to 500 words per minute) and the rate of speaking (100 to 150 words per minute). The gap between these two times allows you to listen carefully and at the same time to think of an appropriate response, the former being the most important.

PUBLIC SPEAKING

Although we seldom encounter technical managers who are polished public speakers, these skills have become more and more important in recent years. Just as each technical manager needs to be skilled as a one-on-one conversationalist, group (large and small audience) public speaking skills are equally valuable. These are acquired skills; few, if any, of us are naturals in this arena. While becoming more polished, be mindful that nearly everyone has some degree of stage fright that they need to overcome. The best, and probably only, way to get over this fear is to get up and do it. With practice comes both ability and confidence.

When speaking to others, there are really just two key concerns: **eye contact** and **volume**. Actually, these same elements apply to both intimate and group communication. Whether speaking to an individual, small groups of three to five people, or to a large audience, always maintain eye contact. This simple technique helps both audience and presenter to relax and makes communication more comfortable for everyone. In group presentations, the most successful approach is to zero in on one or several members of the group and make direct eye contact with selected individuals. Don't simply look over the heads of those present (or the floor) or stay focused on one person or area for too long. Instead, move your eyes from direct contact to direct contact, attempting to engage all in what you are saying.

Similarly, when speaking to a group, it is important to know your own vocal qualities. We all have idiosyncrasies, both in casual conversation and especially in these more formal situations. Your personal evaluation should analyze both volume and any vocal patterns you might have, such as the "ums, likes, buts, and oks" that frequently interrupt the flow of the message. These little fillers can become irritating to audiences and will greatly distract from your presentation.

If the presentation is held in a formal setting, such as a conference break-out room, and the opportunity is available, practice beforehand in the same space your presentation will be given. Formal settings usually require that we speak in a louder voice than normal; if you think you are talking slightly too loudly, you are probably at the right volume. If a mic is available, check the sound system with the aid of a trusted listener. Mockup exact presentation conditions as much as possible; no shortcuts.

Body language is important, too. Learn to be relaxed and avoid moving around too much, leaning on a prop such as a podium, or being too dependent on notes. Lift your head to facilitate eye contact, and make every effort to enunciate; your diction must be crisp and clear. Be deliberate and conversational in tone, but speak more slowly than you do in normal conversation. Gage your pace so that your audience has enough time for your remarks sink in. Two important rules to keep in mind: first, you owe it to the audience to be prepared; and second, practice, practice, practice.

GIVING DIRECTION TO PROJECT STAFF

The last, but certainly not the least, face-to-face verbal communication skill needed to be an effective technical manager is the ability to **convey direction**, both to individuals and to groups. This task is the principal rationale for the existence of technical management.

Assuming the technical manager is a master craftsman of sorts, most managers target product results equal in quality to what they believe they personally could produce. This goal can only be accomplished by providing clear directions. Commonly, directives include a project overview, instruction in the order and manner of activity expected, and the prudent assignment of individuals and groups to take on the task. Some of the major methodologies are shown in figures 5.5 and 5.6, followed by further description.

When giving directions:

- **Know what you plan to say before speaking.** If indecision and lack of confidence underlie the message being delivered, confusion is the only result.
- **Before starting, provide an overview** of where the project fits into the big picture. Instructions given within a context afford staff a better

---

STEPS FOR GIVING EFFECTIVE DIRECTIONS
- Get the receiver's attention.
- Specify the goal(s) of the task.
- Review visual materials that may be of help—drawings, sketches.
- Be clear about what must be followed precisely.
- Suggest a starting sequence.
- Forewarn anticipated difficulties.
- Review any safety concerns.
- Offer contact information for clarity.
- Have receiver repeat back what he or she has heard.
- Check back for follow-up confirmation and further assistance.

FIGURE 5.5 Giving effective directions

Drawings Have Value in Communication Sharing

A shop drawing or quick sketch can effectively communicate, clearly and concisely, the design and construction elements of a production and their many components. The drawing enables visualization of the project by describing critical information like size and shape and helps to raise questions and provide answers.

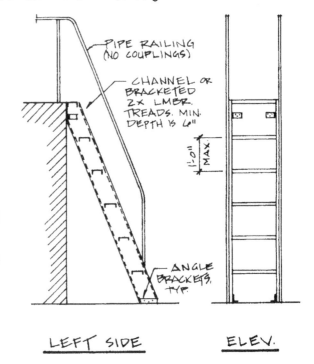

FIGURE 5.6 Value of drawings

understanding of the project, which in turn leads them to be more likely to ask follow-up clarifying questions.

- **Articulate where the assignment fits into the project's priorities.** Stating the priority at the beginning of the process will likely trigger more attentive listening.
- **Follow a logical sequence.** Mentally walk through each step necessary to complete a task and deliver the information in that order. Work from beginning to end, not the other way around.
- **Utilize the K.I.S.S. principle.** "Keep it simple, stupid!" Avoid instructional overload; too much detail will confuse even the most astute staff members.
- **Use visuals to clarify your instructions.** Sketches, models, research photos, and working drawings all serve to rapidly and

comprehensively convey large amounts of information. Quality visuals are a big boon to staff trying to fully understand a project's scope.

- **Accompany your presentation with written and/or graphic instructions**, a.k.a. shop drawings. Paper instructions serve to answer questions when you are not around and provide staff an even greater level of detail than verbal instructions alone allow.
- **Address people by their name.** Nothing helps get people's attention more than hearing their own name. By speaking directly to a person by name, you communicate respect and make the listener even more likely to listen carefully.
- **Have a confirming conversation** with the individuals involved to assure that your message has been perceived correctly. Probably the most effective technique to determine this is to have the person to whom you are speaking repeat what you have said in his or her own words.
- **Solicit staff views rather than issuing directives.** This may seem a minor point, but people are much more responsive being asked rather than told to do something.
- **Divide your instructions into manageable work units.** Logical units of information can be based on the number of individuals assigned to an effort and/or the level of complexity demanded by the project. The entire group of workers requires the overview, but once done, specific instruction to each team of two will advance the project more quickly.
- **Refer to source materials** that support the intended plan. The technical manager is under no obligation to justify his or her action plan by sharing the entire history of the project to the crew. However, a few background statements reinforcing the origin of the plan give the staff a different level of understanding about the project.
- **Show your appreciation** throughout the effort. Perhaps two of the most important phrases in any technical manager's vocabulary are "please" and "thank you." Everyone needs encouragement from time to time, and the recognition of efforts, given with genuine appreciation, goes a long way toward supporting staff and increasing productivity.

As a brief summary of these important verbal communication skills, we ardently note two basic and very important principles that all technical managers should never forget: **honesty** and **respect**. Honesty begets honesty and serves only to reinforce the reputation of the technical manager and the quality of the work environment. Respect is key to all interpersonal contact. Respect sets the tone in which the message is delivered. The question "What is this?" can be expressed with kindness and the inquisitiveness of youth or as a soul-crushing backhand. Learning and addressing a person by name is a good start to assuring staff that their contributions are valued and equal to yours, even if each possesses differing skill sets. Tone makes a difference.

PHONE COMMUNICATION

While there has been much to say about face-to-face communication competences, in today's world there is a whole other side of personal communication. Many—for some people, most—communications are electronic and involve only phone, text, and email exchanges. As a sense of the importance of our voices, strong friendships are often formed by people who speak to each other only on the telephone, folks who have never met in person.

Because technical managers spend so much time researching processes, procuring materials, and coordinating efforts with people outside their personal workplace, developing skills for both incoming and outgoing calls is very important. Before placing a call, take a moment to think though the purpose of the call and determine the best approach to get the information you need. Project in your mind who might answer, what might be said, and how you might respond. Consider the path the call is likely to take (receptionist → contact → supervisor, etc.) and plan accordingly.

When calling a vendor or manufacturer for information, the first person to answer the phone is rarely the person who can provide the needed answer. Provide the receptionist only such information as will help forward your call to the appropriate person. Most vendors would like to know your name; your organization; and the department, material, or service that you are researching. Plan ahead so you can ask your question(s) in a direct manner and subsequently be connected to the right person without being wasteful of everyone's time.

Too often, due to most technical managers' lacking an aptitude for office organization, a scrap piece of paper or individual sheets of a yellow pad are used to jot down the information gathered during a phone call. A more beneficial idea is to maintain a simple phone log of all incoming and outgoing calls. A good tool for this purpose is a center-divided stenographer's pad. Incoming calls and messages can be recorded in the left column, and your response with written notes can be listed on the right. Your log serves as a record of phone activities and helps keep a paper trail of earlier inquiries, contacts, and quotations. Whatever format you choose, be sure that it is a comfortable size and not overly cumbersome. Keep your record keeping simple and make it a daily habit.

Important data to retain is the date, time, and purpose of each call. Never fail to record the name of the person (doesn't hurt to confirm the spelling) who provided you with the needed information. The latter is especially important in purchasing situations since price quotations often vary, sometimes significantly, dependent on the person who gave them.

Since not every technical manager sits at a desk all day, leaving a voice message has become de rigueur. While the process doesn't seem overly complex, the person leaving the message needs to be mindful of several important aspects. One, leave your name and number, speaking slowly and clearly. Those two pieces of information are the most vital being exchanged; they must be distinctly communicated.

When speaking to an electronic device, leave as succinct a message as possible. First, state your name and phone number (taking the time to spell out your name and repeat your number). Proceed with a brief explanation for calling, and indicate your desired response. Finally, just before completing the message, again give your name and restate your number, this time digit by digit.

WRITTEN COMMUNICATION

The very act of reading this book indicates you possess some mastery of understanding written communication. Excellent reading skills are assumed as a prerequisite for success as a technical manager. However, equally important and far more difficult to master than reading skills are writing skills. Examples of typical written communication shared by technical managers are memoranda, specifications, drawing notes, proposals, letters, evaluations, and published articles. Good writing is a skill that takes both a lifelong commitment and daily effort. A technical manager cannot be all talk; each individual leader must have the appropriate paperwork to back up talking points.

The goal of carefully crafted writing in any of its many forms is fourfold, as noted in figure 5.7.

Clear writing involves writing, editing, rewriting, and reviewing. Writing notes and jotting down thoughts may help you personally become more mentally organized, but at the point you wish to share your ideas, you must write clearly. Clarity implies that you have already thought through that which you intend to say, organized the material, and effectively formatted it prior to its distribution. To check for clarity, review what you have written, looking for possible ways in which a message can be misconstrued. If you find a problem, edit and rewrite the statement. Then leave your draft to sit for a time or have someone else look over what you have written. Another pair of eyes, even if not completely

---

WRITING GOALS
Be . . . Clear
. . . Correct
. . . Concise
. . . Complete

FIGURE 5.7 Fourfold goal of writing

knowledgeable of the subject, and the passage of time both afford a different point of view and support a refreshing exam of your work.

- **Correct writing** does not refer to the accuracy of writing but rather a person's compositional skills. A working knowledge of the conventions of punctuation, letter formats, memo structures, and literary citation is requisite to write correctly. Every technical manager should have access to, either on a bookshelf or an electronic communication device, a dictionary, a thesaurus, and especially a style guide such as the *MLA Handbook*; *The Chicago Manual of Style*; or the ever popular Strunk and White handbook, *The Elements of Style*.

- **Concise writing** is important to us all given the overwhelming amount of written material each of us digests on a daily basis— information overload is a likely result. As readers, we expect an author to get to the point and to not lose the message within a framework of "well-turned" phrases. Delivering information in a succinct efficient manner is the goal of concise writing. As a rule, short sentences are preferred over long ones; paragraphs should contain no more than three or four sentences; and prepositional phrases, a.k.a. "qualifiers," should be kept to a minimum. The use of bullets, headings, font changes, and eye-catching physical layouts help readers quickly ascertain the crux of written material and more fully comprehend its supporting material.

- **Complete writing** implies that a writer has fully thought through all the details of the communication. Those ideas are committed to paper in an easily understood form and provide a reader with a logical flow of information and conclusions. Complete writing, as a concept, follows a four-part formula (fig. 5.8) that serves as a mental check when evaluating any written communication. By ensuring that these four parts are incorporated, a technical manager will attain recognition as an articulate writer.

FOUR CRITICAL PARTS TO EFFECTIVE WRITTEN COMMUNICATION

INTRODUCTION	States both the purpose and the context of information being shared
SUMMARY	Outlines the contents of the writing and the desired outcome
BODY	Provides support for the summary and promotes understanding
CONCLUSION	Restates position and identifies next steps

FIGURE 5.8 Critical parts for effective writing

In many ways, **being a good writer means being a good editor**. Personal computers, tablets, and rapidly changing communication technologies have made this task infinitely easier than the time just a few decades past. These electronic tools let a writer copy, cut, and paste text and images, allowing us to rearrange words within a sentence and throughout a work. These gizmos, and the hundreds of others residing in software, make it possible to be more succinct writers and provide a level of finesse that has never before been possible.

Skilled writers create sentences that are stripped of superfluous words, and paragraphs are expunged of unnecessary sentences. The writer's overarching goal is to provide breadth of thought but with economy of expression. Given that much of the writing of technical managers will be specific and at times complex in nature, it is even more important to keep language terse, logically organized, and complete enough to be understood on its own merits. Flowery epithets have no place in technical communications.

Another useful rule of thumb, which will also help tighten up communications, is to use the **active voice** rather than the passive voice. For example, "I recommend" is more clear and concise than "It is my recommendation that . . ." Similarly, "twelve flats are complete" is more effective than "twelve flats have been completed." Again, economy in language is greatly aided by using the active voice.

Although the message usually differs, the form and the purpose for much of what technical managers write are similar in many ways. Subsequently, it is useful for any manager to develop personal or organizational standard formats (commonly called "templates") that will simplify the number of steps required to create a document; the resulting product being similar to a "fill-in-the-blanks" approach. Most word processing programs have built-in functions that support such tasks and make it easy to modify documents rather than start each from scratch. Similarly, a writer can transfer information from one document to another when appropriate, essentially creating personal boilerplate language.

There is another advantage to this approach. Over time, individuals will come to recognize your personal format and be more responsive because they have learned your personal sense of organization. So-called universal formats help readers to quickly identify the communication source and its likely content, even before they take the time to fully read the text. Most organizations employ standard layouts for memos, purchasing requests, company announcements, and similar applications.

Like most professions, the entertainment industry has a language (many languages, in fact) all its own, generated by the vast number of technological specialties in the industry. Technical managers will find **jargon** useful when communicating with colleagues in the same or similar fields, but they must be aware that these terms are unique to that small segment of the industry. When communications are addressed to individuals outside the field, and even more so individuals outside the entertainment arena, either avoid the jargon completely or provide brief definitions to make the terms comprehensible to all readers. Simple words

53

like "gaffer" and "nape" have unique meanings to entertainment electricians and costumers, respectively, but using them in communications with people not in the industry can render a memo or letter incomprehensible. Whenever and whatever you write, carefully consider the audience and write accordingly.

PROOFREADING YOUR WORK

All written communication should be proofread. Thankfully, spelling- and grammar-check features are standard elements of nearly all word processing software, but total reliance on these systems can be dangerous. Each writer is accountable for the content and quality of his or her written communication. Language checking features can't judge the appropriateness of a word that is spelled correctly but misused, insert missing words, or delete nonsequiturs. These all require human judgments. Writers are likewise judged by others when numerous such errors appear in their communications.

While quickly scanning the work before sending it is always appropriate, as noted earlier another approach involves taking some time away from the writing project before you proof it. Once a document is drafted, wait until the next day to finalize and print the letter or memo. This gives the author an opportunity to concentrate on what they have actually written rather than what they think they have written. Better proofreading is possible when some time has elapsed between the time the content was written and the time it is reviewed.

Another helpful tactic is to ask someone else to read the document and comment or mark it up. Unless the information is technically highly complex, finding a proofreader who is somewhat unfamiliar with the subject frequently provides the best results. That person usually needs to read more carefully and is quick to point out sentences that contain errors, both grammatical and contextual. Regardless the approach used, always proofread everything.

ELECTRONIC COMMUNICATIONS

Enormous changes in written communication have occurred due to the advent of electronic mail and text messaging. Currently social media, e.g., Facebook, Twitter, Google+, Linked-In, blogs, and the like, have expanded exponentially with no likely end in sight. Societally, we employ different standards to writing in each of these mediums. Social media is full of phonetic spellings, incomplete sentences and a whole host of issues that would make any English teacher cringe. This discussion focuses exclusively on email since it is the most similar to classical written communication and, for many, has become their primary written form of communication.

The email medium offers several great advantages. Readers control when they will take the time to read and respond to a message, and more information can be transmitted than shared on a phone message, especially when attachments are utilized. Best yet, all the information is verifiable, able to be reexamined as needed. Other advantages include transmission of graphics, as well as attachments, across differing computer platforms, and large "mailing lists" are easily assembled, which allow multiple copies of the same message to be delivered almost instantly at little or no cost. Different contact lists allow individuals to be added or deleted from receiving information intended for select audiences, all with a single click of a mouse or touchpad.

The promise that computer use would result in a paperless society has turned out to be only a myth. As the ease of producing of high-quality graphic material has increased, low content written work has expanded exponentially. Green-minded technical managers will strive at all times to generate as little printed material as possible and become efficient and dutiful filers of electronic documents. Using email whenever possible allows you to add your response(s) directly to initial and follow-up messages and can be inserted into your return copy of the corresponding communique. This practice creates an electronic "paper" trail, resulting in fewer piles of paper that seldom get read again or filed. A limited amount of print communication is necessary in every organization and is often personally useful, but in our current environment most information can stay in electronic form.

When paper copies must flow, their proliferation can be reduced using some shorthand techniques. For example, respond to memos and letters directly on the original, then return it to the sender. Often simply writing the word, "approved" on a request, along with a signature (initials) and date, is all that is necessary as a response. Should a record of your decision be desirable, scan the marked-up original and use the universal medium of a PDF document to electronically store it. Even this step is unnecessary if colleagues retain their original, with your response as a record of your approval. Should you need to refer to the matter again, you can simply request a copy from the sender. Two quick rules of filing: When in doubt, pitch it out, and never file something someone else will be filing.

Present-day server networks, accessed through or without the use of email, have made shared information the currently favored filing system for the distribution and access to routine memos, meeting minutes, and graphic design materials. Electronic storage and connection systems such as Local Area Networks (LAN), the "cloud," and services like "Dropbox" enable all forms of electronic data to be exchanged between users with only virtual storage of the shared material. The data resides elsewhere but is accessible to multiple users who require permission to access it. No physical record of the information actually ever exists. The reader then has the option to determine whether or not to print the document or just keep an electronic record.

EMAIL STRATEGIES

The rules for writing emails remain the same as those previously discussed: be clear, correct, concise, and complete. Some other helpful guidelines that apply include:

- **Keep responses short and to the point.** As a rule, do not exceed one screen full of text.

- **Recognize the tone of your email.** Since body language and vocal inflection are not present, misunderstandings, misplaced anger, and hurt feelings can occur because of misinterpreted tone.
- **Use email address lists** (often called a "listserv") whenever convenient, but as a caution, always confirm to whom you are mailing before you press the button. Many embarrassing exchanges occur by mail being routed to the wrong mailing list as well as the distribution of information to persons who no longer should have access. A similar forwarding tool is the "Reply All" choice, which, when used indiscriminately, distributes communication often best kept private and clutters the mailboxes of folks who don't need or want to know your reply.
- **Avoid forwarding electronic junk mail**, spam, malicious mail, and "time-wasters" that seem to reach our email systems daily. Nowhere has the computer saying "Garbage In, Garbage Out" been truer than in the world of electronic mail.
- **Don't waste electronic bandwidth.** While a smiley-face emoticon may brighten someone's day, it is only part of a whole new language of symbols arising from social media that adds additional layers and clutters up your intended message.
- **Avoid inappropriate writing** such as sexually explicit and vulgar language. Despite the ease of use and the faint possibility of anonymity, write and email only those things that you would be proud to have your parent(s) read.

Presently the most popular electronic communication device is the **smart phone**. This handheld, pocket-sized computer allows users to leave voice messages and, to the point here, written "text messages." Text messaging is good for quick updates such as verifying departure times, quick notes such as "On my way" or just "OMW," confirming appointments, contact information, and the like. Handy as these techniques may be, however, for business practices they should be used sparingly. Longer forms of written communication and direct conversations through phone calls are more effective, easier stored, and far better mediums for the exchange of truly critical information.

GRAPHIC COMMUNICATION

Regardless of the specific field of entertainment technology in which a technical manager is employed, graphic communication plays a huge role. Graphics help us convert three-dimensional ideas into two-dimensional images, which in turn make it possible to envision, organize, and specify the particulars of any project, in some extreme instances perhaps even the entire production.

The ability to visualize objects in space and translate an idea to paper forms the roots of graphic communication. Besides shape descriptions and the accompanying dimensions and finishing specifications found in costume plates, drafting plates, and riser diagrams, organizing information graphically as in a chart or table allows a technical manager to create an effective tool capable of delivering a large volume of material in a highly readable format. These typically appear as forms, spreadsheets, and calendars.

While design professionals use drafting as a way to convey their production concepts and images, drawing frequently serves the technical manager more as a problem-solving tool which is, discussed later in this chapter. This problem solving can be done in a variety of ways, including, but not limited to, drafting, sketches, graphs, or tables. Working a problem out on paper is often one of the first steps a technical manager takes in tackling a challenge.

Today's visual entertainment world is overwhelmingly focused on film, animation, avatars, gaming, and the like. But even the field of live entertainment finds, or dreams, of high-end applications of these digital tools, such as the creation and use of holograms and moving projections. Interesting as these ventures might be, they require expertise and expense that put them far outside the affordability of most live performance companies.

Digital tools are used, however, in efforts to communicate the overall vision to both creative and technical staffs. For several decades now, the architectural world and, by extension, the theatrical world, has been intrigued by "walk-throughs," also known as a "fly-by." The tools are usually CAD programs that allow a 2-D drawing to be converted to a 3-D layout through which an observer, building client, or stage director can be virtually walked through the envisioned space. In the entertainment world, the process is probably overrated since audiences never have the same opportunity or location afforded the director in this exercise, but still it's a neat toy and sales gimmick, and may lead to other changes in the future.

Within the technology fields, the relationship between entertainment design and technology and graphic communication grows ever more important. With the rising mobility of designers and remote locations of many studios, rental houses, and supply companies (necessitated by high rent and land cost within city boundaries), the need to effectively communicate design and technical data on paper, although usually digitally generated, has increased to a degree that any technical manager who is ignorant of, or deficient in, the skills of graphic communication is, in essence, professionally illiterate. Drafting and sketching are essential skills for most any technical manager, regardless of his or her field of employment, be it scenery, costumes, or props, among others.

GRAPHIC COMMUNICATION IN COSTUME FIELDS

Costume managers rely on a wide range of graphic work, usually hand-drawn but increasingly digitally generated, in order to execute designs that transform a person from actor to character. For inspiration, costume designers usually assemble significant amounts of research for each character, often combining details from a variety of source images. When the research begins to coalesce, the designer develops thumbnail sketches, small figures that define silhouette and begin to solidify the design in relationship to other characters. In some cases, sketches are done that show the evolution of a single character over multiple costume changes; in other cases, groups are shown as they appear on stage together.

These first steps are important to the costume studio crew and managers because they provide a visual sense of the whole. Preliminary sketches provide the costume studio manager enough information to start organizing work plans, purchasing materials, and making other appropriate preparations. Following initial sketches, the designer and/or assistant render a series of colored costume plates that are larger than the sketches and include a multitude of techniques to fully describe the costume construction, fabric, and accessories. While the figures are proportional, they are not drawn to an exact scale since the costume staff must adapt each image to the measurements of the actor who will wear the finished costume. Renderings include numerous handwritten (or typed if the designer is using a computer program) notes and enlarged views showing particularly complex construction details. Fabric swatches and a collage of research material may also be attached to the plates as reference.

Although the management and division of labor differs from studio to studio, there is usually one technical manager who takes on the development of brown paper patterns to be used to cut the fabric pieces along with the required stitching allowances. Other studios use drapers and slopers, which are less precise techniques but still suitable to support the construction of many costume designs.

GRAPHIC COMMUNICATION IN SCENERY & PROP FIELDS

Set design graphics serve as the basis for the work of numerous other disciplines in the production process. Like the costume designer, the set designer begins with research into period or art styles that help establish an overall visual look. Next, using a scaled, base drawing of the venue stage groundplan, the designer sketches both elevation and groundplan to begin the process of defining space. Sketches can be drawn freehand with some attention to scale or can be created with simplified CAD-like programs such as Sketch-up. Details such as color, texture, and performance demands can also be cited through the extensive use of notes or referenced research.

From this point, the set designer uses mechanical graphic techniques to develop "working drawings" (a term borrowed from the architectural world which parallels scenic fabrication) that detail all elements of the set design from which a three-dimensional model will usually emerge. All these drawings are scaled drawings, assuring that the size of objects are properly maintained and remain relative to the human body, the standard by which everything is compared. To keep size reasonable, the model is usually 1/8"=1'-0" scale or 1/4"=1'-0" scale, but all the other drawings are typically 1/2"=1'-0" scale, 1"=1'-0" scale for smaller objects and 3"=1'-0" scale for details. Much of the specific techniques involved in creating these drawings can be found in the *USITT Scenic Design and Technical Production Graphic Standard* publication, which identifies drawing processes, line symbols, line weights, sheet layout, and required information.

From the above information, the scenery technical management team creates an entirely new group of drawings, typically in CAD and using the designer's working drawings as a base. These new drawings are most appropriately called 'shop drawings," another architectural term. Shop drawings detail specifications for the construction of the scenic units and/or larger properties and include shop versions of the center-line section and groundplan, assuring that there is room for everything that needs to fit on stage. The scales are similar, but they are sometimes larger than those used by the designer since shop drawings in many instances contain vastly more information than working drawings. While the drawing process doesn't vary much timewise whether drawn by hand or using CAD, CAD makes revisions vastly easier and quicker.

Along with standard drawings, shop technical managers produce calendars, "to-do" lists, scene shift and scenery storage plots, load-in schedules, assignment schedules, and numerous other documents that are combinations of both verbal and graphic (visual) information. Graphics ought to make it easy to see and comprehend blocks of information without requiring lengthy verbal communication. In this way, visual, verbal, and graphic communication tools are all tied together.

GRAPHIC COMMUNICATION IN LIGHTING FIELDS

Lighting designers begin with the set designer's groundplan and section and then create a series of plots and charts that communicate to other members of the artistic team and the lighting technical managers the steps required to create the final lighting design. These drawings are informed by the *Recommended Practice for Theatrical Light Design Graphics* published by USITT. Again we have research; hand-drawn or CAD-generated sketches; then scaled light plots, sections, and cardboards (a cardboard-backed portion of the light plot showing a single boom, lineset, etc. with all the pertinent information, enabling technicians to carry the package of information in their back pockets during the light hang).

Oftentimes, the head electrician (a technical manager) creates the cardboards and lays out the circuit plot using the designer's and the electrician's own drawings. In addition, there are numerous lists to be created, most of which are created in a graphic format: shop orders, circuit assignments, color and template assignments, and mark-ups to the light plot based on changes required by field conditions.

GRAPHIC COMMUNICATION IN AUDIO FIELDS

Like scenery and lighting, the field of **sound** design has developed its own set of graphic standards (*Sound Graphics Recommended Practice*: A Project of the USITT Sound Commission), some of which are based on set design practices but which for the most part resemble circuit-board drawings. The use of consistent "defined" symbols is important, as is the need for everything to be well labeled. These simple line drawings show the connections of cable runs to various audio components and detail how equipment is tied together and the pathway to control panels. Similar techniques are used for microphone arrangements since the use of microphones has become de rigueur in modern day theatre and musical/concert venues.

GRAPHIC COMMUNICATION IN SPECIAL EFFECTS

Although **special effects** technical managers employ graphic communication to guide crews through the assembly and distribution of equipment as well as control, these drawings vary significantly. There isn't an industry standard, and the appearance of such drawings may vary from the sound graphic format to 2-D drawings that use individually devised symbols and many local notes.

Graphics are key to the communication of tasks overseen by entertainment technical managers. To one degree or another, everyone uses graphics in order to guide their work. Sometimes it is a technical manager who generates the paperwork; just as often it is a designer. Regardless, the crew and their managers use a vast array of graphic tools to develop, refine, and record the work required to mount a project or full production. Coordination is required within all areas, even the seemingly standalone costume area since costumes must fit into defined spaces, have provisions made for on-stage storage and change booths, and be protected from edges and surfaces that may damage garments that in some circles may be worth thousands of dollars.

USING GRAPHIC COMMUNICATION FOR PROBLEM SOLVING

While many technical fields use formal communications like drafting, freehand sketching is a communication tool that every technical manager cannot be without. Sketching is frequently used to graphically communicate ideas that are in various stages of elaboration, including some that are not yet fully developed. For many designers and technical managers, sketching is way of thinking, much like speaking out loud graphically.

Additionally, the process of putting an idea down on paper allows for refinement and clarification—or to be readily tossed with only a minimal investment of time. Design and technical solutions that are derived through sketching can greatly improve the quality of projects since a variety of options can be explored quickly. A sketch allows others to contribute more easily to the process when a problem can be shared graphically among many. The freedom to sketch helps many designers and technical managers overcome self-doubt and enables both concepts and solutions to become more fully developed.

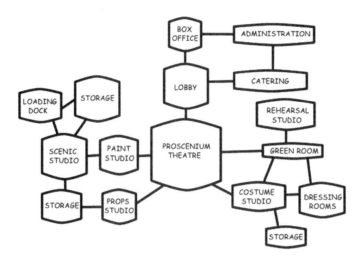

FIGURE 5.9 Bubble diagram

The use of sketching is not limited to drawing objects; it is also a very effective tool to express and refine abstract concepts and relationships. One such highbred sketch is a bubble diagram, as shown in figure 5.9. Bubble diagrams are often used by architects to conceptually identify space relationships in the planning phases of new construction. Similarly, the use of the Time, Talent, Money Triangle image used throughout this text is meant to help the reader more easily assimilate a rather complex concept just by remembering and associating the ideas associated with this graphic image.

"No project is complete until the paperwork is finished."

This sign hangs on the office wall of many technical managers. Instrument schedules, character plots, and cost/cut lists are all examples of forms that graphically assemble complex information (fig. 5.10). Through the use of spreadsheet and database computer programs, most technical managers are already quite adept at assembling information in a row/column format. Once a logical order and layout of a form is determined, information can be collected, recorded, and efficiently communicated. A well-designed form is clear and concise and provides a useful summarization of information to be transmitted.

One of the most common row and column forms in use by the technical manager is the blank calendar. A calendar often serves as the foundation for all effective planning and estimation. In fact, any information that can be transmitted in graphic form will usually be more accessible to the reader than a large block of text containing the same information.

Scenic Constuction Cut List

Show: _____   Plate #: ____   Prepared by:____

Date: _____   Unit Description: _____

Comments:_____

Unit Label	Piece Label	Stock	Qty	Length	Notes	Done

FIGURE 5.10 Scenic construction list form

"What we have here is a failure to communicate."

This famous line, probably said millions of times before and after, is taken from the movie *Cool Hand Luke*, starring the very cool Paul Newman. In the movie, it referred to a prisoner who, by his actions, repeatedly refused to respond as directed by authority. Here the line is mentioned to remind us all that miscommunication repercussions (although unlikely physical abuse such as Luke suffered) are analogous to our own failures to recognize and prepare ourselves to be good communicators.

The entertainment world is among the most collaborative of any occupation in the world, using technology, art, specific skills, unique ideas, and materials to produce beautiful and sometimes inspiring events. But in order to accomplish all this, we rely on people—many people. And what enables us to work together is communication: verbal, written, and graphic. Master these skills and your career will be long and rewarding . . . and successful.

Chapter 6

Specialized Communication

This chapter examines several explicit applications of the communication classifications discussed in Chapter 5, specifically job descriptions, specifications, and grant writing. While only a few will be used on a daily basis, each helps define a train of thought and degree of specificity that will serve any technical manager well.

As the connective tissue of the Time, Talent, Money Triangle, excellent communication skills are a necessary part of the skills maintained by any technical manager. Daily practice and frequent study will, over time, result in a technical manager becoming adept at all the various tips and techniques discussed in this chapter.

COMMUNICATION CATEGORIES

Job descriptions define each person's responsibilities at work, provide a framework for his or her priorities and duties, and detail where that position fits into the overall organization, i.e., worker, supervisor, and so on; colloquially, the organizational pecking order. Correctly framed, the information assists everyone involved by dividing up the workload, resulting in a team-based workplace environment.

Specifications are most commonly associated with the building trades, but in reality they appear in many places in artistic environments in the form of drafting notation, rendering details (costumes), lighting paperwork, and even models, just to name a few. Research materials that find their way into production studios are also specifications. Specification information includes elements such as dimensions, notations, finishes, recommended or required outsourced products, weights, equipment handling protection, colors, and final coatings.

Grant writing is another specialized writing skill that more and more has become a responsibility of technical managers, either in partnership with other staff or as the sole author. A growing number of performance and research projects are being funded through regional and national granting agencies. State arts councils, corporate sponsors, and local foundations are all potential funding sources. Each agency will typically require a specific application procedure or, worse yet, ask that you submit your own individually developed request.

JOB DESCRIPTIONS

Within most organizations, there is a commonly held belief that employees who know what they are supposed to be doing will be better workers. This may seem a rather simple concept, but many in the entertainment industry still take on jobs that come with limited or no job descriptions. Not until they begin their work do workers fully realize the range of their duties and their employer's expectations. Often this scenario backfires on both employee and employer. Too many surprises (or discoveries) after the fact lead to misunderstandings and hostility and ultimately end in a failed working relationship.

One method to inform people as to what is expected of them is a written job description. A good job description simply defines a task utilizing a proscribed format and articulates five functions within an organization: duties, required skills, required training, time commitment, and line of accountability.

Unfortunately, there is no universal format for job descriptions. Despite their recognized worth, in most instances each producing organization has developed a unique methodology for organizing position information. Some prefer a description that follows a timeline format, citing responsibilities chronologically. This format is especially useful with production positions where specific duties change as opening approaches. Another system emphasizes general duties and needed skills coupled with the anticipated time commitment. Volunteer support staff and salaried employees may find the latter format most useful.

Regardless of the format used, all written job descriptions should include the following information shown in figure 6.1.

Element	Description	Example
Duties	Anticipated job activities written in a concise manner, each beginning with an action verb.	The Head Carpenter shall: a) Supervise construction crews. b) Assist in the daily scheduling of work flow. c) Inform the Technical Director of progress
Required Skills	Anticipated competencies necessary for the successful completion of the aforementioned duties. Whenever possible, the skills listed should be measurable by imperial testing.	The Head Carpenter shall be able to: a) Read theatrical construction drawings. b) Operate standard scenic studio tools including the table saw, band saw, and drill press. c) Drive a standard transmission vehicle.

Required Training	This section should refer to specific educational requirements and certifications necessary to hold the job.	The Head Carpenter shall: a) Hold a BA or BFA degree in Theatre. b) Have attended a "Certified Master Rigging Class." c) Hold a Class D chauffeur's license.
Time Commitment	Two aspects of time should be listed.	The amount of time required each week (40–45 hours per week) and any exceptions to that pattern. If possible, cite normal workday as well as the length of the commitment (hired on a nine-month seasonal contract)
Line of Accountability	Identify to whom the employee is responsible as well as which decisions can be made without the consultation of a higher authority.	The Head Carpenter serves as the primary crew leader in the shop and reports directly to the Shop Supervisor and Resident Technical Director. The Head Carpenter is authorized to make routine supply purchases as well as make construction modifications necessary for touring scenery that do not conflict with the overall scenic design.

FIGURE 6.1 Elements of a job description

An assortment of job descriptions for positions involved in a typical theatrical production is provided in the appendix. These samples can be used as is or provide model language and format to any technical manager who is given the responsibility to develop in-house job descriptions. Regardless of the adaptations used, be mindful that the more accurate and direct the job description, the more useful the document will be. Those tailored to the specific positions and personnel within a company are the most useful of all.

PRINCIPLES IN WRITING A JOB DESCRIPTION

In developing a job description, avoid using broad generalities, especially that infamous phrase: "And other duties as may be assigned." Such ambiguous language only serves to raise questions. A better approach, if you wish to keep the description wide open, is to use the statement: "And other duties as determined to be mutually beneficial to both employer and employee." This phase indicates a willingness to discuss any expansion of duties that might come along. In reality, all job descriptions represent a snapshot in time, detailing job expectations as much as possible, and may not reflect each and every expected action.

Well-written job descriptions have a direct connection to the overall mission and goals of an organization, articulating thoroughly who is responsible for what actions in advancing the organization. In addition, they serve as a common standard for planning and evaluation. By utilizing a unified format, direct comparisons can be made in relationship to issues like workload distribution, compensation concerns, and recruitment practices. Job descriptions afford the technical manager a tangible method of planning, which greatly impacts the talent side of the Time, Talent, Money Triangle. Some of the multiple uses of written job descriptions are shown in figure 6.2.

Job descriptions, no matter how well developed, are working documents. As such, each description requires periodic review. When people develop and expand their role power within an organization, without doubt there will need to be some shuffling of defined duties. At a minimum, all job descriptions within an organization should be reviewed annually. This review is especially helpful if it coincides with an annual performance review of staff members, providing a clear and timely opportunity to bring the paperwork into alignment with what is really happening within an organization.

Use	Purpose Analysis
Clarify Expectations	A written job description clearly details both the general and the specific performance expectations for each employee, student, intern, or volunteer.
Planning Tool	As an organization is being formed or reformed with an employee addition or departure, a job description assists in connecting the organizational mission and goals with specific personnel needs.
Recruiting Device	Once written, a job description can be broadcast as a job announcement to which individuals seeking employment might respond.
Memo of Agreement	Once accepted by the employee, a job description forms the contract between the parties involved, enumerating mutually acceptable expectations and responsibilities.
Basis of Evaluation	Routine employee evaluation is critical for the health of any working community. A job description provides an outline of discussion points and identifies sources of comparison to determine relative achievement within the work environment.

FIGURE 6.2 Job description uses

As a part of the annual review, check each position for **job description creep**. Additional duties an individual has either picked up or lost during the year need to be evaluated in light of the whole organization and how they may have been adapted to reflect the respective strengths and weaknesses of the individual currently holding the position. In order to manage effectively the talent portion of the Time, Talent, Money Triangle, the technical manager must be aware of the individual contributions of each associate as well as the collective strengths of all. The review is an opportunity to curtail inappropriate expansion and to encourage appropriate development.

A staff vacancy is a unique opportunity for planning and evaluation that ought not to be squandered. An open position provides an ideal time during which to modify the old job description to conform to changes that have occurred within your organization over time and/or simultaneously support the development of an entirely new staffing vision for the future. At this point, the revision will not be hampered by the opinions or actions of the former position holder. This clean slate opportunity should be thought through very carefully.

Don't limit the annual review of job descriptions to only those associates you supervise. There is much to be gained from a periodic inventory of your personal goals and job performance and a comparison between your expectations and those articulated by your organization. Analyze in what way your job serves the organizational mission, as well as how your job serves your own personal development. A **self-reflective review** is a good check of the time side of the Time, Talent, Money Triangle taken from a personal viewpoint. During this analysis, it is not uncommon to discover that you are spending the majority of your time on some very minor activities within your overall job description. This imbalance, once brought to your attention, can be addressed and more easily rectified.

If your personal job analysis indicates that your responsibilities have stretched far beyond the original scope of the position, you can determine to pass on to others the extra things you have undertaken, accept the new duties with full recognition of their impact on your lives, or decide it is not worth it and move on. Occasionally, a successful job description analysis, if shared with your employer in a positive light, will produce beneficial results such as an increase in pay, promotion, or even a welcome reduction in workload. The result may also be that by personally clearing the decks of the unnecessary tasks, you are able to concentrate more on what is important, allowing you to seek better balance in your life and therefore gain greater satisfaction.

When searching for a new position for yourself, use the posted job description to compare your qualifications with those desired. A quick scan of the skills and qualifications cited can tell you much about your ability to match this organization's need. If you appear either highly overqualified or underqualified, it is still a judgment call on your part as to whether to pursue this potential new employment. Rather than let the lack of a perfect match stop you, use the information gained through job description comparison as a tool to assist you in achieving your own goals.

SPECIFICATIONS

A highly specialized form of written communication is that of specification writing. Specifications serve as the written instructions for detailing building construction and renovation project demands. Although not all technical managers will be called upon to write specifications for a project, most will at one time or another encounter a project that involves written specifications.

Specifications follow a standard form, developed by the Construction Specification Institute, which provides a uniform system for organizing the various technical sections necessary to fully support a building being constructed. For example, Division 11, Section 11060 contains specifications describing theatres and stage equipment.

There are four basic types of specifications (as shown in figure 6.3)—**descriptive, performance, proprietary,** and **reference standards**. All but the latter specify the crucial properties of materials needed for a project.

Descriptive specifications include a detailed written description of the required properties of a product. Often lengthy and tedious, writing these specifications involves researching products and critical features; determining which features to specify; describing critical features; and providing information about submittals, tests, etc.

Performance specifications identify the performance characteristics that must be met by a product or system. Writing performance specifications is a two-part process that includes preparation of a statement of required results and identification of a method for verifying compliance. Avoid use of both descriptive and performance specifications for a single requirement; the resulting specifications are redundant and open to conflicts. Performance must be technically possible.

Proprietary specifications identify desired products by manufacturer name and model number or by a product's unique characteristics and take one of two forms: **closed** and **open**. Closed specifications do not allow substitutions; open specifications allow for proposed alternates, a request often made by contractors bidding work. Funding agency rules and regulations may limit the use of proprietary specifications.

SPECIFICATION METHODS
- Descriptive
- Performance
- Proprietary
- Reference standard

FIGURE 6.3 Methods of specifying

Reference standard specifications are published standard specifications that can be incorporated into project specifications by reference. They are documents created by industry consensus that provide rules, guidelines, and/or characteristics for activities and their results and are published by trade associations, professional societies, standards organizations, governments, and institutions.

SPECIFICATION FORMATS

The formal construction specification follows one of two formats: either the **method system** or the **result system**. The method system fully describes the quality of materials, processes, and expected workmanship in great detail. The method system could be considered a how-to manual for the construction of a building.

The result system focuses on how the resulting work should perform in use conditions by specifying a performance standard that takes one of three forms:

- **A Requirement**—This is a qualitative statement of performance. "The 12" diameter sheave shall be free of holes and casting flaws."
- **A Criterion**—This is a quantitative statement regarding performance. "The 12" diameter sheave shall be made of class 30 gray iron and shall have a minimum hub diameter of 3 7/8"."
- **A Test**—This is an evaluative procedure to assure compliance. "The 12" diameter sheave shall be made of class 30 gray iron conforming to ASTM specification A-48."

The result system leaves the actual process for meeting the specification up to the provider.

INCORPORATING SPECIFICATIONS

Specifications are only useful in conjunction with their related drawings and vice versa. The drawings will show the extent, size, and relative location of parts; detail part sizes and overall dimensions; and often cite material selection. A specification speaks to the type and quality of the materials to be used, the quality of workmanship expected, methods of fabrication and installation, tests and code requirements, and any acceptable alternates.

The reading audience for a written specification varies widely. The primary reader is the contractor who is charged with implementing and directing construction of the final project. In addition, specifications communicate information to estimators who perform cost analysis, purchasing agents who contact vendors and purchase materials and supplies, building owners who seek to know exactly what they are buying, consultants who use the specification as an inspection tool, and the supplier/manufacturer who must know exactly what is to be provided.

The specification serves as a contract between the owner and the supplier as defined throughout the construction process. Typical notation and directions on theatre shop (construction) drawings for a scenic design are mini-specifications in that they communicate similar, if not identical, types of information to individuals involved in the production process. However, standard construction specifications carry the weight of law. When something on a job site goes wrong, the first communication that is examined is the specification. In such light, full specification writing is best left to professionals.

GRANT WRITING

Grant writing requires the technical manager's very best skills of analysis and writing. First and foremost in the development of any grant application is an articulate statement describing the problem being addressed and how that definition relates directly to the goals of the funding agency. The obverse is probably the most common mistake in grant writing: asking a grantor to fund something in which they have no interest. The result in this case is almost certainly a denial of the request.

The writer must carefully analyze the RFP (request for proposal) that typically precedes any round of grant application; a breakdown of common components being shown in figure 6.4. Once digested, the writer works to determine the nature of the potential funding organization and to try to define the proposal to meet the grantor's goals. Generally, responses should be limited to only that information that is specifically requested through the application procedure.

STANDARD PARTS OF A GRANT REQUEST FOR PROPOSALS (RFP)

Statement of Purpose	■ Overall objectives of the grant
Background Information	■ Description of funding agency
Scope of Work	■ Specific funding criteria
Outcomes and Standards	■ Anticipated impact of funding
Submittals	■ Application expectations ■ Inventory of required materials
Terms of Contract	■ Application deadline ■ Funding cycle ■ Renewal options
Evaluation Criteria	■ Procedures and standards for grant awards
Contact Information	■ Grant officer contact and available help

FIGURE 6.4 Parts of a grant RFP

More than one grant has been denied because of an overload of the wrong type of information provided by the grant writer.

Standard practice for grant applications is submission of a concept paper or abstract. This one- or two-paragraph statement should be very carefully crafted using precise language to answer these six standard questions.

- What is the problem to be solved?
- Why is the project needed at this time?
- How is the project going to be conducted?
- What specific resources are required to address this concern?
- What is the expected outcome and benefit?
- How will the impact of the project be sustained?

If it is a struggle to answer any of these questions in light of the goals of the funding agency, then more homework is needed before submitting a request for funds. At any given time, there are only a few possible proposal ideas that are ripe for solution, and there are even narrower groups for which a convincing case for funding can be made. Successful grant writing is a developed skill built upon a foundation of practice. Try not to let your early failures cloud your efforts for future success. Remember, you will never be awarded a grant unless you apply!

As the connective tissue of the Time, Talent, Money Triangle, excellent communication skills are a necessary part of the skills maintained by any technical manager. Daily practice and frequent study will, over time, result in a technical manager becoming adept at all the various tips and techniques discussed in this chapter.

Chapter 7

Professional Practices & Resources

There are innumerable clichés that could be applied to the matter of knowledge. The late 20th century and the early 21st century are called the "Information Age." "Knowledge is Power" is another one. Smart phones, iPads, tablets, netbooks, smart watches, and the Fitbit are all tools that make it possible for us to learn or inform ourselves nearly instantly. Trips to libraries, the use of reference books, and home or office libraries are becoming increasingly quaint.

Technical managers mostly fit into the same mold and are constantly hungry for information to enhance their personal tool kits, making it possible for them to do a better and more effective job. Internet searches have become one of, if not the, most used tool for most technical managers. But we handicap ourselves if we turn only to the Internet and fail to recognize the knowledge we need to possess at our fingertips that will inform all the day-to-day decisions technical managers need to handle. Technical managers need an awareness of the demands they face and a familiarity with the many resources available. Having a baseline knowledge on a wide variety of common subjects greatly aids in addressing the challenges a technical manager faces on a daily basis.

FACILITY OPERATIONAL PRACTICES

As a rule, most technical managers are intrinsically interlinked with the physical facility in which they work. Subsequently, they need an intimate knowledge of their building's capabilities, limitations, points of access and egress, and safety systems, as well as the organization's historical practices and operations. Such knowledge should not be underestimated. A perceptive technical manager knows:

- The space
- The activities in the space

- The occupants and users
- The equipment available to the space

By developing this comprehensive knowledge about a space and its operation, the technical manager can make informed decisions and better serve the parent organization and its events.

HEALTH & SAFETY

In many work environments, technical managers serve as default safety monitors. Technical managers' inherent capacity to define problems, quickly assess a situation, and develop rapid response strategies makes them a natural to fill this role. This group of people approaches each day with an uncommon sense of caution, not fearful of taking risks but exhibiting a willingness to make informed choices despite the range of possible dangers present to themselves and colleagues who work in the entertainment industry. Figure 7.1 provides a list of just some of the challenges workers are likely to face.

The list cited below addresses significant concerns, but where might one look for guidance regarding the noted issues? Fortunately, there exists a variety of safety resources that can assist technical managers in their safety oversight role. Organizations such as OSHA, NIOSH, and A.C.T.S. are in place to help solve these important quality-of-life issues.

THE ENTERTAINMENT INDUSTRY CAN BE HAZARDOUS FOR YOUR HEALTH

- Long work hours are not uncommon.
- Meeting deadlines and managing collaborations can be stressful.
- Less than ideal working conditions are often tolerated.
- Vanity and misplaced tradition ("The show must go on!") force pain suppression or denial.
- Exposure to hazards (chemicals, noise, particulate matter, etc.) can occur.
- Funding is limited to address chronic safety problems.
- Proper training is not always available.
- Many staff members are in poor physical shape.
- A less than ideal diet is often consumed, particularly as deadlines loom.
- Substance abuse (tobacco, alcohol, drugs, etc.) is far too common.

FIGURE 7.1 Ten reasons the entertainment industry can be hazardous for your health

GOVERNMENT HEALTH & SAFETY ORGANIZATIONS

The Occupational Safety and Health Administration, or **OSHA**, is the main federal agency charged with the enforcement of safety and health legislation in the United States. OSHA provides numerous bulletins regarding a variety of health and safety topics, offers a curriculum for personnel training in the application of rules and regulations, outlines worker safety and compliance issues, and enables the filing of complaints against employers that launch investigations to determine if laws have been violated. Information from OSHA speaks to communication standards, workplace practices, response directives, and mandated record keeping.

While OSHA has oversight of most commercial and federal government activities, many state and self-employed individuals are not directly under OSHA control. Regardless, the OSHA structure of information and practices makes common sense for everyone to observe in their workplace. Technical managers need to support the efforts of OSHA and similar agencies whose mandate is to help managers and employees to have safe and secure places of employment. [osha.gov]

NIOSH is the National Institute of Occupational Safety and Health, a branch of the Center for Disease Control and Prevention (CDC). It, too, is a federal agency, but organizational responsibility lies in conducting research and making recommendations for the prevention of workplace injury and illness. Focus areas are Diseases & Injuries, Safety & Prevention, Hazards & Exposures, Chemicals, and Emergency Preparedness & Response. NIOSH is not a regulatory agency but rather focuses on advocacy for workers and the dissemination of scientific information about work hazards. [www.cdc.gov/niosh/]

NONGOVERNMENT HEALTH & SAFETY ORGANIZATIONS

Arts, Crafts, and Theatre Safety (A.C.T.S.) holds the position of being the principal profession-related resource. The organization is a not-for-profit corporation providing health and safety publications for those engaged in the arts. A.C.T.S. offers no- to low-cost consulting for artists and is known throughout the entertainment industry as an outstanding resource to assist in raising awareness about health and safety issues. Additional nongovernmental agencies that are good safety resources include the following:

- **American Red Cross** offers both emergency support and ongoing training activities.
- **National Association of Safety Professionals** (NASP) is a nonprofit membership organization that provides safety professionals with state-of-the-art training and certifications.

- **National Safety Council** (NSC) is a nonprofit resource for information related to the prevention of accidental injury or death. NSC focuses on research and statistics, consulting services, and training and publishes *Safety and Health Magazine*.
- **American Society of Safety Engineers** (ASSE) manages, supervises, researches, and consults on matters of occupational safety, health, and environmental issues in the fields of industry, labor, and education. It is the oldest and largest American professional safety organization.

SAFETY RESOURCES & PRACTICES

A **Material Safety Data Sheet** (MSDS) provides information to both workers and emergency personnel regarding proper procedures for handling or working with a particular substance. MSDS reports include information such as physical data (melting point, boiling point, flash point, etc.), toxicity, health effects, first aid, reactivity, storage, disposal, protective equipment, and spill/leak procedures. These data sheets should be reviewed by all who use the specific material in order to improve one's knowledge about any materials in use. They are a particularly helpful reference when a spill or other accident occurs. By law, a binder of MSDS documentation must be available for inspection by any individuals at work and must contain the appropriate MSDS descriptions for the often wide variety of chemicals and materials used throughout that particular facility.

Basic application of established organizational safety practices includes:

- the proper **labeling** of chemicals and materials
- **maintenance** of equipment, including appropriate application of guards and shields
- developing **emergency response** plans, including the prominent display of emergency contact information
- seeking appropriate **training** to enhance one's skill set
- vigilance in the **documentation** of accidents and responses

Another extremely basic safety practice is the commitment to **keep a clean and organized work area**. All too often in the throes of production efforts, shortcuts are taken that relax normal quality and cleanliness standards, thereby greatly increasing the dangers inherent in the work situation. The same laxness reduces worker efficiency when tools can't be found or materials must be constantly moved from place to place to gain access to necessary work space.

The technical manager's obligation toward workplace safety is paramount. Constant vigilance must be maintained to anticipate hazards, understand responses to mitigate those hazards, address concerns in a timely manner, and encourage all to

75

Personal Protection Inventory	
Items	Notes & (Alternatives)
■ Safety Goggles	(Wrap-around glasses)
■ Disposable ear plugs	(Ear muffs)
■ Industrial grade footwear	i.e., heavy leather uppers, thick soles and ties
■ Gloves appropriate for the task	i.e., do not use when operating equipment
■ Hardhat	(Bump cap)
■ Dust Mask	i.e., facial hair interferes
■ Respirator	i.e., various cartridges for varying needs

FIGURE 7.2 Personal protection inventory

be safety conscious. Accidents will occur, but with a heightened sense of awareness permeated throughout an organization, industrial accidents will be minimized, as will their impact.

PERSONAL SAFETY EQUIPMENT

The value of personal protective gear should not be underestimated. An essential list of useful equipment is shown in figure 7.2. Technical managers are responsible for their own set of self-protection equipment and materials; and need to assure that those they supervise are properly equipped. Possession of personal equipment should be emphasized as the responsibility of each individual staff member. In the instance of visitors or misplaced equipment, there should be a complement of disposable protective gear (ear plugs, particle/dust masks) that can be shared with, or provided for, those unable to provide their own.

INDUSTRY STANDARDS & BEST PRACTICES

Despite the fact that nearly every production-related project has a prototypical nature to it, technical managers can inform their decision making and process/procedural analysis through the application of "industry standards." One type of standard is known as a **material performance standard**; that is to say, these standards describe the expected performance of a product as long as it is used in a proper manner and in accordance with particular guidelines. Performance standards can also be set that

JOB PERFORMANCE STANDARD TYPES
HEAD ELECTRICIAN (PARTIAL)

*Results standard (Emphasize **what** is accomplished)*

- Hang and cable 20 fixtures on a batten safely
- Maintain paperwork to reflect daily achievements

*Behavior standard (Emphasize **how** results are to be attained)*

- Lead crews with attention to safety, accuracy, & positive energy
- Communicate with Lighting Designer daily, prioritizing information to achieve greatest efficiency

FIGURE 7.3 Job performance standard types

describe manager expectations of work effort for various individuals involved in a project. Much like a grading rubric in an academic environment, the performance standard provides an assessment tool to measure quality and to serve as shorthand to instruct others in expectations, supporting clarity, accountability, and advancing the development of quality. Job performance standards (see figure 7.3) can be written as either **Results-focused** or **Behavior-focused**.

The United States Institute for Theatre Technology (USITT) publishes a series of recommended best practices that are intended to aid with communication practices across a production effort and even across electronic lighting control systems. There are recommend graphic practices for scenery, lighting, and in-progress recommendations for audio systems. In one of the entertainment industry's first efforts to create its own standards, USITT members developed the DMX512 protocol, creating a common electronic "language" that enables control and distribution equipment created by differing manufacturers to "speak" to one another. This effort proved to be the stepping stone to numerous new technologies, including many of today's automation control systems.

At an organizational level, any production group can internally develop its own recommended practices for typical construction processes, communication forms, and operational sequences. As with all other best practice development, there must be local ownership and consistent application for such guides to be useful. Local practices need not cover every possible contingency; their simple purpose is to provide a guide for specific and often repeatable techniques, limiting personal interpretation and often increasing productivity. An example is shown in figure 7.4.

Another type of recommended practice is a **certification** standard. Certification standards are used to develop certification criteria and processes

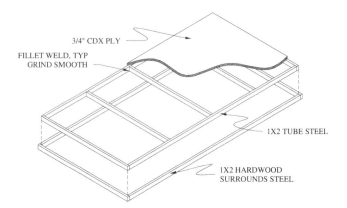

FIGURE 7.4 Page from scenery standard handbook

FIGURE 7.5 ETCP logo

that enable individuals to clearly demonstrate their capabilities through a formal review process. Should they "pass their exam," they are declared certified for that particular operation or field. In recent years, the Entertainment Technician Certification Program (ETCP) has been developed to support such certification programs for the fields of Rigging-Arena, Rigging-Theatre, Entertainment Electrician, and Power Distribution Technician. All are areas of high risk with significant populations working in the entertainment industry (figure 7.5).

Eligibility for ETCP certification is grounded on achieving, and then documenting, a combination of qualifications such as: a specified minimum number of hours of professional work experience, participation in internships or apprenticeships, or completion of an appropriate record of education. Once qualified, the candidate for certification takes a paper or computer-based examination that is evaluated by a qualified psychometrics testing center.

Assuming passage of the exam and payment of fees, the candidate becomes an ETCP-certified Arena Rigger, Theatre Rigger, Entertainment Electrician or Power Distribution Technician. Each certification is valid for a period of five years and can be renewed through payment of a small fee along with a predetermined amount of either ongoing activity in the area of certification or continuing education courses or by retaking the examination. Increasingly, entertainment industry contracts, such as staffing for arenas, convention centers and other public places of assembly and traveling events, cite requirements having ETCP-certified personnel on the jobsite. Subsequently, being a certified technician is becoming more and more of an asset to industry technicians.

CODES, STANDARDS, BEST-PRACTICES AND NETWORKING

In addition to being identified as an official, or often unofficial, safety monitor, many technical managers become involved in building renovation or new construction projects. As such, building codes like the National Electrical Code (NEC), the International Building Code (IBC), and the National Fire Protection Association's Life Safety Code (NFPA 101) are very valuable resources. These industry consensus codes are established through a rigorous national process, serve as directives on how to address certain conditions, and can provide guidance in bringing such projects into compliance. Building codes are adopted, with or without modification, and enforced at the state and local government levels. Familiarity with the codes in effect and meeting with those who enforce these regulations will prove beneficial to anyone involved with such projects.

Codes and standards seek to establish patterns, reduce conflict among various processes, provide guidance in addressing a particular challenge, articulate a firm educational foundation, and address legal compliance. They provide minimum requirements with due regard for function, design, operation, maintenance, structural, and safety issues. Some have the force of law and others simply have the force of organizational agreement. Regardless of the specific type, all fall under the rubric of **best practices** and all are valuable resources for the technical manager.

A recent new set of expectations is sweeping through the entertainment industry that can affect the daily activities of the busy technical manager. As more and more organizations are increasing their environmental consciousness, leadership is needed to promote the issue, seek engagement, encourage knowledge, and promote compliance. Growing efforts in the **greening of the studio** call for the active reduction of toxic chemicals; the intentional conservation of materials; and a commitment to maximize recycling, minimize waste, and commit to the improvement of the overall work environment. By reducing one's environmental footprint, social obligations are met, costs can be reduced, and goodwill is generated.

Joining a member-based organization like USITT opens up a world of networking possibilities for the technical manager. Sessions at that organization's Annual Conference and Stage Expo enable continuing education. Exposure to the latest products and production resources can be accessed by attending the trade show floor where vendor booths are staffed by knowledgeable, helpful representatives.

Publication opportunities abound in both USITT's *Theatre Design and Technology* journal as well as within other special projects such as their biennial Tech Expo catalog. Membership in this organization also sets up networking opportunities to share both triumphs and challenges with other technical managers.

In addition to USITT, technical managers can also find benefit in joining other discipline-based organizations such as the Association for Theatre in Higher Education (ATHE), the Costume Society of America (CSA), the International Federation of Theatre Researchers (IFTR), and PLASA—the leading professional trade association representing worldwide entertainment technology—and others. All of these organizations have member benefits that can prove helpful over a career as a technical manager.

Finally, the development of a personal library of printed technology resources is helpful to any technical manager. Industry standards include: such titles as

> *The Backstage Handbook* by Paul Carter and George Chiang
> *Concert Lighting: Techniques, Art and Business* by James Moody and Paul Dexter
> *The Costume Technician's Handbook* by Rosemary Ingham and Liz Covey
> *Drafting for the Theatre* by Dennis Dorn and Mark Shanda
> *Fabric Painting and Dyeing for the Theatre* by Deborah Dryden
> *From Page to Stage: How Theatre Designers Make Connections between Scripts and Images* by Rosemary Ingham
> *Mechanical Design for the Stage* by Alan Hendrickson
> *Scene Design and Stage Lighting* by R. Craig Wolf and Dick Block
> *Show Networks and Control Systems* by John Huntington
> *Stage Lighting Design: The Art, the Craft, the Life* by Richard Pilbrow
> *Stage Management* by Lawrence Stern and Alice O'Grady
> *The Stage Rigging Handbook* by Jay O. Glerum
> *Structural Design for the Stage* by Alyce Holden and Bronislaw Sammler
> *The Sound of Theatre* by David Collison
> *Theatrical Design and Production* by J. Michael Gillette

Works like the examples above can serve not only as helpful resources, but the ideas they present often function as a springboards for a solution to managers' own technical problems.

Chapter 8

Employment

Production companies are formed to allow people to join their collective knowledge, skill, and effort to achieve greater productivity than individually possible. The performing arts contrast with other art forms in that the product (the art) is formed primarily through collaboration. Unlike the painter who needs only tools and supplies or the composer who needs paper, pencil, and piano, theatre production requires some organizational structure to support the input of many individuals.

The traditional model for understanding theatre organizations is a hierarchical one (fig. 8.1), modified from the business world that in turn borrowed organizational chart design from the military. Rows of boxes with names of positions and individuals are stacked one on top of another with short lines indicating a chain of command and a hierarchy of authority. The higher up the chart, the fewer the boxes until the top of the management pyramid is reached. Generations of theatre textbooks have been published that begin with a chart detailing this presumed order of hierarchical responsibility.

While this traditional model is helpful in understanding formal roles within a production organization, the model does not really reflect the multiple relationships

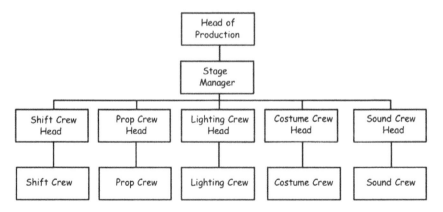

FIGURE 8.1 Performance-run crew organization chart

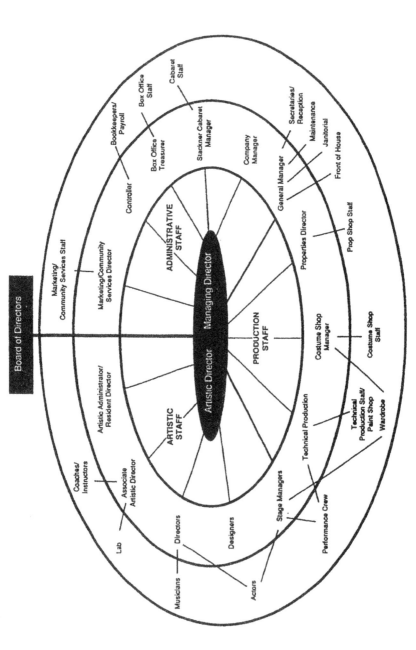

FIGURE 8.2 Facility flow chart

Myers, Sherrill & O'Connor, Sara. *Working Space: The Milwaukee Repertory Theatre Builds a New Home*, 1992, Theatre Communications Group, Inc. New York, NY, p. 7.

present in a live production. The lines of communication, and therefore lines of authority in a producing organization, are structured much more like a spider web (fig. 8.2).

Hundreds of lines of communication facilitate production. This spider web model represents the dynamic of the collaborative effort, far more integrated than the traditional hierarchy model.

In addition to understanding the web model of relationships, one must also consider that producing organizations develop a personality of their own depending on personnel, mission, and goals. Companies develop reputations for being relaxed or tense, disciplined or disorganized, responsive or unresponsive. Organizational characteristics affect season selection, hiring practices, and target audience. Sometimes the most vital information to describe a company is the reputation shared informally throughout the industry.

The specific organizational chart describing any company is far less useful than an understanding of the typical practices of that organization. We divide all producing organizations into three broad categories: resident/regional, commercial, and educational. There may indeed be variations on these three styles, and not all generalities will apply to each, but by focusing on these three broad categories, the majority of all theatre production venues are covered.

	Resident/Regional	*Commercial*	*Educational*
ORGANIZATIONAL			
Mission	Entertainment Outreach Education	Profit	Teaching Learning Outreach
Artistic	Visionary 3–5 yr contracts	Whatever the project demands	Education Goals Distributed Leadership
Season	3–11 months	Project Duration	9 12 months
Performers	Professionals — (AEA) Amateurs Interns	Professional — (AEA) (SAG) Local Talent	Students Guest Artists
Support	Ticket Sales Corp. Sponsors Donors (Friends)	Sales Backers	Ticket Sales Subsidy Donors (Friends)

FACILITIES

Shops	Onsite & offsite	Offsite— all projects ship	Most onsite
Venues	Onsite— Proscenium Thrust, Flexible	Venues vary greatly Tents to Arenas	Onsite Proscenium & multi-form
Rehearsal space	Onsite — Few / Offsite — Most	Offsite	Onsite — Shared Classrooms
Design staff	Some Resident Most hired per project	Hired Per project	Faculty/staff Student Professional Guest

SCHEDULE

Design	Design Team Rarely are artists in one location	Design Team Rarely are artists in one location	3–7 weeks typ. Weekly onsite meetings
Build	2–4 weeks 40 hrs. per week	As project requires Quickly as possible	2–8 weeks Student Labs
Rehearse	1–4 weeks	3–6 weeks	4–8 weeks
Technical Rehearsals	3 to 5 days + Previews	Days to months	7–12 days plus previews
Performances	1–10 weeks +	Few hours to years	1–3 weeks
Estimation/	1 day to a few wks	Few hours — days	Few days to few
Project	Year in advance	Years in advance	weeks to years
Planning			in advance

PERSONNEL

Paid labor	Staff Tech Mgrs. Staff Skill Specialists Staff Labor Hourly Overhire	Staff Project Mgrs. Department Heads In-house Staff Hourly Overhire	Faculty Staff
Minimally— Paid Labor	Interns	Not Applicable	Work Study Teaching Assoc.
Unpaid	Volunteers	Not Applicable	Students Volunteers

Run crew	Union to Volunteer	Onsite rep(s)	Students
Labor	Stable admin.	Stable admin.	Stable admin.
quality	High turnover?	High turnover/	Stable staff
	/long term	long-term	Student
			turnover

MISCELLANEOUS

In-house	Little to none	None — Items sold	Some, but
			limited
stock			by storage
			areas
Communi-	FAX, Overnight	FAX, Overnight	Face to Face
cation	mail	mail	
	E-mail, Phone	E-mail, Phone	E-mail
	Face to face	Face to Face	Phone, FAX

RESIDENT/REGIONAL THEATRES

The growth of resident and regional theatres has been quite remarkable. While professional theatre was once the domain of only New York and Chicago, successful regional theatres are now found in Houston, Minneapolis, Cleveland, Denver, and many other cities. With this distribution of theatre production across the United States has come an equivalent distribution of technical managers who work in these theatres.

Most regional theatres are led by a board of directors who hire a managing director and an artistic director to run the operation and set the artistic agenda. From this strong, shared logistical and artistic administration, a variety of departments are led, including production, marketing, development, education, and outreach. The regional technical manager is usually charged with oversight of the production area and is responsible to both the managing director and the artistic director. The technical manager relates to the managing director in all matters of money and resource management (time and money of the Time, Talent, Money Triangle) and relates to the artistic director in all matters of scheduling and personnel (time and talent of the Time, Talent, Money Triangle).

Working with permanent, professional department heads (technical managers in their own right), the company technical manager (production manager) assumes the lead to produce a season of plays. Department heads perform a variety of administrative responsibilities, overseeing small groups of highly skilled artisans. In most regional theatres, staff are contracted for a season and work on a salaried basis. There is a distinct division of labor between the various staffs and studios, much of which is determined by a combination of organizational heritage and current personnel. Since the staff is paid whether there is work to do or not, one of the primary challenges of the technical manager is to keep the work

85

flowing in a timely fashion. In a similar vein, careful time estimation on projects is necessary to assure that the available staffing level will support the pending endeavor.

When personal resources are not adequate to mount a production, additional local talent may be brought in to help. This practice is known as "overhiring." Overhiring in times of peak need is standard procedure for many companies. The "pick-up" labor can range from union stagehands to theatre-savvy high school students depending on the needs, the venue, and the available labor pool. Being on a venue's "extras list" is a common entry vehicle into the world of paid theatrical employment. Many a successful theatre artisan's first paid experience was through the overhire door.

Although it is not uncommon for regional theatre staff members to change theatres from season to season, there is a very limited amount of upward mobility within the regional theatre spectrum. Department heads often remain stable for several years, while lower-level staffing changes are common season to season. One trap many department heads discover over time is that in order to advance financially in an organization, they must become part of the management structure. A move into a management position can be a good thing; however, often it represents a loss as a person is no longer doing the hands-on things he or she enjoys the most and is most proficient.

The physical facility of each regional theatre dictates much of that organization's work pattern. Most have control of a performance venue, but many of these same companies may have remote construction studios as well as remote rehearsal, costume, and storage spaces. Many are located in adaptive reuse buildings, which sometimes provide less than ideal working environments. Possibly more than any other type of venue, regional theatres are limited in their available storage and therefore rarely build up a large stock of items. At best, a nearby warehouse is rented to provide storage for properties and furniture.

Like nearly all performing arts organizatiions, there is constant money pressure in the regional theatre. Most hold a not-for-profit legal status, but they still must generate enough income to support the staff, pay union actors, and fund materials for all production-related construction, equipment, and facility expenses. Unlike the academic environment where there is little much less danger of the doors closing on a program, the regional companies must constantly battle for financial viability. As a result, fundraising (development) is a major activity among most theaters, and cultivating corporate sponsorship for individual productions is common.

One decades-long trend in light of these financial pressures is the advent of the shared production whereby two or even three regionals jointly produce a work, sharing expenses, the physical set, and sometimes even cast members. These joint productions, as well can be imagined, present a whole new level of complexity when it comes to scheduling, planning, personnel management, and accounting, but—when well planned—the cost savings can be significant.

Regional theatres tend to buy materials on a per-show basis. Since purchases are directly related to income flow, capital purchases are difficult to make because the payback is so far into the future. As a response to this dilemma, technical managers frequently develop a stock of equipment by buying reusable components for such things as automation and scenic movement within the confines of individual production budgets. Over time, this stock of components becomes invaluable in meeting future technical challenges and allows the regional theatre to take on larger and more ambitious projects. This same approach is common in academic theatre production as well.

Fortunately, many communities recognize their regional theatres as a valuable asset, adding to the quality of life and favorably impacting the local economy. Subsequently, although both diminishing corporate sponsorship and rising costs continue to fiscally challenge regional theatres, these companies remain a source of employment for technical managers and other production personnel.

COMMERCIAL STUDIOS

Profit is the driving force for a commercial studio. A primary goal for technical managers who work in this environment is to assure that there is no downtime in workload and that there is a positive cash flow at the end of a project. To earn a profit, these facilities can fabricate or rent costumes, scenery, properties, curtains, sound and projection equipment for stage and film production; hold conventions, trade shows, and industrials; host fashion shows and product launches; and even offer space for parade floats and party décor, responding to whatever a client's vision needs, often competitively bidding against competing studios to acquire the work.

The commercial environment is very competitive as studios actively bid on multiple projects to ensure a winning number of contracts to keep the work steady. Demand for the services provided by such commercial studios expands greatly when the economy is strong, and the wide variety of entertainment options for the consumer also increases. For studios, large or small, the stakes are very high.

As a technical manager (frequently called a project manager in this sector) develops a bid for a commercial project, attention is paid to the proposed schedule, the available labor pool, and the capacity of the studio. The anticipated markup (profit) on a project can range from a low of 10% over anticipated expenses to over 100% of expenses depending on the studio's desire and/or need to take on the project as well as the technical manager's confidence in the proposed project's design. Many times the decision made by a commercial studio as to whether or not to assume a project is based on the personnel involved. Over time designers or design teams develop a reputation that is widely shared among studio owners. The anticipated ease or challenge with which a project may come to fruition is a strong determining factor in a commercial studio's willingness to take on a project.

Some commercial studios specialize in specific aspects of fabrication. Given the rapid speed with which current ventures are designed and built, it may be necessary for various parts of a production to be produced at completely different facilities. When this is the case, the technical manager is further challenged by coordinating the efforts of these various units. Logistical challenges may dictate that the first time all of the components of a production are assembled is load-in. At that late date, surprises are very costly to correct.

Should the technical manager of a commercial studio also be the owner, much of that individual's time will be spent generating future business. Rarely do such individuals participate in hands-on construction. Rather, their daily routine involves information gathering, reviewing project status, planning for what's next, and preparing bids for future endeavors. Commercial studios can get so busy with work and/or have such a short turnaround time between learning of a project and a bid deadline that the task of bid preparation is divided up among the staff. Here again, the technical manager must be a coordinator of extraordinary skill to maintain the integrity of the whole and to assure that nothing has been overlooked.

Labor costs are by far the most significant portion of any commercial studio bid. Often only 30% to 40% of the entire bid is material costs, with the balance being labor charges and shipping. With labor costs as the highest expense on a project, "outsourcing" (buying a ready-made product direct from another manufacturer) can generate significant savings, resulting in a better bid and larger profit. Purchasing ready-made products from others rather than taking the time and developing the talent to produce something directly reduces both the time and the talent portion demands of the Time, Talent, Money Triangle. Products such as moldings, columns, furniture, and carvings items that can be ordered directly from a manufacturer are commonly outsourced.

Once accepted, a bid is the foundation for a working contract. The bid, in conjunction with the design drawings upon which the bid was based, may be the only paperwork exchanged between the owner of the project and the studio other than a confirming letter of agreement. The letter of agreement usually states what is being provided, on what schedule, and in response to what payments. A well-written letter of agreement confirms the understandings of all involved and serves as a binding agreement.

As is common in theatre production as well as other forms of fabrication, changes may occur as production unfolds, which impact the construction process. A practice borrowed from the construction industry, the "change order" has become a standard method of exchanging information. Change orders formally request that a change be made, documents the nature of the change, and seeks signatures noting approval regarding both artistic and financial concerns. This necessary paper trail serves all and is supported by the direct involvement of a technical manager.

Rarely does a commercial studio invest in something that will become stock. Each project, once complete, becomes the property of the owner and not the supplier. Occasionally, a commercial studio will invest in a mechanical device or specialized unit (Like Audrey II from *Little Shop of Horrors*) that has future rental potential. If such a project comes along, the studio may commit additional resources in anticipation of these future revenues. All projects are further constrained by shipping costs and container sizes. Almost all objects produced at a commercial studio must be able to be shipped in a standard shipping container (air freight, semitrailer, sea container, etc.). Once an object is loaded, it becomes the property of the owner. The commercial studio may send a representative to the theatre at load-in, but more than likely its employees are already onto their next project. Build, pack, and ship are three standard activities for the commercial studio.

ACADEMIC THEATRE

There are hundreds of academic theatre departments throughout the country, ranging from one- person programs all the way up to schools and conservatories having 50 or more faculty and staff. The primary mission of academic programs is the education of students either as an aspect of liberal arts training or professional training. Most academic departments, large or small, are in some way dependent on box-office income. As such, they walk a fine line between providing community entertainment and meeting educational goals. The challenge of the academic season is to serve student educational and developmental needs while generating sufficient income.

Public performance at colleges and universities requires production work to be done by somebody. Typically this work is supervised by a technical manager and is primarily done by students with limited experience levels. While in most instances much production work is performed by a few zealous individuals, even if the actual number of bodies able to work is plentiful, the skill levels of the majority may be quite low. As a result, the academic technical manager often chooses to rely on the time side of the Time, Talent, Money Triangle to meet production demands. A longer build time allows for both the necessary education in construction methods to take place with an ever-changing workforce as well as provides an opportunity for the progressive skill development of the handful of stalwart student technicians over multiple projects.

Another way the Time, Talent, Money Triangle is manipulated to assist the academic environment is through the reliance on stock resources, including costume collections and accessories, flats, platforms, and equipment inventories in the areas of lighting, audio, and automation. Many programs extend their assets well beyond their established funding sources through the creative use of stock and reuse of materials salvaged from prior endeavors. Salvage costs are kept low due to the availability of student laborers but are also limited by available storage space.

Most academic programs hire several technical managers (technical director and costume shop supervisor), although it is not uncommon for these jobs to be combined with other duties—most typically design responsibilities. Oftentimes the existence of these plural duties cause for shortcuts in the planning phases and even more in the preparation devoted to bringing a production into the construction phase. As such, it is an environment where technical managers are frequently tempted to assume construction duties in addition to overseeing the work of those they supervise, i.e., coworkers rather than managers.

A major challenge for technical managers in the academic environment is to become skilled at estimating time demands for an unskilled labor pool. As a rule of thumb, everything takes longer than originally anticipated. Additionally, an allotment of time must be budgeted to redo poorly done or incorrect work. If they are not successful in their estimation, there often isn't sufficient time or opportunity to do trial assemblies, which affect load-in activities and can further affect preparation for productive technical and dress rehearsals. Production facilities often double as classrooms, and overlapping scheduled projects further complicate the work environment.

Despite some shortcomings, one distinct advantage of the academic environment is that a kind of shorthand can be established between the various directors, designers, and managers who work together over and over again in the same roles on multiple projects. Since the faculty and academic staff are most often in positions of leadership, individuals get to know one another over time and discover their own and their colleagues' working methodology.

BUSINESS OR CORPORATE THEATRE

Any theatre company may find itself involved in producing corporate theatre. A rise in the desire of the business world to incorporate multimedia presentations along with live spectacles has given rise to this relatively new genre. Trade shows, gala celebrations, and convention display booths are all embodiments of corporate theatre. Some observers refer to these types of presentation as "flash and trash," although as budgets grow bigger and clients gain sophistication, corporate events can be quite spectacular.

Time is usually the major constraint on a corporate event, often accompanied by seemingly unreasonable demands and overly high expectations. Facilities are rarely available or affordable far enough in advance to support rehearsals. Additionally, unclear project goals and scattered management contribute to the challenge. Success in this highly charged environment is based on flexibility and organization.

The biggest challenge is often the identification of the individual(s) who really has authority over the project. Corporate theatre is marked by unclear lines of authority with too many bosses, many of whom lack sufficient knowledge of the production process and who lack specificity for the desired end result. A common expression heard is "Just keep showing me something and I will know it when I see it." Despite the frustration, a technical manager may realize some advantages of working in corporate theatre.

Often, price is no object. Unlike the operations profiled earlier that seem to have to pinch every penny, corporate theatre is supported by much deeper pockets. The object is to get the job done on time, and thus the money portion of the Time, Talent, Money Triangle becomes the most flexible. Not only does this translate into better materials and products, greater access to the latest technology, and highly skilled personnel, corporate theatre often leads all others in the ability to fiscally compensate the technical manager. Because of the higher level of salaries, many educational and regional theatre technical managers eventually move into the corporate theatre world.

Corporate theatre events happen in all sorts of venues—from ballrooms to boardrooms. The fully equipped theatre is a rarity, and the creative problem-solving side of the technical manager is put to the test. As noted, rehearsal time is often limited and/or nonexistent. Producers will demand that everything be ready on time but rarely can afford to take the time to fully walk through the plans. As a result, the technical manager must hone his or her skills to the very sharpest edge for live performance. Often the result is great fun (if you don't develop ulcers first)!

COMMUNITY THEATRE

One other unique environment that employs technical managers is community theatre. These groups are organized around a love for the art and are made up primarily of many members who have limited or no formal training in theatrical production. Although on paper most community theatres appear to be hierarchically organized, the majority function with a strong core group of individuals who rotate among the various leadership roles. There are rarely restricted working departments and even more rarely are budgets large enough to support the artistic vision of the group.

The technical manager in this environment must often play the role of cheerleader, touting the many opportunities for backstage service and community fellowship. The one commodity that all community theatres have plenty of is enthusiasm. One would be hard pressed to find more steadfast volunteers. Although financial rewards may be minimal, the social structure of community theatre may indeed make the experience well worth it. The rehearsal time portion of the Time, Talent, Money Triangle is often elongated greatly to compensate for the less-skilled talent and the constant pressure for financial resources (money). However, the additional time being used may increase rental costs for the rehearsal and performance venues. The most important outcome of the technical manager's efforts in most community theatres should be enjoyment and development for all who participate. Great satisfaction can be gained by channeling individual passion into effective skill development.

Part Three

Strategies

Chapter 9

Planning & Scheduling

As stated earlier, a technical manager's major planning function is to think ahead, to anticipate and solve problems, or to at least arrange in advance for their proper handling. This is the role of the technical manager as scheduler. Using a variety of planning tools, the manager must be able to coordinate numerous aspects of the many processes needed to produce production elements. To name just a few, these tools include material and labor estimation forms (discussed in detail in Chapter 10), project lists, calendar(s) and charts, logs, and reconciliation forms. Using the procedures associated with these forms enables a technical manager to estimate and schedule project work and personnel, identify available facilities, share information with staff, and provide staff development.

Who and what is involved in production planning? The answers are complex since, given the collaborative nature of production projects, many individuals must be involved in a variety of capacities, some of which are not always aligned. Some are involved by the authority of their job responsibilities; some are merely gadflies who feel compelled to offer their unique perspective. Thankfully, most involve themselves as proactive members of a production staff who work collaboratively to meet a common goal: usually the successful opening of a performance run. The latter best describes the recommended role for the technical manager because this role is the one most likely to yield the most positive results.

The decision to mount a production is made months and sometimes years in advance. The producing organization works hard through proper planning to guarantee that all the elements of live performance—performers, costumes, scenery, lighting, house staff, and audience members, among others—will be in place when the day and hour of opening finally arrive. To ensure that this goal is met successfully, there are two levels of projection to which the technical manager must devote attention, these being the **season schedule** and the **production (or project) schedule**.

THE SEASON SCHEDULE

Season schedule development is a planning phase that usually takes place months before any actual work begins on any single production. During this period, managers examine production activities from a global viewpoint rather than the very detail-specific approach used during individual production (project) planning.

The season scheduling process begins by identifying likely performance dates, including performance runs. The most specific and important target is opening, although close attention must also be given to societal calendars that coincide with the project schedule. As both the workforce and the audience population become more diverse, greater awareness is needed regarding observed religious holidays, national holidays, and scheduled academic calendar breaks (if working in an educational environment). Many unhappy surprises await the technical manager who fails to recognize the specifics of those days of conflict since they often affect employee, and therefore work, and performance schedules.

Once initial available dates are projected, the planning system works backward, usually from closing and strike. Step one is to identify the fixed date requirements necessary to produce the desired production. Among others, these standard requirements might include design submission deadlines, technical drawing (planning) deadlines, rehearsal start dates, fabrication and assembly periods, load-ins, and technical/dress rehearsals dates. In this arena, it is the responsibility of the technical manager to assure that all aspects of preparation activity are given adequate time to meet each respective goal. While the process is sufficiently complex for even a single production, the inherent difficulties are geometrically exacerbated when multiple productions are involved, as happens with a season playbill. To be certain that all scheduling requirements are identified and allotted sufficient time for their completion, a technical manager is wise to employ planning tools. Portions of two examples of organizational scheduling formats are shown in figures 9.1 and 9.2 to illustrate possible layouts. The full version of these guidelines is provided in the appendix.

Documents such as these two are useful in making certain that no "standard" activity is overlooked, noting that every project has its share of "nonstandard" requirements. While it is impossible to be specific about nonstandard activities during the proposed schedule period, all technical managers are well advised to listen carefully to discussions by the artistic and managing directors about "unique opportunities" or "special celebrations (promotions)" that are being proposed as part of the upcoming season. Such events almost always require additional resources. The technical manager needs to recognize the potential

96

	TECHNICAL PRODUCTION GUIDELINES	

Time Prior to Opening	Event	Definition
16 weeks	Director's Written Concept Statement	At the first production meeting for each show, the director shall present a prepared, written concept statement to the production staff. This may include anything that he/she feels will aid in the understanding of the concept. The designers take this information and begin work toward an initial design, in ongoing meetings with the director and project advisors they progress to their final product.
16 weeks	Budget & Production Parameters Outlined	At the first production meeting for each show, the production coordinator shall present an overview of the budget, the schedule for the production, and in consultation with the Producer, shall identify specific parameters under which the production is to be planned. Production team members should keep all of this information in mind as they progress toward opening.
14 weeks	Preliminary Set Design	On this date the following items are to be presented at the production meeting. • A drafted floor plan • Pencil sketches of the set • Color samples of the set and major props • Sketches of any special or unusual units • Designers initial properties list • Any other special items requested to aid in the budgeting process Student designers must have their project advisor's signature on all drawings and related design materials prior to submission to the production staff. No construction will proceed without the sign-off indicating that the student and the advisor have discussed the design and any changes made through the process.
13 weeks	Preliminary Prop List (from Director)	This should include all of the props the director envisions for blocking and action during the production, including a minimum three part description (size, color/texture, use), the number needed and any consumables.

FIGURE 9.1 Partial Ohio State University technical production guidelines

impact of these newly identified needs and adjust the Time, Talent, Money Triangle resources in a manner to sufficiently meet any needs imposed by these auxiliary goals.

New works (new and reworked scripts) are a project category for which the "blueprint" approach is not always a good fit. While the blueprint tool remains an

WEEK	DATE	PERSONS INVOLVED	PURPOSE
BLUEPRINT of a PRODUCTION			
12 weeks prior to construction		Stage Manager	Collect scripts, audition cards & schedules from the business office
9 weeks prior to construction		Costume, Set, Light, Sound Designer, Director	Designers meet with director individually for brief working sessions
DSGN MTG #1 8 weeks prior to construction		Producer, Director, Assist. Director, Technical Director, Costume, Set, Light, Sound Designer, Business Manager, Music, Director, Stage Manager, Faculty Advisors	Director presents mise en scene including remarks on design elements, Discussion with designers presenting ideas, All area budgets are presented and reviewed, Production schedule is reviewed, Future meetings scheduled, Production parameters presented
DSGN MTG #2 7 weeks prior to construction		Producer, Director, Assist. Director, Technical Director, Costume, Set, Light, Sound Designer, Music Director, Stage Manager	Set & Costume designers formally present: (1. Research, 2. Preliminary sketches, 3. Preliminary prop list, 4. 1/8" or 1/4" groundplan/section or thumbnails), Sound designer present preliminary plot, Director presents 1st draft props & sound list, Initial discussion of color pallet, Following this meeting - compile prop and sounds lists, Designers meet individually with Director
DSGN MTG #3 6 weeks prior to construction		Producer, Director, Assist. Director, Technical Director, Costume, Set, Light, Sound Designer, Music Director, Stage Manager, Faculty Advisors	Designers present:(Rough 1/4" or 1/2" scale model, Revised groundplan and section, costume sketches), Discussion of props noting complex or exotic, Identify special challenges (effects, movement issues, install concerns), Identify run crew needs, Preliminary cost estimates for all designs, Confirm colors, Schedule visit to light lab

FIGURE 9.2 Portion of University of Wisconsin–Madison blueprint of production

effective checklist, experience has shown that works-in-progress strongly resist any attempts to adhere strictly to preassigned dates. The new works model often requires the decision-making process to be extended, up to and including the day of opening (and in some instances, even throughout the run). Producing organizations should embrace the opportunity to develop new work, but technical managers and their staffs must be patient, grit their teeth, and recognize that "the projected schedule" exists only to enable a successful production and not stifle creativity.

To work in this mode, without undue agony, most technical managers have to adopt what has been coined as the "sandbox" approach to production.

In the sandbox model, a production is provided with a known physical space and a set of design components that can be integrated into the show. These components are designed with the full understanding that some, all, or none may ultimately be used in the final presentation. The sandbox (performance space) and toys (production components) are provided; the utilization of both is up to the performers, artistic staff, director, and producer. While the construction of the toys can be scheduled, the timeline of potential use cannot.

PRODUCTION SCHEDULE

Step two of the planning process is the **production (project) schedule**. This term suggests, and in fact does involve, the planning of events around a single production or project. Before getting into a detailed discussion, readers should understand that for most performance companies, this situation never actually occurs. More often than not, each technical manager is involved simultaneously in planning and expediting three or four, perhaps even more, events. Often this need for a global overview is the nemesis of a technical manager. Given the split focus that this sort of juxtaposition demands, many technical managers find it hard to feel that any project is really complete since there is always another project either on the horizon or already at the front door. Still, while acknowledging this turgid environment, our discussion centers on the planning aspects of the mounting of a single production for the sake of simplicity.

The production-schedule phase is actually a combination of a number of distinct phases, each subset of which involves specific actions that confirm the project can be successfully completed within established production parameters. These actions are the same regardless of the scale of a project, their only distinction being the level of resources allocated. In fact, so-called small projects can actually require more planning time than building time.

TECHNICAL DESIGN

Many visual artists in the performing arts freelance, working as independent contractors. As such, their schedules either are or have to be flexible as to when they can begin a project. In general, the artistic design phase enjoys more flexibility than those involved in technical design. The latter must adhere to a timetable as to when projects must be prepared for the respective studios to begin fabrication and assembly. This critical preparation period for the realization of a design is a process that begins shortly after initial design ideas are presented and runs through the opening of the production. Most technical managers advocate for "starting early" on both the artistic and technical design processes in an attempt to get items into the studios sufficiently early to assure their completion when needed.

At the time of the first formal design meeting, the producer, often with the assistance of one or more technical managers, presents the project parameters. These include the specifics of both time and money budgets, the proposed schedule and any other important factors like venue, restricted times, and potential scheduling conflicts. Later in the design phase, the technical manager can become more specific in planning, developing further fabrication plans, fabrication and assemblage schedules, and establishing purchasing priorities. These aspects are identified in figure 9.3.

Task identification requires that a technical manager be a good listener during the initial design discussions, asking only an occasional question to clarify a point. To be effective, a technical manager must understand the project's concept and scope, while establishing his or her presence as a full participant in shaping the effort.

- **"Big picture" view** refers to the need of the technical manager to think globally, comprehending the various elements and aspects of production within one's own area of expertise, while equally recognizing the impact that area will have on the work of other departments. Taking the big picture view requires considering multiple factors beyond just the Time, Talent, Money Triangle to assess a design's viability and to respond appropriately.
- **Preliminary estimations** are important for purposes of evaluating the reasonableness of a project given the resources of time, talent, and money. Estimations and research demonstrate that a technical manager has begun the problem-solving process and honed an understanding of the way(s) that the proposed project will likely affect the personnel and facilities involved. Such involvement also assists a technical manager

---

TECHNICAL DESIGN FACTORS
- Task Identification
- "Big Picture" View
- Preliminary Estimations
- Resource Availability
- Prototypes

FIGURE 9.3 Technical design factors

clarify the project's true scope since project design materials may, or may not, be submitted as a complete package prior to entering the build phase.

- **Resource availability** checks are activities that permit the technical manager to keep the upcoming project on the front burner without investing great amounts of time and money. The results of such investigations often directly influence design decisions by confirming that production parameters will, or will not, allow sufficient time for the delivery or fabrication of certain elements.

- **Prototyping** is a means by which a technical manager can mock up one or more possible solutions to a specific challenge that has emerged during design meetings. Rather than waiting until the design element becomes a *fait accompli*, prototyping makes the technical manager a sort of associate designer, a much preferred position than that of an adversary.

- In the scenic area, as the design is being finalized, the technical director begins to prepare the necessary construction drawings. These drawings detail the actual construction techniques to be utilized (figure 9.4). Supporting documentation usually consists of material and labor estimations and a detailed construction schedule

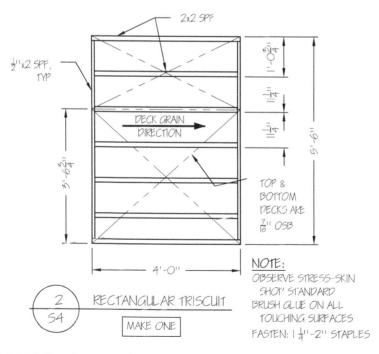

FIGURE 9.4 Sample construction drawing—top view

THE UNIT BREAKOUT LIST

When the technical manager is initially presented with a series of design (working) drawings for a production, the amount of information received may seem overwhelming. (The opposite situation is also overwhelming in those instances when the designer fails to produce the working drawings on time.) After that initial sinking feeling has left, the technical manager's first step is to analyze the project and to break this seemingly very large task into a series of smaller, more manageable tasks. Usually this takes the form of a **unit breakout list**. The unit list is simply a cataloging of each of the major components of the design. Using scenery as an example, such units might include: deck, walls, stairs, drop, masking, etc., as illustrated in figure 9.5.

The unit breakout list becomes a primary reference list supported by the graphic information prepared in the drawings. Eventually, the list can be further broken out in each of the broad categories originally established. Walls become: "Wall A," "Wall B," or "Wall C." The unit list and its various secondary lists are typically developed during the preparation of the estimation (material and labor) spread sheet. Each unit is identified, along with both associated time and money costs. The integration of talent within this equation is also the responsibility of the technical manager, i.e., the marriage of the right workers to the right task.

CALENDARS

Directly linked with the identification of tasks and the corresponding assignment of personnel resources is the need for scheduling the resource of time. While frequently not acknowledged as such, without question time is the most precious of the three parts of the Time, Talent, Money Triangle. The most basic resource for scheduling is a blank calendar featuring the appropriate months and days. Whether hand drawn or computer generated, the calendar serves as *the* primary planning tool. A thoughtful analysis of a blank calendar can be a humbling experience; there is no way to expand this time-based resource. There are only 24 hours each day, and there is a finite amount of time between the present day and opening. The only way a technical manager can affect this time dilemma is by making the passing time more effective through careful comprehensive planning and scheduling.

Any standard calendar that fits on a single sheet or screen (with plenty of room to write) is the best place to start since it provides the technical manager an overview of the entire period under examination. This format allows a technical manager to plan using a broad brush, before fixating on the minute details that need to be incorporated into the final schedule. The aforementioned unit breakout list is a useful accompanying tool since it provides an overview of all the elements that must be completed with the available work hours. As an interesting side note,

WALLS	Width	Height	Notes
A	1'-6"	12'-0"	
B	19'-6"	12'-0"	2 @ 12-light windows, French doors with sidelight panels
C-1	8'-0"	12'-0"	Arch opening
C-2	7'-0"	12'-0"	Arch opening
H	12'-3"	12'-0"	Door with 2 shutters w/upper window panel
J	1'-0"	12'-0"	
K	8'-0"	12'-0"	
L	1'-9"	12'-0"	
BB-1	10'-3"	12'-0"	Brick texture, double hung window
D	14'-0"	12'-0"	Single door shutter
E	12'-0"	12'-0"	
F/G	2'-0"	12'-0"	
HH-1	5'-0"	11'-0"	
HH-2	4'-3"	11'-0"	Single door shutter
HH-3	23'-0"	11'-0"	
CYC	22'-6"	11'-0"	Framed, Seamless Muslin

Doors

B			French Panels 2, Sidelights 2
H			2 Panels with upper window panels
D	Stock		Single shutter with 3 raised panels
HH-2	Stock		Single shutter with 3 raised panels

Molding

Cornice	100 linear feet	
Picture rail	90 linear feet	
Chair rail	90 linear feet	
Base Board	70 linear feet	

Platforms

Stage left			+8" height, assemble from stock
Stage Right			+12" height, assemble from stock
Step SL			+4" height
Step SR			+8" assemble from stock - One at +4", one at +6" and one at +8"

Windows

B-1			
B-2			
K			
BB-1			
Balustrade	12'-6"	3'-0"	

FIGURE 9.5 Unit breakout list

keep in mind that effective scheduling not only establishes start and completion dates for projects but simultaneously defines opportunities for elements or decisions still under discussion to remain undefined for an extended period before a final decision is necessary (figure 9.6).

A rule of thumb that may assist in preparing a build plan is that all construction tasks require the efforts of one key individual with the occasional assistance of another. By applying this rule, the technical manager can avoid the problem of overstaffing a task. This mistake is frequently made in the educational environment where many students arrive for a lab experience and their work opportunities are limited by both space and material availability.

THE CRADLE WILL ROCK - BUILD CALENDAR

SUNDAY	MONDAY	TUESDAY	WEDNESDAY	THURSDAY	FRIDAY	SATURDAY
26 FEBRUARY	27 LUMBER DELIVERY / UNLOAD & STORE LUMBER IN SHOP / CONSTRUCT LAYOUT TABLE / BUILD -8' STEP PLATFORMS / BUILD +0' MAIN DECK PLATFORMS / HANG BACKDROP ON PAINT FRAME	28	1 MARCH / PAINT BACKDROP	2	3	4 / BOWEN RENTAL
5	6 / MODIFY DS EDGE OF BOWEN DECK & INSTALL NEW +0' PLATFORMS / INSTALL -8' STEP PLATFORMS & FACINGS / PAINT BACKDROP	7	8	9	10 WINTER CLASSES END	11
12	13 WINTER FINALS / PAINT BACKDROP	14 WINTER FINALS	15 WINTER FINALS	16 WINTER FINALS	17	18
19	20 SPRING BREAK	21 SPRING BREAK	22 SPRING BREAK	23 SPRING BREAK	24 SPRING BREAK	25
26	27 SPRING CLASSES BEGIN / BUILD +9' BAND PLATFORM / BUILD +30' CENTER PLATFORM / BUILD +38' DESK PLATFORM / BUILD +36' JAIL PLATFORM / BUILD CENTER STAIRCASE	28	29	30	31	1 APRIL / BOWEN RENTAL
2 BOWEN RENTAL	3 BUILD WALLS	4	5	6	7 BOWEN RENTAL	8 BOWEN RENTAL
9 BOWEN RENTAL	10 BUILD WALLS / HANG BACKDROP / INSTALL +9', +30', +38' & +36' PLATFORMS, SUBFLOOR, SHOWFLOOR & FACINGS / INSTALL CENTER STAIRS	11	12	13	14	15
16 EASTER SUNDAY	17 INSTALL WALLS A THRU L & ATTACH ALL MOULDINGS / BUILD WINDOWS (X5) / BUILD DOOR	18	19	20	21 BOWEN RENTAL	22 BOWEN RENTAL
23	24 INSTALL HANDRAIL / INSTALL WINDOWS & HANG DOOR / INSTALL ESCAPES / PAINT - PAINT - PAINT / SCHEDULED SET LOAD IN	25	26	27	28 CLEAN BACKSTAGE / ADJUST MASKING	29 CRADLE LIGHT FOCUS
30 CRADLE CUE WRITE	1 MAY CRADLE CREW WATCH	2	3 CRADLE 1ST TECH	4 CRADLE 2ND TECH	5 CRADLE 3RD TECH	6 CRADLE 1ST DRESS
7	8 CRADLE 2ND DRESS	9 CRADLE FINAL DRESS	10 CRADLE OPENS	11	12	13

FIGURE 9.6 Sample build calendar

Christopher Zinkon, Resident Technical Director, Ohio State University

BAR CHARTS

A handy and very effective visual tool to illustrate project management is a bar or Gantt chart. Gantt charts, named after management consultant Harry Gantt, illustrate a project schedule, detailing the critical relationship between tasks, including start-to-start, start-to-finish, finish-to-finish, and finish-to-start. The various stages of a project are laid out in a sequential, linear fashion and visually stacked on top of each other, indicating the dependent relationship between necessary actions. Start-to-start indicates the simultaneous launch of two actions, start-to-finish projects the anticipated length of time necessary to complete a task, finish-to-finish is the simultaneous completion of two tasks, and finish-to-start shows the necessary completion of one task before another can begin. For example, a finish-to-start relationship is the need to complete the assembly of all the flat frames before covering and painting.

There are many computer applications that support the creation of Gantt charts with software functions that enable the visual tracking of characteristics like critical paths, slack time for noncritical activities, task duration, percentage of completion, current project status, and the embedding of detailed notes. An effective Gantt chart is a daily reminder of what has been completed, the number of tasks left, the schedule of what lies ahead, and the remaining time before a project must be finished.

Figure 9.7 is a very simplified bar chart version of *The Cradle Will Rock*'s build calendar featured in figure 9.6. Inspired by GANTT chart practices, this bar chart is an effective visual reference, revealing resource overlaps, competing deadlines, time demands, and underutilized opportunities as well as illustrating possible space conflicts. When shared with workers, this bar chart calendar indicates to the entire staff the technical manager's expectations and can give a quick yet full view of build plans and progress.

When creating a bar chart, be mindful of the hours previously established during the estimation phase as being necessary to build each unit, as well as the availability and skill levels of labor resources. This process requires a thoughtful assessment of the skills and schedules of the respective members of the labor force. Be careful to be as realistic as possible regarding the actual amount of work that can be accomplished within a given time span. In some instances, it is better to view time as hours, while in others it might be more fruitful to use half-days as the unit of measure. Include catch-up and contingency time in each week of the build phase, thereby allowing some slack time in the timetable to make certain that everything stays on schedule as much as possible. Do not leave all this time to the very end; this frequently results in an accumulation of either half-completed projects or projects that never got started at all. And through all this, the technical manager must be aware that even with the most carefully crafted plans,

CRADLE WILL ROCK – BUILD CALENDAR
(Partial) 15-Jan-14

Task	Staff assignment	S 26-Feb	M 27-Feb	T 28-Feb	W 1-Mar	R 2-Mar	F 3-Mar	S 4-Mar	S 5-Mar	M 6-Mar	T 7-Mar	W 8-Mar	R 9-Mar	F 10-Mar	S 11-Mar	S 12-Mar	M 13-Mar	T 14-Mar	W 15-Mar	R 16-Mar	F 17-Mar	S 18-Mar	S 26-Mar	M 27-Mar	T 28-Mar	W 29-Mar	R 30-Mar	F 31-Mar
Unload Lumber	Lab Students	X																										
Construct layout table	Jim		X																									
Build 8" step platforms	Sue		X	X	X	X	X																					
Install 8" step platforms & facings	Sue			X	X	X	X			X	X	X	X	X														
Build main deck platforms	Chris	X	X	X	X	X	X																					
Hang drop on paint rack	Robert	X	X																									
Paint backdrop	Robert				X	X	X			X	X	X	X	X			X	X	X	X	X							
Modify stage edge & platforms	Jim									X	X	X	X	X														
SPRING BREAK																						S P R I N G — B R E A K						
Build 9" band platform	Sue																							X	X	X	X	X
Build 30" center platform	Jim																							X	X	X	X	X
Build 38" desk platform	Chris																							X	X	X	X	X
Build 36" jail platform	Robert																							X	X	X	X	X
Build center stair case	Sally																							X	X	X	X	X

FIGURE 9.7 Bar chart example

circumstances and absences will occur that hinder (hopefully only temporarily) the desired rate of output.

Many components of the production process are dependent on another, and the technical manager must stay on top of all of these aspects. Keep in mind that scenery needs to be constructed before it can be painted, props and costumes built before being used by actors, and the stage spatially defined prior to light hang. A rough priority to use in laying out the schedule would include:

1. Items that must get to the painters;
2. Items that affect the performers that would be helpful if received earlier than first tech (doors, tables, and chairs, etc.); and
3. Pieces that must get onstage to provide shape, mass, and tonality for the lighting designer's focus and level-set sessions.

The build phase is further informed by the priorities developed through rehearsal. The technical manager is responsible to respond in a timely manner to "requests" as they come. Each request needs an honest appraisal as to whether the timetable will permit its inclusion and completion. If time is tight, treat each request using the principle of the "change order" long established in construction industries, i.e., every change brings the risk of additional cost or a need to reestablish priorities.

The technical manager needs to be available to receive reasonable progress reports during the production process. Keeping a check on progress allows for quick schedule revisions and improved planning. Avoid giving today's answers to yesterday's problems. A daily to-do list, taken directly from the build calendar as well as shop notes, and weekly review of the bar schedule are requisite.

SCHEDULING STAFF

To assist workers in understanding their role within the producing unit, the technical manager should strive to instill in everyone a goal, rather than a task, orientation. Workers should be informed of the relationship of the particular project on which they are working to the whole production and to participate in checking off the completed project on the master schedule (calendar, bar chart, or project list) when each phase is finished. Such involvement helps to keep everyone aware of the timetable and gives each crew member a sense of team effort, task completion, and personal satisfaction.

Even someone assigned to complete a long series of cut lists will perform the task with more concern if he or she knows how the pieces being cutting will be incorporated into the design. Through stressing the relationship of each part to the whole, the technical manager encourages a stronger level of personal investment in the production. In addition, an informed worker who completes a task is likely to recognize that there is more to be done and will be more inclined to ask, "What's next?"

The technical manager also must ensure that there is sufficient work to do. Because of the law of human nature that states that work expands to fill the time available, the technical manager must constantly battle the tendency to underestimate the needed time. There is nothing that can turn workers off more quickly than not having something to do. Even more to the point is that ineffective use of time resources can have devastating results as opening approaches. Remember that there is no such thing as "just a simple set." Be prepared.

Another concept not to be lost in the scheduling process is the need to allow time for staff development. Developing and honing worker skills is the mission of educational institutions and is an approach that greatly enhances the commercial environment as well. When tasks are assigned, time should be allocated with the full expectation that the worker performing the job will need to learn aspects along the way. The opportunity for skill development improves worker morale, provides appropriate challenges to long-term workers, and decreases the technical manager's reliance on the same person for particular techniques. Variation of task assignment aids professional development and expands the portfolio of skills within a given shop.

What drives the decision to assign certain workers to specific projects? Most shops have two levels of workers: laborers and skilled or semiskilled craftspersons. By learning and appropriating the particular skills of each member of your workforce, you can assign tasks with confidence that the assignment can be completed successfully and on time. When matching workers to tasks, begin by listing each person or group of persons, e.g., students in similar skill-level groupings, by name. With this list of names, you can associate a particular set of strengths that will be brought to bear on the project. For example, Michael, your master carpenter, may be the best finish carpenter you know, but he may also possess the strongest welding skills. Through careful matching, the project succeeds and the worker is affirmed and the technical manager is able to consider what needs to be accomplished, where it is to be done, what process is needed to get there, and what problems might be faced. As noted earlier, decision making should not turn into micromanagement where all the choices are made by the technical manager. A far better situation is one where, through planning, the technical manager develops a comprehensive understanding of the project and makes it his/her responsibility to provide the tools and resources necessary to enable workers to complete the task.

SCHEDULING FACILITIES & EQUIPMENT

The Time, Talent, Money Triangle is inherently connected to facility and equipment issues as well. Limitations created by the amount, type, condition, and availability of space and equipment have great impact on the production process.

The effective technical manager stays vigilant in planning where raw materials are stored and projects will be assembled, painted, and eventually loaded into the theatre. Offsite locations may be necessary, and temporary storage of finished goods may also be a consideration. Regardless of the size of the available studio, physical space remains at a premium. Technical managers also become extremely conscious of architectural challenges such as narrow doors, long hallways, and low ceilings. Access to specialized equipment such as a welder, paint hood, or personnel lift can also be a significant factor in project planning. Just as time cannot be expanded beyond our given 24 hours a day, the laws of physics cannot be bent or broken to better enable construction, finishing, and installation. Constant and open communication with those directly involved in building the project and an intimate knowledge of every square foot of space that is available to achieve the production goals is yet another responsibility of the technical manager. Effective visualization of traffic patterns and workflow is a critical part of the scheduling and planning process.

Chapter 10

Analysis & Problem Solving

Comparisons between the desired design and the available time, talent, and money are integral to the design phase. If the design scope works within the allotted resources, approval of the final design becomes easier. If the design does not fit within the available resources, then a period of design refinement must begin. During these discussions, a technical manager can be of considerable assistance by offering specific alternative suggestions that may enable the completion of the project to move forward without unduly sacrificing the integrity of the design concept. This is sometimes referred to as value engineering.

During the technical design phase, a technical manager consciously needs to avoid any subjective tendencies to limit a perceived challenge too closely. For the sake of the project and for the team, grant yourself and the production team the opportunity to examine as many alternative approaches as possible, doing your best to ignore any limiting personal boundaries—be they creative or structural. Try to isolate real problems from imagined ones, and above all be judicious, even generous, in your comments about early ideas. By definition, the design phase in the performing arts is a collaborative effort. Acknowledge the talents of others to inform the process.

No prescription is available to equip a technical manager with the skills necessary to become an effective problem solver. Even though the exact path will vary from individual to individual, effective problem solving does, however, rely on using a specific pattern through which information progresses. This template organizes the myriad of details that affect each decision and provides a path to follow to reach a decision in a timely fashion (fig. 10.1). Good reasoning, backed with a thorough technical understanding, forms the foundation for effective problem solving.

1. Define the problem. Although seemingly simple, coming to an agreement on a problem definition within the collaborative structure of production is often one of the technical manager's biggest challenges. Seeking a corporate definition as to what lies ahead involves clarity of thought, in-depth dialogue, and effective questioning. A good starting point is to identify firsthand desired outcomes by simply asking, "What is it that we are trying to achieve?"

A common understanding of a universally accepted goal goes a long way toward building up the confidence of a production team and establishing open lines of communication early in the process. Each individual and/or organization needs to know what is to be accomplished before deciding the best way of achieving that goal. Defining the Time, Talent, Money Triangle parameters of each problem as well as examining the task from the perspective of each collaborator is also helpful. Agreement on basic objectives lays the groundwork for all of the additional steps of the necessary analysis. If a problem faced cannot be clearly articulated in one sentence, most likely the problem has not been adequately defined. Ingenious solutions depend on properly describing a problem and allowing adequate examination time to reach an effective decision.

2. Establish the criteria and identify the obstacles. Once a problem has been defined, by what measurements will the relative success or failure of the endeavor be judged? The criteria phase places the potential decision within a context (fig. 10.2). As this context is established, the original problem definition

---

PROBLEM ANALYSIS
- Define the problem
- Establish the criteria and identify the obstacles
- Research
- Brainstorm
- Analyze and Hypothesize
- Decide
- Evaluate the action

FIGURE 10.1 Problem analysis

CRITERIA QUESTIONS
- What will the results look like?
- Who else should be involved in the decision-making process?
- What are the available parameters of the Time, Talent, Money Triangle that may be applied to this solution?
- What stands in the way of success?
- Who or what will have to change to successfully achieve this challenge?
- What are the guideposts necessary to observe along the way?

FIGURE 10.2 Criteria questions

111

is further refined. Each piece of new information narrows the path to achieving a viable solution and moves the effort closer to a satisfactory conclusion.

Although a technical manager is unlikely to foresee every circumstance, establishing the whole criteria for a problem is essential. In touring, for example, all units must be constructed not only to fit on the back of a truck but also must fit through the smallest loading door on the tour. Both of these pieces of information individually affect the construction of a unit, but taken together they have an even greater impact on a unit's required design. Ongoing conversations with the production staff regarding both form and function greatly assist in defining parameters.

3. Research. Research is simply the process of asking questions, seeking answers, and creating new knowledge. When asking a question that has not been asked before and then vigorously seeking an answer to that question, the evaluator cannot help but find and create new knowledge. Research inherently follows a variety of paths and feeds itself, spooling off all sorts of important data that may be of use immediately or may simply inform the technical manager for future challenges. Research demands a commitment to rigorous methodology. Research often starts with a careful examination of the work of others who have faced similar challenges. Published sources of previously solved production challenges can be found in the *USITT Tech Expo Catalog* collection; the *Theatre Design and Technology* magazine archive; the costume poster session archive of USITT; and the three-volume *Technical Design Solutions for Theatre: The Technical Brief Collection,* edited by Ben Sammler and Don Harvey of the Yale School of Drama.

Accumulate as many facts as time permits, and write them down. The mere act of writing things down assists in seeing patterns and making connections. Throughout this data-collection phase, avoid defining your research too narrowly, too early. Be open to many ideas; you never know what one thing may prove to be of value in seeking a solution. Play with the wording of your original question and you may discover a different solution. The answer one gets is directly related to the questions that were originally asked.

Research requires too much time and effort to be selfish with your discovered knowledge; share the challenges and discoveries with the creative talent of your production team. Hearing someone else's perspective on the task ahead may just open a new door, possibly providing a different path toward the development of a solution. Never underestimate the contributions that others can make to your process. One of the joys of the collaborative nature of the performing arts is that problem solving is not vested in one person. Most colleagues are also fully engaged in the production process. They all have the ability to make effective contributions, if the technical manager grants them that opportunity and the power to influence decision making.

4. Brainstorm. Another good technique to generate potential solutions is to brainstorm ideas. Brainstorming involves a temporary shutdown of any judgment with the goal of developing a quantity of options with little concern for quality. Brainstorming is especially effective as a group problem-solving technique. By allowing undeveloped ideas to be shared, new options are discovered, and superior results are achieved. If you are too critical too early, flexibility of thought and freedom to form new associations is suppressed.

In brainstorming, ideas are generated and listed as fast as possible. The wilder the idea, the better for expanding ideas; creative solutions are often found beyond perceived boundaries. During this process, there should be no idea, policy, or tradition too sacred to question. As assumptions are altered as to what can be done, the traditional or commonplace is broken, opening new possibilities both for solving specific problems and for meaningful development.

Newly formed ideas are quite fragile and may require some time for incubation. Fragile new thoughts that are given support often lead to other ideas that can bear positive results. After generating a long list of possibilities, take some time away and simply let the challenging features process in your head. This background thinking gives your brain the freedom to explore and can be very successful. Many colleagues cite that some of their best solutions are discovered while sitting in traffic or taking a shower, not by directly thinking about the problem.

5. Analyze and Hypothesize. With the problem well defined and information gathered, the next step is to begin to play out "What ifs?" Compare and contrast alternate solutions. Forecast what the outcome might be with each potential solution path. At this juncture, for the first time, practicality can become a concern. What will the true impact of this solution be as analyzed using through the Time, Talent, Money Triangle?

In the analysis phase, ask these two questions: "What is the worst thing that will happen if we make this choice?" and "What is the best thing that will happen if we make this choice?" A time-honored approach is to write out a list of the issue's pros and cons on a single sheet of paper divided with a line down the center. The resulting contrast between loss and benefit serves to focus thought. This analysis rarely results in identifying a single perfect option, but as your degree of confidence in any one solution arises, that solution will move to the forefront of best options.

Often helpful during deliberations is to look at a second "right" answer, somewhat analogous to the much-referenced Plan B. As the problem-solving process progresses, no doubt one solution will rise to the top as the most viable. Do not cut the process short at that point; look for another option. History has shown that the first solution is not always the best, nor viable later on as the process moves forward. Often, the second right answer proves to be the best approach in achieving the desired goals.

Creativity is the watchword. Mentally playing out the possibilities in collaboration with others is frequently cited as some of the most satisfying work performed by a technical manager. In being creative, one must avoid such stumbling blocks as fear of failure, pressures to conform, reluctance to face a challenge, and habitual behaviors. The more open the mind of a technical manager remains, the greater the potential for success.

6. Decide. Indecision is a form of procrastination, which, in the performing arts, can prove to be catastrophic since the deadline never moves forward to provide more time. The entire problem-solving process is meaningless if a clear decision is not reached. Indecision examined through the lens of the Time, Talent, Money Triangle shows that there is simply too little time to squander, staff talent is diminished by forcing hasty action, and the inability to reach a decision will undoubtedly cost money. Bad decisions are forgivable, but indecision simply is not acceptable.

The compulsive perfectionist is typically overly cautious in decision making. There will never be enough data nor enough time to satisfy this type of individual. To be a success as a technical manager, a person must be aware of the problem and be careful never to fall into this behavior pattern. When working with others who fit this type, a manager is well advised to develop strong skills in bringing challenges to a timely conclusion. If nothing else, the technical manager is often in a position to establish a deadline for gathering and analyzing data and identifying the point at which a decision must be made. A good technical manager learns to judge the necessary time allowed for deliberation and recognize the point where action is required.

Most decisions made during the course of a project are in fact quite small, but collectively they determine the overall success of a project. Sensitivity to the unique time demands of each decision is key. Knowing when to force matters to a decision point and when to allow the process to continue a bit longer comes with experience. Keeping perspective on the magnitude of each decision as it affects the production process aids the development of a technical manager's perception by others as a problem solver.

Once a decision has been made, inform everyone involved. Be aware, however, that the way in which you articulate your decision can be as important as the decision itself. Give some thought to how your decision will be accepted among your colleagues. The validity of your decision will only be determined if it is recognized by others and then implemented.

Equally important is that a manager realize that the further one is from a decision-making level, the harder it is to appreciate the logic and quality of the decision made. Additional background may need to be provided, or you may simply need to rely on the authority you hold within your organization to carry the day. Certainly not everyone will agree with you, but everyone must move forward to implement the plan. In any event, a sensitivity to both the message and the messenger must be developed.

7. Evaluate the action. Although there never seems to be enough time to look back at the choices made, ongoing evaluation is vital to the development of both an organization and the people within that group. Only through evaluation is a technical manager able to recognize both the triumphs and the mistakes from the past and learn from them. Was the choice made effective? How could it have been improved? Will I ever do that again? What went right? What went wrong? What piece of information that I did not have at the time would have affected the decision I made?

Evaluation is not second guessing. A decision has been made, and the consequences have already occurred. This is not a time for regrets; rather, it is a time to recognize the learning that has taken place and to apply this new found knowledge in future opportunities. Evaluation with a recognition of what has been learned in hindsight is the true benefit of experience.

The evaluation of the success or failure of a decision implies a comparison to some sort of standard. Common standards include issues such as safety, function, economics, and industry practices. No decision will hold up to the detailed scrutiny of all of these factors; each evaluation is seen as an opportunity for growth.

TWO DYNAMICS THAT PLAY A SIMULANTEOUS ROLE

Throughout the seven steps of the problem-solving process, two other factors are at work. The first is **projection.** Simply put, projection involves a constant awareness of what comes next. At each problem-solving step along the way, the technical manager must remain mindful of the desired outcome while simultaneously looking ahead to the completion of this task and moving onto the next. None of the steps of the process are approached in a vacuum. The "big picture" remains always in the foreground. Only during brainstorming sessions should projection be set aside.

The second factor is **feedback.** Feedback involves the constant flow of new information that is generated as time passes. Finding a solution has to be viewed as an ongoing process. Throughout the examination, new information will become available that will, in turn, impact earlier steps. Still, the goal is to make a decision. At some point, a decision must be made and the technical manager must move on. However, along the way, late-breaking information should not be overlooked or ignored.

Examples of tangible feedback are all those changes that come out of rehearsals as opening night approaches. Some are minor and must simply be shared. Others can be quite major and have significant impact, resulting in redesign or rebuilds. While a technical manager needs to keep the whole project in perspective and seek ways to soften the impact of changes on others, maintaining an attitude that every problem can be solved goes a long way in assisting others to deal with change.

The problem-solving process described above works just as well on a micro level, such as when making such decisions about what to have for lunch or what movie to see, as on a macro level, such as when thinking about season selection or individual production development. The steps involved can take weeks or months or can be compressed into just a few moments.

Chapter 11

Budgets & Quality Control

One of the more significant contributions a technical manager provides to the production process is the projection of costs and labor hours and, as a part of that process, the determination of material and labor methodologies to be utilized in the fabrication and finishing of a theatrical product. Be it costume, scenery, props, sound, lighting, rigging, multimedia, or special effects, all require similar effort and use the same principles. However, to cover them all is beyond the scope of this book; to simplify our discussion, we use the example of scenery to illustrate the various aspects of the estimation process and the characteristics and tools of the technical managers involved.

Estimation is a process that many technical managers find problematic. Unfortunately, the natural reaction of many technical managers is to see the challenge awaiting them and attack it head on; they start to execute the selected design before thoroughly examining the task. They want to move forward immediately and dismiss the need to first examine project feasibility to see if can be completed given the parameters or restraints that control projected resources. The task of estimation holds us back; it holds up the project. But without the assurance that we have the needed resources, our work is likely to risk incompletion and create dissatisfaction among many constituents.

The preparation of a time-and-materials estimate clarifies the Time, Talent, Money requirements for a project, measures project needs against available resources, and allows technical managers to become intimately familiar with the entire project or production. The resultant estimates greatly assist a technical manager in the future decision-making process. Thorough and accurate estimation activities assemble information sufficiently in advance of actual decision making –providing time to manipulate the production components to fit within "fixed" company parameters. Labor and materials estimates enable value comparisons of production design components. "We can either afford the requested disappearance trap for the end of the show or the revolving bookcase for the entrance in act II but not both. What do we want to do?"

QUALITIES OF AN ESTIMATOR
- Thoroughness
- Experience
- Detail-specific knowledge
- People skills and knowledge
- Organizational skills

FIGURE 11.1 Qualities of an estimator

Later there is a discussion of various estimation systems that might be used, but regardless of the specific estimation system chosen, each technical manager must possess a critical set of skills or attributes to successfully complete this duty (fig. 11.1).

- **Thoroughness** refers to a methodical approach to identify and analyze every element within a project. Each design component—e.g., (in scenery) framing, subsurfaces, finished surfaces, and detailing such as molding; (in costumes) slopers, mockups, costume fabrics, fasteners, and accessories; and (in lighting) equipment and accessory inventories, power runs, repair parts, and color media—must be considered. In addition, the estimator must provide identical, or near identical, information about each piece to assure that every aspect has been covered.
- **Experience** recognizes all the various steps and pitfalls likely to be incurred during the construction of a piece. Experience helps the estimator read between the lines and to foresee the problems inherent in completing a project. This characteristic is very much tied-in with . . .
- **Detail-specific knowledge**, which requires that the estimator know specifics such as standard dimensions of materials, their availability, sources, fastening methods, technical design issues, handling methods, purchasing practices, and costs.
- **People skills** help the estimator understand the physical and psychological boundaries of the crew. The technical manager must be aware, when making assignments and when determining actual work output, of such issues as everyone's need for, and right to, respect and recognition and that each individual has personal strengths and weaknesses.
- **Organizational skills** are, of course, probably the most basic and often the most assumed of the five characteristics. Scheduling materials and personnel, maintaining records, and procuring resources are

the major organizational challenges of management. The practice of estimation has two principal phases: the budget projection phase and the cost estimation phase.

ESTIMATOR SKILLS AND TOOLS

Having the necessary characteristics is not really enough. Each technical manager's background is different, but what they have in common is that they work in a field that is as custom as the finest homes built to client specifications. That translates into technical managers having tool sets and personal resources that make them experienced in making choices. For technical managers, being able to make decisive and successful choices is key to their value to the company.

Technical managers initiate and oversee custom projects. Much of the construction required is unique to a production, or more precisely to a specific designer's visual interpretation of a specific script. Since no two productions of the same script are identical, each technical manager must determine the specific materials and assembly techniques that best fit the designer's intent and optimize the talents of the crew while still remaining within the projected parameters of the project.

One of the specialized skill sets that a technical manager must develop are those involved in purchasing materials and supplies. Even if the lead manager is no longer involved in this activity on a daily basis, understanding the purchasing process and knowing the wide variety of materials that are available greatly increases the resources that can be brought to bear on problem solving. Knowing what goods and services are available opens the technical manager to a much greater variety of potential solutions.

PURCHASING RESOURCES

Most technical managers collect catalogs featuring all manner of products, although they collect fewer with the rise of the Internet. Catalog files would be organized either alphabetically by corporation name or arranged by subject headings based on some self-developed system. In addition to catalogs, product samples collections, including molding pieces, fabric swatches, paint cards, and plastic shapes, remain common and always useful.

A quick scan of the purchasing resource files of any technical manager will reveal the five or six primary sources utilized. These dog-eared works are identified by quickly scrawled notes on the cover and pricing sheets inserts that have been carefully dated. Clearly identified on the front of each catalog will be a contact name with whom the technical manager has worked on a prior purchase. In addition, a wide variety of product retailers will also likely be bookmarked in appropriate folders on the technical manager's computer.

Catalog and sample files are not only useful when making product purchases, they also serve as an idea repository. When technical managers face a particularly complex technical challenge, they will often thumb through related product catalogs to generate ideas. Over time, they often develop a relationship with a several or more vendor representatives and will contact them directly for advice. Even in totally unrelated fields, sales people can be great sources of free information. Many become fascinated with the challenge presented by a performing arts project and are more than willing to share their expertise in the efforts toward a solution.

Developing a personal relationship with a vendor also has another benefit in that the vendor's goodwill can shave some time off the Time, Talent, Money Triangle. By expediting a purchase, sometimes prior to the actual paperwork being processed, many a vendor has "saved" a theatrical production. Personal relationships with vendors are developed through conversations over the telephone and at trade shows, as well as through maintaining good records of prior transactions.

PURCHASING TIME FRAMES

Material availability is a major factor in the scheduling of work. In the broadest definition, the materials are identified as part of the "money" portion necessary to complete the Time, Talent, Money Triangle for a project. Because a lack of needed materials can bring a project to a grinding halt, ordering supplies far in advance of their need is highly recommended. In planning, the technical manager must be mindful of both local availability and necessary shipping and compensate for these time factors.

There is usually the possibility of accruing some cost savings through volume buying of commonly used goods. Many vendors provide generous price breaks on large volume purchases. However, there is no cost saving by overbuying. If the quantity necessary to receive a price break exceeds the amount of material you would be likely to consume within a reasonable time, e.g., a single fiscal year, or the space available for storage, then quantity buying becomes a poor choice.

VOLUME PURCHASING

Quantity buying can be problematic also from both materials handling and shelf-life viewpoints. The price of glue, for example, can be greatly reduced if purchased in 55-gallon barrels; however, these barrels are bulky, very heavy, and inconvenient when dispensing the product. The shelf life of many reactive chemical products such as molding and casting materials is also rather short. For any project suggesting the application of these materials, buy them when you need them and not months in advance.

In purchasing large quantities of natural materials like wood, be aware of the effect of building climate conditions on even the short-term storage of such items. The moisture content of lumber is radically affected by the storage conditions at both the lumberyard and within your production facility. The warping caused by drying wood has resulted in many a "sled runner" being forced into some semblance of true in flat construction.

Commercial theatres rarely have the storage, desire, or capital to invest in large quantities of materials and as such are even more at the mercy of availability. Educational facilities are sometime hampered by the overall purchasing policies of their parent institution.

The materials estimate, when prepared for a project, serves as the master shopping list of items to purchase for a project. By staying aware of the wide variety of materials available and maintaining a good working relationship with a variety of vendors, technical managers are able to be more creative problem solvers. The hunger for information discussed earlier in the chapter on technical manager personal characteristics extends to include the tools and equipment available, as well as the techniques that may be utilized, and is the foundation for developing an extensive knowledge base.

ESTIMATION METHODOLOGIES USED BY TECHNICAL MANAGERS

Figure 11.2 illustrates the **three principal estimation approaches** used by most companies and serves as a good model for the estimation work prepared by entertainment technical managers. They are each unique and, at the same time, both

Estimating Approaches	Definition
1.0 Similar	Useful when little is established or even known, as is often the case early in development. Although a quick and relatively easy method, it's not terribly accurate. Compares the current project with similar past projects; best if we can remember or have recorded them.
2.0 Metric	Most useful for estimates that are measurement based, e.g., $/SF or #units/day. This is The National Construction Estimator model. While a fairly simple method, not every activity or cost can be estimated quantitatively. Here's where the M.U.F. approach can be used.
3.0 Piece-by-piece	Useful when there exists significant detail about a design. The most accurate method of estimating this system is also the most time-consuming and expensive.

FIGURE 11.2 Estimating approaches

useful and not. Time and temperament probably serve to guide the choice of which is used by a manager, but all carry the element of risk. How much risk can the technical manager handle? How much risk can the production company withstand?

Approach 1.0—**Similar**

Although every technical manager hates to be trapped into giving a "ballpark" estimate, the Similar Method is perhaps the only organized response that can be given. Mention has been made of the usefulness of "as-built" record keeping, but time does not always permit the opportunity or resources to do so. All that remains is our personal and sometimes collective memories to provide guess-timates as to the costs of comparable projects. The response is not something a technical manager wants to be held to, but it does allow some information upon which a project can move forward. Caveats aside, our best hope is probably that we won't be bitten by poor judgment. Using the Similar Method is a time to apply a generous but reasonable contingency.

In standard estimation practice, a contingency percentage is determined either by organizational policy or by the estimator's perceived complexity of the project. Given a reasonable level of confidence in the calculations and the use of standard fabrication techniques, a figure of 10% of the total material, labor, and overhead charges is normally assigned (fig. 11.3). If the project is complex and/or involves unfamiliar circumstances or fabrication techniques, the contingency used by most estimators is 15–20%.

Subflooring Studding

Craft@Hrs		Unit	Material	Labor	Total

Studding Per square foot of wall area. Do not subtract for openings less than 16' wide. Figures in parentheses indicate typical board feet per SF of wall area, measured on one side, and include normal waste. Add for each corner and partition from below. Costs include studding, nails. Add for plates from the section above and also, door and window opening framing, backing, let-in bracing, fire blocking, and sheathing for shear walls from the sections that follow. Labor includes layout, plumb and align.

Door Opening Framing Wall stud framing, 2" x 4"

Craft@Hrs		Unit	Material	Labor	Total
2" x 4", Std & Btr					
2" x 4" studs, 16" centers, per MBF	--@.000	MBF	675.15	--	675.15
12" centers (.73 BF per SF)	B1@.031	SF	0.49	1.36	1.86
16" centers (.54 BF per SF)	B1@.023	SF	0.37	1.01	1.38
20" centers (.45 BF per SF)	B1@.020	SF	0.30	0.88	1.18
24" centers (.37 BF per SF)	B1@.016	SF	0.25	0.70	0.96
Add for each corner or partition	B1@.083	Ea	1.45	3.65	15.09

FIGURE 11.3 Studwall construction

National Construction Estimator, 63 edition, 2015, Craftsman Book Company, Solana Beach, CA, p. 42.

Approach 2.0—**Metric**

This is the system most common to contractors and architects. This foundation of all estimation methodology comes from an examination of each unit to be constructed and the assignment of an appropriate cost factor incorporating the Time, Talent, Money Triangle. This foundation is also the basis for the following three methods discussed. While each requires attention to detail the amount of time necessary to conduct the estimate differs, the certainty of accuracy is directly proportional to the steps in the order of their listing.

Although we are not aware of any similar published formal approach regarding aspects of the performing arts currently available, construction estimators and contractors have been using cost (time and materials) information from publications such as *The National Construction Estimator* for most of the past century. The arts would be well served if such a set of guidelines were available, but the custom nature of the work makes this approach too general to ultimately be useful. Still, individual companies, where certain factors such as skill levels, venue restraints, and available labor fit into a sort of constant, may lend themselves to the creation of an "in-house" standard. Appendix vi—Scenic Construction Estimation Guidelines is a sample of one such document that focuses only on time issues.

Industry publications, like *The National Construction Estimator*, provide a more inclusive application that includes both time and materials. Each listing provides a description of the job; the material(s) employed; the number of square feet or cubic feet involved in "unit cost"; and the cost of the materials, labor, and equipment necessary to complete the task. The table below is a sample of the kind of information typically provided by this estimation manual (fig. 11.3).

Each category is introduced by the material and process covered by the figures provided, then a variety of options are given such as the material and its spacing. Intended to be used nationwide, *The National Construction Estimator* provides general information but permits substitutions to reflect local conditions. The series of statements from *The National Construction Estimator* (fig. 11.4) nicely summarizes the reasoning behind such guidelines.

As noted above, no current "estimator" is available for the entertainment industry, nor is the development of one anticipated. The lack of a theatrical estimator is due to two factors: the wide variety of producing situations and the "custom" nature of each project produced. However, familiarity with the *National Construction Estimator* provides a model for the organization of estimation information and can assist technical managers to develop some personal "rules of thumb" for their own process.

Figure 11.5 is a sample of an estimate created using a *National Construction Estimator* estimate sheet. The craft "B1" refers to a combination of one carpenter and one laborer, with an average hourly rate of $34.56, a figure that includes wages, benefits, sick leave, vacation, welfare, and all tax and insurance charges based on wages. Note that the expense of "supervision" is not included among these labor costs but is estimated and applied separately—the very model of what we discuss later in the Labor Estimation section.

How Accurate Are These Figures?

As accurate as possible considering that the estimators who wrote this book don't know your subcontractors or material suppliers, haven't seen the plans or specifications, don't know what building code applies or where the job is, had to project material costs at least 6 months into the future, and had no record of how much work the crew that will be assigned to the job can handle.

You wouldn't bid a job under those conditions. And we don't claim that all construction is done at these prices.

Estimating Is an Art, not a science. On many jobs the range between high and low bid will be 20% or more. There's room for legitimate disagreement on what the correct costs are, even when complete plans and specifications are available, the date and site are established, and labor and material costs are identical for all bidders

No cost fits all jobs. Good estimates are custom made for a particular project and a single contractor through judgment, analysis and experience.

This book is not a substitute for judgment, analysis and sound estimating practice. It's an aid in developing an informed opinion of cost. If you're using this book as your sole cost authority for contract bids, you're reading more into these pages than the editors intend.

FIGURE 11.4 The *National Construction Estimator* quotation

National Construction Estimator, 63 edition, 2015, Craftsman Book Company, Solana Beach, CA, p. 5.

Using as a resource only the relevant data of the estimation table in figure 11.8, here is an example of an estimate for an 8'x8' 2x4 stud wall using 24" centers.

	Craft@ Hrs	Unit	Material	Labor	Total
Wall stud framing					
2" x 4" (at $510 per MBF), Std & Btr					
24" center (.37 BF per SF)	Bl@.021	SF	0.28	0.54	0.82

Summary Chart below:

8'x8' = 64 square feet @ .28/SF	Total materials estimate	$17.92
8'x8' = 64 square feet @ .54/SF	Total labor estimate	$34.56
Materials of $17.92 + Labor of $34.56	**Total cost of wall**	$52.48

FIGURE 11.5 Estimate for 8' x 8' 2x4 stud wall, based on figure 11.3 guideline

Alternative Approach 2.1—**the quick and dirty theatrical version**
Inspired by the system detailed above, theatre technical managers have used a similar but significantly simpler system for years that also involves the development of a unit cost. The technical manager compiles over a period of time either a worksheet or a diary that lists projects generically, itemizing certain assumptions such as commonly used materials and their associated costs, along with background (notes) as to how these materials might be used in a recognized construction technique. Armed with this knowledge base, the technical manager performs rough square foot calculations for each unit that meets the fabrication criteria.

The cost of an incoming unit can now be easily determined by placing the object within a rectangle large enough to enclose the entire entity, regardless of its particular irregularities, curves, and cutouts. If there are large cutouts and extreme extended arms, some allowance can be made, but in most instances, such negative space requires extra framing that more than makes up the difference that an estimator might assume would be saved. The overall cost of each unit (subtotal) is determined by multiplying the total square feet by the estimated cost per square foot. The cost of the entire project is then determined by the sum of all the subtotals. On the positive side, this method is quick. On the negative side, the system is not specific and consequently not very accurate. This system overlooks specific details that often prove costly.

Alternative Approach 2.2—**an even quicker theatrical version**
Even more specific and, presumably, more accurate estimates can be generated by development of a square foot (SF) cost for like units within a *single specific project*. In this scenario, a technical manager estimates one unit, using the piece-by-piece approach (discussed in approach three), and determines a SF cost for that particular unit. The same SF factor is then applied when estimating the remaining project components.

Alternative Approach 2.3—**a shortcut to assign SF costs**
In yet another variation of this approach, the technical manager could make a detailed estimate (see Approach #3 below) of several sample units and then use the average of their cost per square foot to estimate the entire job.

Approach 3.0 —**Piece-by-piece**
The third unique approach is the piece-by-piece estimate, universally accepted as the approach that provides the highest degree of accuracy. Greater accuracy is possible since this format is based on current conditions and specific details of the project, affording the estimator the opportunity to explore many choices

and providing a detailed inventory (shopping list) of required material and labor resources. Figure 11.6 demonstrates a spreadsheet program adapted for such a use. The program contains an interactive material cost list and labor cost information guide that can be easily modified and updated.

The piece-by-piece approach is a preferred choice because it allows the technical manager to keep unit costs as subtotal sheets that are in turn complied into a summary sheet. While a computer provides ease of use and accurate calculations, the same results can be readily achieved using pencil and paper. The paper form can have many different looks, including an "in-house" printed form, ledger sheets

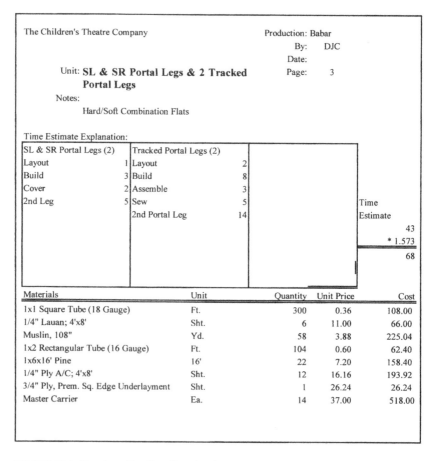

The Children's Theatre Company			Production: Babar	
			By: DJC	
			Date:	
Unit: **SL & SR Portal Legs & 2 Tracked Portal Legs**			Page: 3	
Notes:				
Hard/Soft Combination Flats				

Time Estimate Explanation:

SL & SR Portal Legs (2)		Tracked Portal Legs (2)		
Layout	1	Layout	2	
Build	3	Build	8	
Cover	2	Assemble	3	
2nd Leg	5	Sew	5	Time
		2nd Portal Leg	14	Estimate
				43
				* 1.573
				68

Materials	Unit	Quantity	Unit Price	Cost
1x1 Square Tube (18 Gauge)	Ft.	300	0.36	108.00
1/4" Lauan; 4'x8'	Sht.	6	11.00	66.00
Muslin, 108"	Yd.	58	3.88	225.04
1x2 Rectangular Tube (16 Gauge)	Ft.	104	0.60	62.40
1x6x16' Pine	16'	22	7.20	158.40
1/4" Ply A/C; 4'x8'	Sht.	12	16.16	193.92
3/4" Ply, Prem. Sq. Edge Underlayment	Sht.	1	26.24	26.24
Master Carrier	Ea.	14	37.00	518.00

FIGURE 11.6 Scenic unit estimation sheet

Children's Theatre of Minneapolis, courtesy of Dan Culhane, Technical Director

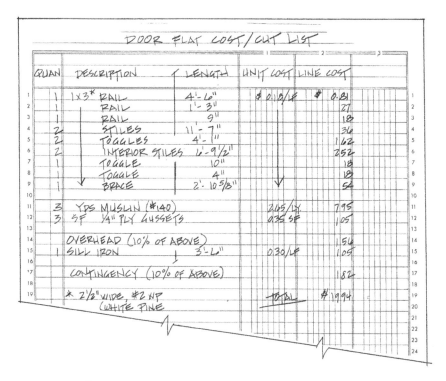

FIGURE 11.7 Scenic unit estimation (handwritten)

(available in any office-supply store) (fig. 11.7), or simply a legal pad. While neatness does count, particularly if the estimate is to be presented to others, the most important issue is to be thorough and consistent.

Having the piece estimate sheets detailing projected costs enable discussions with directors and designers when trying to figure out how to come in on budget. "The walls stage left at 14'-0" in height are costing us $375 dollars in materials, but if we can drop the height to 12'-0", the cost drops by over $125 and gets us within the materials budget. Construction time is not really reduced, but can we make that change to help with our current material costs overage?"

PROJECTING A BUDGET FOR A PROJECT, A PRODUCTION, OR A SEASON

Here's the point where the entire estimation process starts. The budget projection phase is established by the organization administration, employing the expertise of permanent staff that usually involves all technical managers. The phase usually occurs well ahead of the cost estimation phase, often six months or more prior to the start of the design process. As to its purpose, the projected budget is a target for designers and technical managers when choosing how best to achieve the collective vision of both the artistic and business management teams.

Information from past records serves as a point of departure, establishing a "ballpark" figure of anticipated costs, e.g., last year's season costs were 5% greater than the previous. However, although financial records can be of great value in substantiating often clouded memories, the most specific and current data for the projected budget is likely contributed by key technical managers.

The task of projecting a budget is best performed by one or more experienced persons who, ideally, have some history within the company, i.e., technical managers. In the performing arts, production costs vary widely because of factors such as venue size, expected production values, and directorial choices. Record keeping sufficiently itemized to assure accurate detailing of all previous expenditures is simply impossible; subsequently, instinct plays a major role in evaluating needed resources, thus the term "guesstimation," a.k.a. WAG, Wild Ass Guess, or SWAG, Scientific Wild Ass Guess.

Like the cost-estimation phase that will be discussed later, the budget projection phase is a "best guess" process. Following several careful readings of the script (scenario) and preliminary discussions with the artistic leadership, the technical manager identifies the project requirements within his or her area of expertise—such as costumes, props, scenery, stage mechanics, unusual staging, nontraditional lighting sources, and the overall "scale" of the production—and assigns an anticipated budget amount.

Experienced technical managers have some guidelines, either formal or informal, upon which to base their determinations. These guidelines reflect historical spending patterns as well as current on-hand resources and traditional allocations for line items such as overhead, expendables, maintenance, permanent staff, overhire staff availability, and materials. Guidelines must also recognize the priorities of the organization's artistic and/or managerial leadership. Since at this point the budget is only a "best guess," each technical manager should include a contingency of between 5–10% of the overall projected costs to support unanticipated needs.

If a technical manager identifies specific concerns early in the planning process, budget allocations can be adjusted to assure that these anticipated expenses will be addressed. If the budget projection numbers indicate resource needs greater than planned, the technical manager must strongly argue the case for appropriate funding. In particular, technical managers must be careful not to jeopardize, purposely or unknowingly, any aspect of their respective departments that might influence productivity and morale.

Once all the budget projection data has been assembled and debated, the resulting figures become the official budget projection. This set of numbers then serves as a target against which the demands of individual projects and productions must fit. As preliminary design material is presented for discussion, the ongoing responsibility of the technical manager is to investigate each project component thoroughly to determine how these specific estimates align with earlier projection.

Every aspect of the budget-setting process involves educated guesswork, even establishing the required profit margin if the project is commercial in nature. There is no real way for the budget setter to know so far in advance all the specifics of what will be proposed by a production's visual artists, producer, and director. Even more to the point, often a project and its budget are established prior to engaging the services of any or all of the above. Every step of the production process involves an ongoing inclusion of information to an ever-expanding knowledge pool. A good budget projection anticipates and accommodates most unknowns.

Regardless, the guesswork involved does not diminish the importance of budget projection. The more educated and informed the guess, the greater the chance the actual costs incurred will fall within the acceptable target range of plus or minus 5% of the projected figures. Most projects commence without any assurances that actual costs will meet budget projections. The value of a projected budget is the boundaries established that allow both artistic values and financial bottom lines to coexist.

ESTIMATING PRODUCTION COSTS

In the last 15–20 years, a majority of technical managers, regardless of venue size or company organization, have come to recognize the importance and usefulness of preparing by-show or by-project estimates. Tangible benefits can be derived from the seemingly tedious number crunching, including increased quality and productivity, more effective use of resources, heightened morale, and improvements in the working environment. Staff who are not repeatedly asked, i.e., required, to work overtime are more likely to be enthusiastic about their work; have greater respect for their employer, supervisor, and fellow workers; and enjoy a significantly higher level of morale. Taking the time to develop accurate estimates is one important way in which technical managers demonstrate their leadership and support the staff for whom they are responsible.

Unfortunately, despite the recognized importance of estimations, too many technical managers devote little, if any, time to the preparation of written estimates. Many insist that there is no time in their already overwhelming workday for such frills as budget preparation and calendar scheduling. Some say there is barely sufficient time to complete a production before opening! Regardless, overlooking the benefits of careful estimation bypasses an extremely important planning tool.

Estimates enable a technical manager to embark on a project with foreknowledge that both the timetable and resources are either sufficient, or for that matter insufficient, to support the expectations of the artistic team. Additionally, with that knowledge comes an understanding of the positive or negative impact that the current project can have on other projects or productions to which the company is committed. A host of problems occur when the requirements of a season's initial project exceed expectations, problems that affect the cash and time allocations budgeted for each succeeding project. The resultant cascading effect is a "catch-up" mentality that threatens the quality and calm of the remainder of the season.

To anticipate that a designer (and director) will create a design that meets the projected budget on the first go-around is naive. As discussed above, the projected budget is an estimate of available resources. This is the basis against which the proposed design is analyzed to determine if sufficient funds are available for the actual materials and labor required to realize the project as proposed. The process that next unfolds is bringing these two sets of figures into alignment within the Time, Talent, Money Triangle parameters. The difficulties in doing so often result in the need to increase resources in some areas and decrease expectations in others until a stable time and money commitment are agreed upon. Unless a company has an unlimited source of funding and an infinitely flexible schedule, the process of fitting a design to meet the assigned fiscal and time parameters is a multiple-step procedure requiring an initial estimate followed by one or more revisions.

Often technical managers, while analyzing the projected wants, develop a prioritized list of options that range from essential to desirable. This list of prioritized options, along with the associated materials and labor estimations, are shared with the production team. The aim is that all work toward the goal of getting the project realized with a result of "on time and within budget." What discourages many technical managers is that despite hard work and great effort, even arduous negotiation may result in a final estimate that only approximates the projected budget figure. Matters will not improve, however, unless proactive behavior enters the estimation process

ESTIMATION ELEMENTS MATERIALS

To some, the process of estimating the materials and equipment necessary to execute a project is seen as complex. Actually, the process is quite straightforward, if approached in an ordered manner. Complexity enters the picture largely because of the level of detail required to produce accurate calculations. Because most of the work required to mount a project is custom in nature, it is hard to create an accurate picture without examining the project's elements in detail.

While there are as many ways to do something as there are people to do it, some approaches are more successful than others. Common to any approach is that the technical manager must identify and consider the resource needs of each element, enter them on paper or in a computer spreadsheet, then sum up the sub-total costs of each unit, and finally total the entire project. Each material estimate customarily includes these four elements, although for commercial projects, a profit margin must also be considered (fig. 11.8).

In standard estimation practice, a contingency percentage is determined either by organizational policy or by the estimator's perceived complexity of the proj-ect. Given a reasonable level of confidence in his/her calculations and the use of standard fabrication techniques, a figure of 10% of the total material costs and overhead charges is normally assigned (fig. 11.9). If the project is complex and/ or involves unfamiliar circumstances or fabrication techniques, the contingency used by most estimators is 15–20%.

ELEMENTS OF A MATERIALS ESTIMATE

Materials	Fabrication supplies, hardware, novelties, paint, color media, accessories, and transportation
Rentals	Tools, equipment, garments, prefabricated units
Overhead	Costs ranging from administrative and facility expenses to legal fees and other fixed operating expenses
Contingency	A percentage of the unit's overall cost that is established to cover unanticipated expenses such as cost overruns or added elements

FIGURE 11.8 Elements of a materials estimation

UNIT "A" ESTIMATE	COST
Materials	$273
Overhead (10% of materials)	$27
Subtotal of above	$300
Contingency (10%) of subtotal	$30
Total Cost of Unit	$330

FIGURE 11.9 Sample of contingency use

When estimating materials costs, keep in mind the following (not listed in priority order):

- **Enter an estimated number for every component or material**, even if prices seem too trivial to seek exact pricing. Assigning some funding saves having to use contingency funds to cover the full cost of an item.
- **Have current price quotations readily available.** Don't put off gathering prices. Request from suppliers or develop your own data that list the dimensions and prices of materials commonly used in your studio. Price sheets that are updated monthly, or quarterly, are probably adequate for most estimation work. Significant price jumps are possible but unlikely in these short time intervals. However, the price and availability of many products such as plywood can shift radically due to hurricane or flooding, causing immediate increase in demand and reduced supply. Vigilance in monitoring materials pricing is important.
- **Work visually.** Most technical managers have been trained to communicate visually. Use simplified sketches of objects that need to be fabricated, listing the overall dimensions and finish notes. Don't let the sketch become a piece of drafting, but do use it as a guide to prepare the estimate.
- **Know standard sizes and quantity packaging.** In the case of lumber, it is unwise to place an order specifying a linear foot (LF) total when half of the total needs to be 12-foot long pieces, one-third in 18-foot long pieces, and the balance in 8-foot lengths. Be as specific as possible, and be sure to communicate this information to the crew members at the time of construction to ensure materials are used effectively.
- **Never compromise the technical design by employing untested techniques**, inferior materials, untrained staff, and inappropriate tools and equipment. If a process is unfamiliar, build a prototype prior to actual construction.
- **Components must meet ALL of the project's needs.** Each product or component must function as promised, be sufficiently durable to complete the project run, and be ready in time for the actors to use prior to first tech.

LABOR

For all technical managers, labor is the most difficult resource to estimate. The process is filled with unknowns and made even more complex because a work schedule is necessary to effectively match labor resources with tasks. In most instances, given the custom nature of the work, the question is not merely how many hours are needed but rather will the right kind of labor be available when desired. In the performing arts, like in many other industries, employees have distinct specialties, e.g., carpenters seldom alternate as scenic painters, stitchers rarely substitute for cutters, and the skills of the light hang and focus crews cannot be substituted for those of the lighting designer. Consequently, many technical managers do not attempt to do a labor estimate and simply hope that their crew either will be able to finish the project within the amount of time available or that everyone will just work longer hours without additional compensation until the project is completed. NOTE: Hope is not an effective management strategy.

Labor cost estimation requires several factors to be considered. These factors include variability in laborers' skills, difficulty in anticipating individual work output, tardiness, absences, and failed or unavailable equipment. The situation is made even more difficult in that projects often need to be estimated so far in advance that the estimator neither knows the identities nor the abilities of the crew members who will eventually perform the work.

In most performing arts organizations and for-profit studios, labor resources include a range of individuals who fall into one of several categories (fig. 11.10).

Before determining the labor and time resources needed for a project, the technical manager must identify the specific pool of available labor and the total number of work hours each can provide within a given time frame. Regardless of the difficulty involved, technical manager must allocate the "correct" balance of human resources with the time estimated to complete a project.

LABOR RESOURCES

Paid	■ Union
	■ Nonunion
	■ Permanent staff
	■ Overhire staff
	■ Contractor/supplier
Minimally paid	■ Interns
	■ Student help (e.g., work study)
Unpaid	■ Students
	■ Volunteers

FIGURE 11.10 Range of labor resources

Evaluation of Labor Resources

Area	Hours Needed (Estimate)	Available Hrs. [1] (Based on Enrollment)	Student Hours Available					
			Lab 1 [14]*	Lab 2 [5]*	Lab 3 [3]*	Stgcrt Lab [8]*	Paint Lab [4]*	Paid W.S. [3]
Set	710	600	240	90	90	150	—	30
Props	300	390	90	135	135	—	—	30
Paint	350	414	90			42	192	30
TOTAL	1460	[2] 1264	420	225	180	192	192	90

Notes:
1. These individuals are not included in the above labor pool:
   - Graduate teaching assistants (lab supervisors)
   - Technical director (manager/oversight).
   - Assistant technical director (drafting and paperwork asst.)
   - Master carpenters (crew leaders)
2. 1,404 hours minus 140 hours (10% contingency)
3. Although all of the students above attend a four-hour lab session, only three hours is counted as being productive time. The fourth hour is consumed in startup time, group break time, individual breaks such as rest room visits, and cleanup.
* Bracket numbers indicate class enrollments.

FIGURE 11.11 Labor resources worksheet

While exceptions do exist, in most instances, experienced workers (those who have worked on similar projects previously) and paid workers (financially motivated employees) will create more product in a shorter period of time than inexperienced workers. Experienced workers are also more likely to perform the job correctly the first time. In short, neither the enthusiasm nor the fervor of volunteers, interns, or students can equal the value of experience. Despite this axiom, performing arts organizations often push technical managers to use lower-paid and less-experienced workers yet still expect results similar to those provided by higher paid, experienced craftspersons.

A labor force with low pay and limited experience is not ideal but not without some advantages, too. By paying lower wages, limited financial resources can be used to purchase better or more appropriate materials, secure rentals, subcontract fabrication, and even increase the size of the labor pool. Additionally, inexperienced workers are often less rigid in scheduling their time, providing increased flexibility for the technical manager coordinating the activities of several departments and phases of preparation. However, it is worth noting that inexperienced labor will likely require greater personal sacrifice on the part of a technical manager. In many cases, the technical manager serves as the only "expert" in the group, leading to the unavoidable circumstance in which the technical manager must contribute labor time in addition to meeting managerial responsibilities. Clearly, this is a situation to be avoided or at least carefully watched.

Figure 11.11 provides an example of one method to determine total labor resources. The headings are based upon an educational institution model that uses inexperienced, experienced, and paid student services.

LABOR ESTIMATION GUIDELINES

- **Assign a labor cost to everything.** In education, community, and many regional groups, warehoused items, e.g., "stock" platforms and costumes, play a significant role. There is a temptation for the technical manager to pass over these elements and not include them on estimation worksheets.

  However, "stock" items often require modifications that do have associated costs. While additional material costs can be apparent, the labor involved to secure, alter, or install a stock piece can often be as, or even more, labor intensive than creating a piece from scratch.

- **Label everything.** In order to reference components, a labeling system is a must. Labels can take a variety of forms, but avoid using lengthy or "cute" names. The labeling system should facilitate quick notation and readily locate the components on drawings. Figure 11.12 shows several systems commonly employed.

135

Label Systems

PROPER NAMES	■ *"Fisbee, Act 2 rock"* ■ *"CS Turntable"* ■ *"HL speaker"* ■ *Marley, backlight special*
ALPHA-NUMERIC CHARACTERS	■ *A letter, a numeral, or combination, e.g., "P"* ■ *"Cane-1" (Cane, Act I)* ■ *"SLW-1" (Stage Left Wagon, Act 1)* ■ *"P3-12" (Pipe #3, instrument #12)*
SYMBOLS (w/alpha-numeric characters)	■ *Circles, pentagons, triangles, & similar polygons are useful as a way to group units, which are then given their own identity by use of the alphanumeric figure.*

FIGURE 11.12 Piece identification techniques

■ **Acknowledge the direct relationship between the quality of materials and the amount of labor required.** Poor quality materials require added labor to create a satisfactory product. Sometimes, if paid labor is utilized, the resulting costs are higher than if a more expensive but better quality material had been used in the first place.

■ **Develop "rules of thumb" for estimating the amount of labor required** to complete a project. While increasingly even the performing arts finds itself supported and/or directed by specific codes and standards (e.g., USITT, PLASA, IBC, NEC, etc.), the area of estimation remains outside this world. Each estimator invariably develops an understanding of the time required for his or her crew to complete typical activities. These rules guide a technical manager's decisions when determining "reasonable" labor resources to assign to projected tasks. A sample table of estimating guidelines is provided in the appendix.

■ **Use a Multiple-Unit Factor (MUF)** when estimating the construction of identical pieces. A MUF takes into account that less total time is needed to produce multiple identical objects than multiple distinct objects. This efficiency is made possible when materials can be gathered, cut in bulk, and assembled using a set-up fixture rather than having to produce an individual item.

■ **Avoid assigning the technical manager as a laborer.** Much of a technical manager's effort must go toward the instruction and coordination of the crew, making it difficult to focus on lengthy and complex tasks. This does not prevent the manager from participating in construction work, but in those cases where the technical manager does plan to actively participate in construction, the manager's work time should only be considered as an added contingency to the overall labor estimate. Such participation comes with the possible danger of the manager being seen more as a coworker than a supervisor.

- **Assign automation or similarly complex projects to a single individual.** When working on a technically complex project, technical managers often are viewed as the individuals most qualified to undertake the challenge. If the project requires the specialist's full attention, the manager is in a poor position to supervise multiple people and projects. Complex projects should be assigned to a specific member of the labor pool, freeing the technical manager to focus on management.
- **Assign only one person to each task and assume they can complete it.** Encourage your crew to seek help from each other when needed, but empower each person to work individually to complete tasks. When individuals are assigned, there is increased ownership and overall satisfaction with the project.
- **Review material and assembly choices thoroughly in light of available resources.** Provide honest and well-thought out answers to questions such as "Does the available staff possess the skills and/or knowledge required to produce the quality needed?" and "Is there adequate equipment, in ratio to staff levels and their skills, to employ the chosen technique?"

QUALITY CONTROL

The technical manager serves as the primary quality control officer of any production project. As such, they personally set the standard of performance expected by all. Although quality is a subjective judgment, everyone needs clarity of expectations to define the level to which they should strive.

Quality results and high expectations go hand in hand. An effective technical manager is impatient with unacceptable results and unused potential. There is a constant drive to improve personally and inspire colleagues to a higher standard of achievement. The technical manager is always looking for both personal and corporate strength upon which to build.

Live performance events have a quality standard directly related to the venue size and performer/audience relationship. The workmanship and materials used in a proscenium style production are often less demanding than those that will be viewed in an arena-stage event. That is not to say that both are not expected to look their best; rather, the viewing distance affords the opportunity for a greater or lesser audience examination of the final product.

Technical managers in direct collaboration with the appropriate designer and the director establish the quality standard for what is and is not acceptable to appear on stage. Many an educational institution struggles to find a balance between featuring the work of many untrained students and the audience expectation for quality entertainment. A common sense inspection by the technical manager of all work, whenever possible, is the best means of setting an acceptable quality standard.

All work must be judged in terms of accuracy and appropriateness for the project. Specifically, the work is evaluated in comparison to designers' drafting sheets, models, and painted elevations as well as a quality standard for the venue. Sometimes it may be necessary to redo the work should it fail this evaluation. By being uncompromising in the effort to produce quality, the technical manager aids all in advancing the project and develops a good reputation as a desirable colleague.

One good technique for raising quality standards is to set a variety of known control points along the production process. At each step of the way, whether in design development or actual execution, mutually agreed upon points of evaluation are established. A formal sign-off and approval to proceed may be necessary early on, eventually replaced with an overall awareness as to when the technical manager should be consulted and when it is not necessary.

The goal is not to be an overbearing task master but rather a guide by the side who works with all toward self and organizational improvement. Empowering others to take personal responsibility in maintaining quality in support of the project is an admirable goal. With careful scheduling, detailed problem solving, and clear expectations, we'd like to believe most anything is possible

Chapter 12

Putting It All Together

All of the planning, scheduling, analysis, technical design, estimation, purchasing, and fabrication phases come to a head about the time a production project is ready for installation into the assigned venue. There is a significant shift in energy for the technical manager as well, for the amount of hands-on contact with the project is increased, decision making comes at a more rapid pace, and the end goal of a successful opening is ever more looming. The better the advance work of this time period, the smoother this concentrated burst of productivity for all involved. The effective technical manager truly shines by maintaining a level of calm and an infectious positive attitude. All the more critical is the effective use of each hour of stage time that has now become a most precious resource.

The load-in and installation phase is probably the most stressful phase of completing a project in the performing arts, for performers and technicians alike. Stage space and time are at a premium, especially since few organizations have exclusive control over a venue and its availability. Opening is drawing near and unquestionably some project elements are behind schedule, while others remain uncertain, undecided, or perhaps not even yet realized. Stress causes most of us to think more selfishly, especially people in positions such as technical manager, who have both people and gear to employ as effectively and efficiently as they can. Teamwork tends to focus closer to home than seeing the "big picture" that we all see as our end goal.

Load-in involves the transfer of equipment and fabricated units to the performance venue. This can be as simple as moving across a hallway to the far more complex (and normal) situation of moving across town or across great distances as do touring shows. Not only must all pieces be accounted for, safely loaded and unloaded, stored, and positioned, some groups have to transfer a shop-load of tools, materials, and supporting equipment as well. Home is relocated, and all its conveniences are less accessible or perhaps nonexistent. People are equally affected, but more on that later.

During this period of time, technical managers must continue to be vigilant about personnel safety. With all the changes, there is bound to be confusion and

La Traviata Load In Track Sheet
Page 1

Decking
- ☐ Layout Down Stage Black Groundcloth (Tape, Carpet Tacks)
- ☐ Tape Down Stage Masonite
- ☐ Nail Down (4d nails) Up Stage Masonite

Platforming
- ☐ Install Legs (3" Drywall screws)
  Note: Special Legs for the Center 4 Platforms
- ☐ Bolt 4x8's Together (3/8" Bolts)
- ☐ Set 1'-2" Platforms Into Place
- ☐ Nail 1/2" and 3/4" Ply Strips for Low Platforms
- ☐ Set 7" Platforms Into Place
- ☐ Install Decking (4d nails)
- ☐ Install Screen Door Molding (4d Nails)
- ☐ Install 1/4" Masonite Facing (4d Nails)

Upstage Steps
- ☐ Install with Leg Anchors
- ☐ Join with Loose Pin Hinges

Rolling Unit
- ☐ Deck With 1/4" Masonite (4d Nails)
- ☐ Install Recessed Handles
- ☐ Roll Into Place
- ☐ Install Barrel Bolts

Panels
- ☐ Assemble Steel Rigging
- ☐ Crosby safetys
- ☐ Attach Legs (Conduit w/ 1/4" Bolts)
- ☐ Attach Valences (Black Gaffers)
- ☐ Roto Lock To Pipes
- ☐ Install Eyebolts for Safetys (3/8")
- ☐ Safety Chain to Battens
- ☐ Test and Fly Out

Cartouches
- ☐ Install Additional Hangers
- ☐ Set Dog Clips (1/8" Nicopress)
- ☐ Label to Match Legs

Mirrors
- ☐ Attach Bases (Loose Pin Hinges)
- ☐ Install Sconces
- ☐ Wire Sconces
- ☐ Install Beads on Sconces
- ☐ Install Improved Stage Screws if Necessary
- ☐ Spike In Place

FIGURE 12.1 Load-in assignments

miscommunication. Installation is best designed to flow in a progressive and linear manner (fig. 12.1). Once in the venue, or perhaps even before most of the equipment arrives, any overhead rigging must done. Flown pieces must be installed first, before the stage decking and all that rests on the deck.

Overhead rigging is a time-consuming activity that requires skilled labor and a stage clear of equipment and people. A pre-rig call prior to load-in is usually scheduled to prepare the space for the efficient installation of incoming scenery and equipment. The lighting and sound load-in typically follow pre-rig, followed by deck-mounted scenery and finally props and costumes. The reverse of this sequence occurs during strike.

Once the flown equipment is in place, the remaining pieces of scenery, props, costumes, and other stage-level pieces are loaded and positioned. If it's a show that has been previously assembled and reassembled such as tours, installation can go quickly and smoothly. If it is an initial assembly and/or installation, the process takes more time and better coordination between the various departments. Technical managers need to stay on top of progress, recognize existing and upcoming issues such as overlapping space and time needs, and be efficient in how they manage their crew time. Usually the only certainty is that everything will take longer than expected, necessitating patience and compromise on the part of all, but a firmness in assuring that staff will meet the major schedule milestones is needed.

Invariably there will be pressure to get the actors into the actual performance space as soon as possible. The offstage rehearsals held in taped studio halls have increasingly become less productive. The need to be on stage working in the real scenic environment to ramp up the energy toward opening is now paramount in the eyes of directors and choreographers and, in some instances, producers.

One useful solution can be to provide a "guaranteed" onstage time for stage management to facilitate the cast to at least walk the stage prior to starting onstage rehearsals. This date can be set months in advance during scheduling. That makes the activity realistically achievable and, since anticipated, it frequently can be met earlier than announced. Directors and staff will appreciate an early arrival on stage far more graciously than they will tolerate a delay.

Like a broken record, the primary concern prior to allowing actors on stage is safety. As the scenery assembly nears completion, the technical director and lead carpenter should walk both onstage and backstage areas, including Front of House (FOH), at the end of each day, focusing on all actor paths. Trash must be removed; exits cleared; rough surfaces cleaned or covered; trip hazards rectified; and scenery, especially working parts, checked for stability. All escape stairs must have railings, and all known hazards must be minimized and well publicized prior to allowing the performers to take the stage.

If installation schedules are falling behind and performer stage time is being compromised, a guided walk-through by the technical manager and the stage manager with the cast and crew of the unfinished and unavailable set can help set aside some anxiety. A technical manager walk-through with the cast is a good practice to help build an effective working relationship with the actors; if the costume technical manager can be included, so much the better. In addition, it may be possible to secure a portion of the stage for a particular group of complex

---

11/15/14 —Scenery—To do

1. Paint moat floor black.
2. Fix white tape on bottom three house steps in North & South seating.
3. Remove ship ladder to grid.
4. Chair check-in center section after tech tables struck.
5. Construct new autopsy tabletop.
6. Tape all seams of ground row for light leaks (vertical & horizontal).
7. Fix curl at top of ground row near center.
8. Cut out bottom of big crate (à la what we did for light box).
9. Paint work onstage.
10. Paint new autopsy tabletop.

FIGURE 12.2 Work list for day

scenes that need to be worked during a rehearsal without turning over the entire stage. However, the goal should remain that the performers have full access to a safe and secure stage at the originally scheduled "guaranteed" time.

As opening looms closer and closer, rehearsals shift focus from acting rehearsals to the introduction and integration of all production elements—technical and dress rehearsals. Typically, first tech involves actors, lighting, sound (effects and microphones), set (projections and video), special effects, and props, while tech/dress adds the elements of costumes, wigs, and makeup. All throughout this period, installation continues as finishing touches are added to all the production elements (fig. 12.2).

Another critical planning event should occur before the technical rehearsals start, and that event is known as a "paper tech." Paper tech is a gathering of all of the critical production staff and verbally walking through all of the cue and shift sequences of the show. With the production director present to confirm that his or her vision is being met, and the stage manager writing into the prompt script the calling details of the show to assure consistency, the lighting designer, sound designer, scenic designer, and technical manager bring their own prepared sequencing and incorporate all the ideas into one projected production flow.

Starting with an audience member's arrival at the venue and then projecting through to their departure, the group works through minute by minute, identifying the specifics of the audience experience. The paper tech can start with the question: "When the audience enters the venue, what do they see?" Hopefully all of the sequencing questions have been raised before in design and production meetings as well as in individual conferences between director and design staff, but now all must come together seamlessly. The paper tech is a tool to lay out the ideal plan. The technical manager's ability to ask critical questions and confirm production priorities also helps to get the plan off to a great start.

Some academic venues hold an onstage run-through of the production for the student crew in order for them to become familiar with the show. This crew watch occurs just before going into technical rehearsals and may provide the only time that all assigned backstage will be able to enjoy the production from an audience perspective. Crew watch is also a time during which the entire company, which will now be working together for the performance run, can get to meet and know one another. This occasion also provides the director a chance to address the group—to welcome them aboard and to inspire their contributions to the success of the whole.

To avoid surprises before things get started, in a less public venue, the wise technical manager informs the director and other appropriate production staff of the completion status of all production elements. For example, if a prop is still being constructed, those involved should be made aware of the situation and an adequate stand-in provided for use during the technical rehearsal. In addition, the director and those actors affected by the missing prop should be told when the real prop will arrive and plan accordingly. Free flow of accurate information can greatly reduce tension between the various parties coming together during this critical time in the production process.

Technical rehearsals can take a variety of formats and, depending on the particulars of a given production, any one or a combination of styles may be used, as displayed in figure 12.3.

Dry tech rehearsals involve only technicians and are held in the performance venue to sort out problems such as timing, correctness of shifts, and the placement and clarification of cues. The more complex the actions of the crew to enable the shifts, the greater the value of a dry tech. Performers often return to the rehearsal studio during a dry tech to run lines, work out specific performance details, or simply earn a well-deserved night off. If performers are being used to execute scenic and property shifts, there is no point in holding a dry tech; a cue-to-cue rehearsal is a much better option.

Cue-to-cue rehearsals involve both actors and technicians and are held for the purpose of concentrating on specific cue-intensive portions of the script, usually skipping over large blocks of dialogue in favor of rehearsing the transitions. A heavily cued portion of the production can be run repeatedly during a cue-to-cue to "set" the sequence for all involved in its execution. Should a cue sequence need to be rewritten, a brief pause can be taken to make the necessary adjustment. The stage manager may wish to target a five-minute hold as a maximum, recognizing that both lighting and sound are being crafted during this rehearsal and may

143

	Goal	Conditions	Personal	Type
Dry tech	Create smooth, functional visual transitions; sort out timing, shift correctness, and cue placement	All scenery & all props (or suitable substitutes)	Personnel involved in shifting them, which might include actors	CUE-TO-CUE w/o actors
First tech	Timing and coordination are the principal goals	Problem makeup, costumes, costume props, and quick changes	Performers, run crew, costume crew as needed, technical managers	STOP & GO . . . unless a large number of cues; then CUE-TO-CUE
Dress tech	Integrate costumes, costume changes, makeup, wigs, body mics	Scenery & props painted & functional; full makeup and costumes	Everyone	STOP & GO
Dress & final dress	Simulate performance with a halt called if safety or conditions warrant.	Requires all scenery, props, full makeup and costumes	Everyone	RUN-THROUGH
Preview	Conditions are the same as for a performance.	Everything	Everyone	PERFORMANCE

FIGURE 12.3 Types of technical rehearsals

require additional time. If the sequence is critical to the action and will likely take more than five minutes to resolve, performers and crew can take a break while stage management walks the stage to support those making the necessary changes.

Stop-and-go rehearsals involve all production personnel and are conducted in "performance mode," stopping only when a significant problem occurs. Clear lines of authority need to be established as to who is empowered to stop the rehearsal, but all such requests should be communicated only by the stage manager, who by definition is in charge of rehearsals. The stage manager's authority over the production is being established during these early technical rehearsals and supports his or her voice as the single voice that can call "hold please," adding to their credibility. Holds should only be called if the problem that has been encountered involves coordination of moving scenic elements, critical props shifts, costume quick changes, or performer and crew safety. Lighting, sound, and projection needs typically do not warrant a stop; instead, a note can be taken and the corrected sequence run at another time.

Run-through rehearsals include final dress and preview performances and are run in performance conditions, typically with the same curtain and intermission times. Except in cases where real or potential personal injury might occur, these rehearsals are not stopped. Problems may be attended to during intermission, provided that doing so does not interrupt the anticipated scenic, costume, and properties change timing.

Technical rehearsals are often the first time that the control board operators; scenic, rigging, and properties crews; and costume run crews begin their engagement with the production. The technical manager, working in concert with the stage manager, should have already talked through shift assignments, found the best locations for crew placement, and developed a training protocol to prepare the crew. These specific duties of preparing the backstage team are shared among stage manager, assistant stage managers, and technical production staff. Clarifying who is responsible for what training serves the technical manager well.

The number one goal of any of the technical rehearsal formats is to use valuable performer, technician, and facility time as effectively as possible. Simply stated, avoid wasting time. However, the pressure to remain efficient should not preclude the successful completion of special rehearsal goals such as flawlessly executing a given group of cues. Take the time (if the concern can be resolved in approximately five minutes or less) during the technical rehearsals to really solve problems. Each rehearsal closer to opening night adds an increased level of complexity to the production, and habits, good or bad, begin to establish themselves and are not easily modified. As a rule of thumb, remember that there is no time like the present to resolve current problems.

Should the venue in which the production project is being presented be supported by union crews or involve unionized dancers, musicians, or performers, the technical manager needs to be aware of the contractual limitations placed on the production. Union rules and regulations are established to protect both the employer and the employee from abusive practices and are quite specific about work hours, required breaks, and shifting compensation scales that increase as the work day gets longer and longer. Sample contracts with specific requirements are available online, but local variances should also be confirmed with venue staff.

The technical manager works hard to balance the production needs while adhering to all of the wage and hour requirements and keeping the project within budgeted expenditures. Both advance planning and keeping the lines of communications open among the various unionized employees and their onsite management is critical for success. Respect begets respect, and the successful technical manager celebrates the working role with all of these entertainment professionals.

During this stressful time in the production cycle, a technical manager must be ever more vigilant in keeping the lines of communication open. A good practice is to gather production personnel together for the last 15 minutes of the rehearsal block to review what has occurred during rehearsal, assess priorities for each department, and to revise the specific stage time assignments for the next day. All departments (scenery, lighting, costumes, sound, stage management, director) should briefly share their primary concerns of the challenges that they face, and achievable priorities should be set. The technical manager often serves as broker for allocating what can be mutually exclusive time demands. Being conscious of when noise can be made (construction/installation vs. sound design), when the stage will be dark (lighting vs. construction/installation), and when there will be limited stage accessibility (painting vs. house cleaning) can help make the next day's work schedule more productive for all.

Tech/dress and dress rehearsals integrate the costumes, makeup, and body mics (if any) into the production. These rehearsals must approximate actual running conditions as much as possible since costume changes and mic exchanges often are dependent on a real-time sequence. Ignoring or circumventing the real-time aspect schedule can have disastrous effects on a production. Pausing the rehearsal briefly to walk through a costume change, run it a half-speed, then return to run it at full speed may be a useful strategy despite the interruption.

When opening occurs, there is often much relief as well as much to celebrate. This is a good time for the technical manager to express thanks to those involved in the production, to gather project documentation for archival purposes, and to take a few moments of personal assessment. Asking basic questions like what worked, what didn't, and what was learned by this project and making brief notes summarizing the answers are an easy way for the technical manager to continue his or her own education and advance skill development.

During the **performance run phase** of a show, the technical manager keeps tabs on all technical aspects through careful communication with the stage manager. Performance logs, prepared by the stage management staff and distributed to all technical managers, indicate where technical assistance may be needed. There are a variety of software packages that can aid in distribution of these reports as well as provide support for other planning and scheduling efforts. During this postopening period, the technical manager remains somewhat "on call" to assist in the coordination of problem solving and major repair needs during the performance run. However, by this point, the production run crew should be prepared and empowered to address minor technical problems.

The **strike** of a production (project) is often the last entry, but one of the most critical times, on the technical manager's calendar. Often scheduled immediately following the final performance, the combined efforts of the crew (and in some cases the cast) are required to assist in clearing the stage and transporting or disposing of pieces and equipment. However, if circumstances allow, it is preferred practice to conduct the strike during normal working hours because crew members are sure to be more alert, less fatigued, and more safety conscious than they would be during the wee morning hours. If, due to venue demands, the strike must occur following an evening performance, establishing a hard stop for the cast and crew that were directly involved with the performance and leaving the final restoration to a fresher crew can help with safety.

The technical manager is responsible for the careful planning of the strike, applying the same skills for overall planning identified earlier. Matching workers to tasks, linear progression scheduling, and effective operations management all come to bear at this critical time (fig. 12.4).

Following the strike, the technical manager reviews the stage space, checks on storage areas, verifies the return of borrowed items, and secures production documentation. Hereafter follows a period known as restoration when items are returned to storage and the performance venue returned to its "normal"

The Fantasticks Strike Assignments					
	Kate	**Jen**	**Mary**	**Robert**	**Mark**
Capacities	Head Carpenter	Outstanding Rigger	Works in School of Music	Head of Properties	Stage Management
Task #1	Pull up deck	Fly out all goods	Move piano and stand lights	Put all hand props in trunk	Get costume pieces to studio
Task #2	Disconnect platforms	Release banner cables	Gather up all music	Take truck with props to remote storage	Clear out dressing rooms
Task #3	Unbolt legs and put platforms in storage	Restore grid and house plot	Take down lobby display	Pick up pizza for after party	Sort hardware and salvage

FIGURE 12.4 Strike work plan

configuration and rigging. The space must be cleared of all nonvenue items as quickly and safely as possible since most venues have other groups or events that will want to occupy the space as soon as possible. Stage space is valuable; the best preparation takes place in the actual event venue.

Poststrike is also a time for careful evaluation. Through evaluation and analysis, both successes and failures can be identified to inform future endeavors. Records that are properly reconciled can provide useful information for future estimations of Time, Talent, Money resources. Then it is on to the next project.

When a technical manager is connected to a touring production, this same sequence of events repeats itself over and over again. Required technical rehearsals are reduced to the minimum number of hours that can support the desired finished production in each new venue. Load-in and strike times are also limited to create the highest efficiency possible. Time is indeed money when it comes to touring, so as a tour progresses, the production will develop a rhythm for the load-in, rehearsal, performance, and strike sequence that is further supported by the logistics of company travel and venue length of stay.

The combination of production-specific and local support crews can add some additional challenges, but a well-planned tour led by a strong technical manager will take it all in stride. While touring, the professional image of our industry truly shines as all of the professionals involved show up prepared to work with the requisite skill necessary to serve performance. Learning can occur with each stop along the way, but a well-executed touring schedule is a significant accomplishment for all involved.

Part Four

Wrap Up

Chapter 13

Looking Back as We Look Forward

In the process of realizing a production, drawings are drafted, lists are generated, calendars created, invoices collected, and results are often documented through photographs and archive videos. The task of gathering and assembling this project's byproducts and archiving them as a means to inform future endeavors can fall into the job description of a technical manager. The American Theatre Archive Project has produced a fine manual entitled *Preserving Theatrical Legacy* that outlines a proactive approach for any theatre organization to document their heritage [AmericanTheatreArchiveProject.org]. Maintaining such an archive of documentation potentially supports and reinforces all three aspects of the Time, Talent, Money Triangle. Time can be saved by avoiding a repeat of past mistakes, talent can be enhanced by expanding the information base of current conditions, and dollars can be stretched by offering examples of previously successful solutions.

Although requiring an initial investment of time to get organized, developing a systemic approach to record keeping will serve any technical manager well. Such stored records can provide a wealth of knowledge about past practices, reinforce connections to vendors and contractors, enable historic connections to be honored, and relieve staff from relying solely on their collective institutional memory. By following best practices such as those suggested by The American Theatre Archive Project, conscious decisions can be made regarding what to keep and what to toss. The surviving materials can be organized in an intentional manner, enabling both current users and future historians to benefit from its existence.

On a personal level, keeping calendars, purchasing records, and even process documentation can prove an invaluable help on future projects. By referencing the past, fewer mistakes will be repeated and momentum is built as each previous project informs the next project as it comes along. Many a time-tested solution can be found in the personal files of the effective technical manager, but only if the files are organized and accessible.

LEVELS OF ASSESSMENT
■ Season Level—Expected Season Outcomes (ESO)
■ Project Level—Expected Project Outcomes (EPO)
■ Personal Level—Personal Performance Objectives (PPO)

FIGURE 13.1 Levels of assessment

As with the need to be intentional about record keeping, rapidly moving from project to project can prevent the technical manager from taking the necessary time to evaluate what has been accomplished. However, such an investment of time in assessment and evaluation is central to both continuous personal development and the refinement of future practices. We recommend assessment and evaluation on at least three levels (fig. 13.1), noting that a commitment to deliberate evaluation is key to the success and satisfaction of any technical manager.

1. **Season Level:** A producing organization makes choices about both what and when to produce over a fixed time scale known as the season. Season assessment compares anticipated goals of presenting a series of projects with the actual results and impact of those presentations. The question is asked: "Did the season achieve the goals as outlined by the company?"

2. **Project Level:** The typical unit of assessment at the project level is the individual production, although the project level can be broken down even further to include individual contributions to a greater whole. From script selection to strike, each production, as a building block of a season, develops an identity and in the best of circumstances was chosen to achieve a specific set of goals. Ideally, the entire production team is made aware of the production goals before the start of work so that they can make informed choices along the way, comparing options to the agreed-upon goals. At the conclusion of the project, an evaluation can be made contrasting anticipated goals with actual results.

3. **Personal Level:** As one contributes work effort to any endeavor, a common question asked is: "What's in this for me?" Or an alternate focus might be, "What have I gained by being involved in this endeavor? How do I define success in my contributions to what has been accomplished?" Each technical manager possesses an inherent desire for self-improvement and only through personal assessment can one identify strengths, articulate weaknesses, and develop a plan to celebrate the former and address the latter.

SEASONAL GOALS

The reasons a theatrical season is selected are as varied as the talented individuals who bring a season to life. Seasons can be selected based on a theme (Great American Harbor dramas), a time frame (Span the Centuries), or a concept (Shakespeare's canon, in order, with no repeats), or they can even be based on the specific skill set(s) and desires of the artist involved ("I've always wanted to direct *Our Town*, and this time it's my turn to pick."). Regardless of the baseline reason, once a season is selected, those involved should understand the **expected season objectives** (ESOs) so that informed choices can be made. Expected season objectives (ESOs) can include goals such as those shown in figure 13.2.

Any selected season will likely have multiple ESOs. Ironically, as anyone involved in theater production knows, often there are equally desirable but mutually exclusive ESOs at work within any season plan. Regardless of this challenge, in order to support a suitable evaluation of a season, knowing the reasons a particular script combination was selected is essential. Once known, and the undertaking completed, a conversation should be had that addresses questions such as the following:

- Did each production accomplish what we set out to achieve?
- If yes to the above, how well? If no, why not?
- What measures should we use to determine our success (ticket sales, testimonials, research questions answered, company growth)?
- How did we do with each of the above metrics?

EXPECTED SEASON OBJECTIVES (ESOS)

- Presenting a specific genre
- Responding to audience trends
- Expanding diversity
- Educating audiences
- Challenging company members
- Exploring new interpretations

- Engaging guest artist(s)
- Boosting ticket sales
- Exploring a particularly timely issue
- Celebrating a significant anniversary
- Partnering with other community groups
- . . . and the list can go on . . . and on

FIGURE 13.2 Expected season objectives (ESO)

- What would we change if we were to do this same season over again?
- How closely did our results align with our anticipated outcomes?
- What unforeseen complications occurred over the season?
- What was our biggest mistake and what can we learn from it?
- What was our biggest surprise?

PROJECT GOALS

Within producing organizations, project-level assessment is often a subset of a larger endeavor like a season or a production, while in ongoing endeavors such as tours perhaps the gauge is the fiscal year. Regardless, by starting with Expected Project Outcomes (EPOs), a foundation can be laid that will focus insights for the future and provide a means to measure success. Just as a season should have some underlying purpose, so can each production/project. EPOs can include a variety of metrics such as those shown in figure 13.3.

Expected Project Outcomes are often slightly easier to define than season or personal ones; they fit well within the technical manager construct and, because of their scale, probably have fewer inherent conflicts. Therefore, a closer attempt at real and effective evaluation can occur. Each anticipated outcome can be directly compared to the results achieved, resulting in a possible qualitative evaluation as well as the expected quantitative evaluation. Some associated questions might be:

- What production goals did this project address?
- How was our overall effort advanced by this project?
- How did all involved perform on this project?
- What would we change if we had to do this project over again?
- How could we have more effectively deployed labor for this project?
- What additional resources would make this project more successful next time?
- Where did we make wrong assumptions and where were we right?

EXPECTED PROJECT OBJECTIVES (EPOS)

- Desired audience reaction
- Performer growth
- New techniques applied
- Research questioned answered

- Effective materials used
- Sales and marketing goals
- Partnered achievements (working well with others)

FIGURE 13.3 Expected project objectives (EPO)

PERSONAL GOALS

Most of us, technical managers included, desire both achievement and advancement in our lives. How we might measure our success would be more useful if done during our careers than after the fact; thus, asking ourselves critical questions along the path will help bring clarity to how we see our personal growth. Unlike project and season assessment, where a subset of expected outcomes is established in advance, personal assessment is frequently measured after the fact, in comparison to one's own values and experiences. If limited to an afterthought, we miss the satisfaction of how our contributions assist our own happiness and the differences we have made in the lives of others: those who we work for, alongside, and with as a supervisor. For example, figure 13.4 lists a few possibilities for Personal Performance Objectives (PPOs).

Effective self-evaluation has a variety of benefits that go well beyond just feeling good about one's efforts. Unrecognized or forgotten achievements can be brought back into our personal awareness, enabling a person to better measure his or her personal impact and contributions. Job duties can be analyzed, watching for possible mission creep or perhaps a growing disconnect between responsibility and reward. Points of pride can be identified, enabling colleagues and supervisors to both celebrate and be inspired. Often when true personal evaluation is conducted, one's state of mind or attitude toward a work effort can be more clearly understood. An introspective process can also uncover previously unrecognized differences of opinion. Lastly, but potentially most important of all, growth and personal development plans can be identified that will assist in engendering even greater satisfaction in future endeavors.

For many, there is a moment as a technical manager where taking stock is necessary, a practice that we wholeheartedly endorse. In a field where the risk of burnout seems always right around the corner, we have avoided that fate through our personal recipe.

The moment of satisfaction for both of us often came just before opening. Sitting in a semidarkened theatre slightly before the actors were called, we surveyed the stage that just a few short days earlier had been bare and now contained a

---

PERSONAL PERFORMANCE OBJECTIVES (PPOS)

- Have fun
- Learn
- Grow

- Overcome a challenge
- Feel satisfied
- Identify something that we need to work on to improve in the future

---

FIGURE 13.4 Personal performance objectives (PPO)

world that only a few short weeks ago had only been a drawing or model developed as a result of a designer's imagination. Invariably this moment gave us time to reflect on the journey that had been taken with our crew, to see the results that we had achieved by working together, and to admire the accomplishment seen before us. In our personal evaluations, we could ask:

- Did we complete the work on time?
- Did we complete the work within the established cost and labor budgets?
- Did we (and I) have fun?
- Did we achieve the artistic goals of the designer and the artistic team?
- Did I learn anything?
- If I could do anything over, what would I do differently?
- Where did I succeed? Where did I fail?

Again, back to the burnout issue. One of the major challenges for technical managers in employing effective evaluation is setting aside their personal connection to a project, something that frequently can cloud anyone's judgment. Neither the celebration of opening nor the joy in closing a production are a good time during which to truly evaluate ourselves; the project is often still too emotionally precious to withstand the level of critical analysis needed.

Immediate postproduction analysis sessions (postmortems, lately referred to as "lessons learned") can take one of two directions. First, they can become mutual admiration societies where we determine that everyone did great and performed beyond expectations; only good can be seen in what has been accomplished. Second, the opposite happens, and the postmortem turns into an opportunity for everyone involved to voice their complaints about what they have just experienced. The latter effect can be detrimental since any colleagues too close to the source of the emotional outburst will leave the session feeling their ongoing work relationship has been damaged. Neither outcome is desirable or an effective evaluation.

Therefore, while greatly advocating the need to evaluate and assess, diligent attention to timing is also required. Revisit a personal project or season effort several weeks after the start of engagement when the next effort comes along. Or do an initial evaluation and then revisit the work after some time has passed. Often it is only while working on something new or sufficiently different that we can most accurately evaluate a previous endeavor.

CONCLUDING ON A PERSONAL NOTE

Working as a technical manager is both a commitment to the arts and a calling that can serve as a source of personal fulfillment. The challenges are many and the financial rewards can be limited, but through the successful application and understanding of the Time, Talent, Money Triangle, success can be achieved on many levels. The opportunity to wear the mantles of artist, creative thinker, colleague, planner, and positive leader bring new challenges every day but also much opportunity for delight. Technical management enables collaboration with other talented individuals and accomplishes much over the lifetime of a career.

Technical Production Guidelines

Time Prior to Opening	Event	Definition
16 weeks	Director's Written Concept Statement	At the first production meeting for each show, the director shall present a prepared, written concept statement to the production staff. This may include anything that he/she feels will aid in the understanding of the concept. The designers take this information and begin work toward an initial design, in ongoing meetings with the director and project advisors they progress to their final product.
16 weeks	Budget & Production Parameters Outlined	At the first production meeting for each show, the production coordinator shall present an overview of the budget, the schedule for the production, and in consultation with the Producer, shall identify specific parameters under which the production is to be planned. Production team members should keep all of this information in mind as they progress toward opening.
14 weeks	Preliminary Set Design	On this date the following items are to be presented at the production meeting. ■ A drafted floor plan ■ Pencil sketches of the set ■ Color samples of the set and major props ■ Sketches of any special or unusual units

(Continued)

Time Prior to Opening	Event	Definition
		■ Designers initial properties list ■ Any other special items requested to aid in the budgeting process
		Student designers must have their project advisor's signature on all drawings and related design materials prior to submission to the production staff. No construction will proceed without the sign-off indicating that the student and the advisor have discussed the design and any changes made through the process.
14 weeks	Preliminary Costume Design (from Designer)	On this date the costume designer will present sketches of all costumes and costume pieces in the production, including personal props. On each should be a note explaining whether it is to be pulled, rented, or built, and as many color swatches as possible.
13 weeks	Preliminary Prop List (from Director)	This should include all of the props the director envisions for blocking and action during the production, including a minimum three part description (size, color/texture, use), the number needed and any consumables.
13 weeks	Preliminary Technical Statement	Following approval of the preliminary design, the production technical director will prepare and submit the following: ■ Preliminary materials estimate by scenic unit ■ Preliminary labor estimate ■ A list of stock items to be used ■ A list of suggested materials and techniques ■ The costumer will provide a similar estimate for costumes

Time Prior to Opening	Event	Definition
		If the design is within the allotted resources, the Production Coordinator will give approval for continued progress toward the final design stage. If the budget is not within the resources, specific suggestions will be offered as alterations which will enable completion without unduly sacrificing the integrity of the design. Agreement will be reached between the designers and the Production Coordinator as to what changes are necessary before progressing to the final design stage. It should be obvious that to budget the production accurately, all three of these preliminaries must be on time and as accurate as possible. No approval will be forthcoming until all three designs have been submitted and approved.
13 weeks	Final Set Design	On this date the completed set design will be presented. It shall include as a minimum: ■ Finished, drafted floor plan in $\frac{1}{2}'' = 1'-0''$ ■ Rendering or color model ■ Drafted elevations of all scenic units ■ Detail drawings of any unusual units to be built ■ Full furniture plots including motes on whether items are to be built or found ■ Hanging section ($\frac{1}{4}''$ or $\frac{1}{2}'' = 1'-0''$) ■ Final prop list, including director's updated list, sketches of all items, and notes whether items are to be built or found ■ Painter's elevations of all painted scenery
10 weeks	Set Design Drawings Complete	$\frac{1}{2}''$ scale front elevations and sections of all scenic units, Finished ground plan and section, Annotated cut sheets or drawings of all properties

(Continued)

Time Prior to Opening	Event	Definition
8 weeks	Set Construction Drawings Complete	½" scale technical ground plan and section, rigging plot, technical elevations and construction details with cut lists, shift plot, materials/cost estimate, labor estimates, construction schedule
7 weeks	Set Construction Begins	The production technical director shall meet with the Scene Studio supervisor and outline the production, make assignments, and assemble all needed materials. The first "to-do" list should be submitted to the supervisor at this time. Weekly updates and adjustments should take place each week following.
6 weeks	Preliminary Sound Cue List	This list should include the sound cues which the director feels are necessary for his/her action and concept. It should include a brief description of each cue and an approximate length needed. In the case of underscoring, pre-show, intermission, and post-show sound. The description may be as specific as individual selections of music or as general as the period which the sound design should evoke.
6 weeks	Final Costume Sketches Complete	The final costume design shall include full color renderings of each costume, with appropriate fabric swatches, a written costume plot, and specific notes on unusual construction or fabrics, and other items as requested by project advisors.
5 weeks	Costume Construction Begins	The production costume designer shall meet with the costumer and outline the production, make assignments, and assemble all need materials. Weekly updates and adjustments should take place each week following with the costume studio staff.
5 weeks	Preliminary Prop Viewing	The director, stage manager, prop head, scenic designer, technical director, and producer will meet to look at all the properties which have been pulled and or built based on the initial prop list. At this time specific choices will be made as to the proposed for use in the production.

Time Prior to Opening	Event	Definition
4 weeks	Preliminary Lighting Design	The preliminary lighting design shall include: ■ A written paper outlining the designer's approach ■ A light plot showing the major acting areas as broken down into lighting areas ■ A color key
3 weeks	Final Prop List	This is the final list of properties, prepared by the director and the stage manager. It should be as complete as possible and include numbers as well as detailed descriptions of all items.
3 weeks	Final Light Plot	All lighting design must be submitted for approval a minimum of three days before the light hang. The design materials must include: ■ A ½" = 1'-0" light plot with accurate line plot and time ■ A rough section in ¼" or ½" scale. A working drawing that indicates the set, all lighting positions, borders with trims, and sight lines. Design approval requires a section view. ■ A compete hook up, but without circuit information ■ A designer's cheat sheet for use at tech table to design cues ■ A script with cures indicated ■ A list of cues indicated page number and action The script and list of cues must be submitted no later than three days prior to the first technical rehearsal. The set designer should be notified in ample time in order to provide a the required section drawing for the lighting designer's use.

(Continued)

Time Prior to Opening	Event	Definition
3 weeks	Final Sound Plot	This plot should include the cues from the director's sound cue list as well as additional cues which the sound designer envisions after discussions with the director. All cues should be recorded and complied for playback. In addition, written cue sheets indicating operation and placement should be completed.
2 weeks	Load-In	All scenic elements will be moved from the scenic studio and placed in their proper location on stage. Once installation is complete and safe, the director and stage manager will be informed by the Technical Director and rehearsals may move onto the set. Prior to this date, no guarantee is made that the stage will be rehearsal ready.
12–14 days	Light Hang	Crews will be called to hang, cable, and focus the designer's lighting plot. No stage time will be available during this period for other uses.
12 days	Final Prop Viewing	The director, stage manager, prop head, scenic designer, technical director, and producer will meet to look at all final properties prepared for the production. No additions are to be made following this viewing and cuts which prove to be necessary will be made at this time.
9 days	Crew Watch	This is a run through on stage which gives the crew members their only chance to watch the production. Cast and crew introductions will be made, and the directors concept repeated prior to the start of this run-through.
7 days	Dry Tech	Involves technicians only. The rehearsal may be run either by the technical director or, preferably, by the stage manager. The purpose is to sort out problems such as timing, correctness of shifts, placement, and the sorting of cues. Dry techs are called if in the opinion of the technical director, they are necessary. A Cue-to-Cue rehearsal may be held instead of or in conjunction with the Dry Tech date on the master schedule.

Time Prior to Opening	Event	Definition
6 days	1st Tech	May take one of two forms: either Cue-to-Cue or Stop and Go.
		■ **Cue-to-Cue**—Involves technician and actors both. This rehearsal is run by the stage manager. The Technical Director participates only to the extent that his/her help is required and only when requested. Cue-to-Cue tech is for the purposes of polishing timing and exactness. No single problem within a Cue-to-Cue should delay cast and crew more than five minutes. If a problem takes more time to solve, the rehearsal should be completed and the problem solved later. The production is run by skipping major portions of the script and only performing that which is necessary for each cue.
		■ **Stop and Go**—Involves all production personnel. The stop and go is for timing and creating the performance sense of a production. The rehearsal is run by the stage managers and should be stopped only by them. Again, the five minutes problem rule should be enforced. The production is run in its entirety with stops called only when problems occur.
		The number one goal of either technical rehearsal format is to not waste the time of the many artists involved.
5 days	2nd Tech	Usually a stop and go or straight run-through, run by the stage manager.
4 days	1st Dress	Run through with actors in costumes for the first time.
2 days	2nd Dress	Actors in costume with make-up, run by the stage manager with stops occurring only if a major problem occurs.
1 day	Final Dress	All production personnel respond as if the rehearsal were a performance.
	Opening	Stage manager begins to file production reports with all personnel.

(Continued)

Time Prior to Opening	Event	Definition
	Run	Stage manager files production reports following each performance and coordinates issues with appropriate personnel.
	Strike	All members of the production are required to participate in strike. Immediately following the closing performance, all costumes and stage properties are struck and returned to their appropriate studios. At the next appropriate day, crews will work to clear the stage of all scenery, stake the lights and restore the theatre.
1 week after closing	Post Production Evaluation	An opportunity for designers, advisors, and design/tech staff to evaluate the project and identify opportunities for future improvement. This conversation also affords the producer to hear suggestions for how the production system cold be improved.
Production Notes		The stage manager is responsible for keeping production personnel informed during the rehearsal period and through the run of the show. Notes should be directed to the appropriate production team member when necessary.

Blueprint of a Production

WEEK	DATE	PERSONS INVOLVED	PURPOSE
12 weeks prior to construction		Stage Manager	Collect scripts, audition cards & schedules from the business office
9 weeks prior to construction		Costume, Set, Light, Sound Designer, Director	Designers meet with director individually for brief working sessions
DSGN MTG #1 8 weeks prior to construction		Producer, Director, Assist. Director, Technical Director, Costume, Set, Light, Sound Designer, Business Manager, Music Director, Stage Manager, Faculty Advisors	Director presents mise en scene including remarks on design elements, Discussion with designers presenting ideas, All area budgets are presented and reviewed, Production schedule is reviewed, Future meetings scheduled, Production parameters presented
DSGN MTG #2 7 weeks prior to construction		Producer, Director, Assist. Director, Technical Director, Costume, Set, Light, Sound Designer, Music Director, Stage Manager	Set & Costume designers formally present: (1. Research, 2. Preliminary sketches, 3. Preliminary prop list, 4. $\frac{1}{8}$" or $\frac{1}{4}$" groundplan/ section or thumbnails), Sound designer present preliminary plot, Director presents 1st draft props & sound list, Initial discussion of color pallet, Following this meeting—compile prop and sounds lists, Designers meet individually with Director

(Continued)

WEEK	DATE	PERSONS INVOLVED	PURPOSE
DSGN MTG #3 6 weeks prior to construction		Producer, Director, Assist. Director, Technical Director, Costume, Set, Light, Sound Designer, Music Director, Stage Manager, Faculty Advisors	Designers present:(Rough ¼" or ½" scale model, Revised groundplan and section, costume sketches), Discussion of props noting complex or exotic, Identify special challenges (effects, movement issues, install concerns), Identify run crew needs, Preliminary cost estimates for all designs, Confirm colors, Schedule visit to light lab
5 weeks prior to construction		Producer, Director, Assist. Director, Technical Director, Costume, Set, Light, Sound Designer, Music Director, Stage Manager, Crew heads	Week is devoted to problem solving, Staff meet as required to resolve questions and bring concepts in line with production parameters, Set designer drafts ½" scale plans, sections, & elevations, plus scaled props drawings or photos, Sound designer presents preliminary plot and cue samples
DSGN MTG #4 4 weeks prior to construction		Producer, Director, Assist. Director, Technical Director, Costume, Set, Light, Sound Designer, Music Director, Stage Manager, Faculty Advisors	FINALIZE ALL DESIGN ELEMENTS, NO MAJOR CHANGES FOLLOWING THIS MEETING, Set designer presents final drawings & paint elevations or painted model, Costume designer presents finished color renderings with swatches, Final cost projections presented, Updated props & sound lists, Color decisions finalized
Week of casting		Director, Assistant Director, Stage Manager, & hopeful actors	Auditions

WEEK	DATE	PERSONS INVOLVED	PURPOSE
3 weeks prior to construction		Producer, Director, Assist. Director, Technical Director, Costume, Set, Light, Sound Designer, Music Director, Stage Manager, Crew heads	Completed design drawings distributed to: Production technical director, Prop head, Studio copy, File copy, Stage manager, Director, Lighting designer; Design & technical staff discuss drawings & construction techniques, Lighting designer meets with director to review instrumentation and cue sequences
2 weeks prior to construction		Technical director, Assist. Technical director, Head carpenter, Stage carpenter	Technical staff prepares construction drawings & schedules, Makes crew assignments, Orders materials
1 week prior to construction		Technical director & studio staff	Complete all remaining construction drawings, Review stock materials, Order materials & supplies
PROD MTG # 1 1 week prior to construction		Producer, Director, Assist. Director, Technical Director, Costume, Set, Light, Sound Designer, Music Director, Stage Manager, Prop head, Costume supervisor, Production electrician, Scenic artist, Head carpenter, Stage carpenter	Introductions, Director's remarks, Designers present to staff, Review crew needs & assignments, Review calendar
3 days prior to construction		Technical director, Head carpenter, Prop head, Studio supervisor	Construction drawings complete & all materials ordered, Check crew assignments, Review schedule, citing deadlines, sequences, & anticipated challenges

(Continued)

WEEK	DATE	PERSONS INVOLVED	PURPOSE
Evening of 1st Rehearsal		Costume, Set, Light, Sound Designer, Director, Cast Stage manager	Introductions of production staff, Director presentation on choice & interpretation, Designer presentation of renderings, models, Actors introduced, Schedule distributed
4–5 weeks prior to load-in		Scenery & costume crew & staff	Explain project scope & procedures, Begin construction
PROD MTG #2 3 weeks prior to load-in		Producer, Director, Assist. Director, Technical Director, Costume, Set, Light, Sound Designer, Music Director, Stage Manager, Crew heads	Director remarks, Area reports, Publicity photo scheduled, Set and sound deadlines, Review theatre use schedule
2 weeks prior to load-in		Director, Prop head, Technical director, Set, Light, Sound Designer, Head electrician, Stage manager	Final prop list from prop head distributed to Director, Set designer, Stage manager, Light plot complete, Light designer & Head electrician discuss light hang, Technical director & Stage manager finalize shift plot for scenery & props
PROD MTG #3 1 week prior to load-in		Costume, Set, Light, Sound Designer, Director, Cast, Stage manager	Publicity photo shoot, Sound cue review, Props viewing, Light hang prep, Review load-in, paint & lighting stage time demands, Distribute revised paperwork from all areas
PROD MTG #4 Week of load-in		Producer, Director, Assist. Director, Technical Director, Costume, Set, Light, Sound Designer, Music Director, Stage Manager, Crew heads	Light hang & focus, Scenery installation, Floor painted & touch up, Actors on stage following safety walk through, Problems solved

WEEK	DATE	PERSONS INVOLVED	PURPOSE
8 days prior to opening		Director, Assist. Director, Technical Director, Costume, Set, Light, Sound Designer, Music Director, Stage Manager, Crew heads, Run crew, Board operators	Crew watch, Run crew assignments
5–6 days prior to opening		Director, Sound, Light designers, Board operators	Set sound & lighting levels
5 days prior to opening		FULL STAFF	Technical rehearsals (no work past 12:00 am)
4 days prior to opening		FULL STAFF	Tech-dress, costume & make-up
3 days prior to opening		FULL STAFF	Dress rehearsal with full make-up
2 days prior to opening		FULL STAFF	Final dress rehearsal, Photo call
1 day prior to opening		FULL STAFF	Preview
Opening		FULL STAFF	Performance
Last Performance		FULL STAFF	Costume & properties strike
Day after last performance		Studio & production crews	Scenery & lighting strike, restore theatres
Within 3 days following strike		Crews & crew heads	Return all equipment, Send out thank you letters

Sample Student Job Descriptions University of Wisconsin-Madison

JOB DESCRIPTION: BACKSTAGE LAB STUDENT

The **Backstage Lab Student or Volunteer** assists the Master Carpenter (MC), and other crew heads in the scene studio in the fabrication of scenery, props, etc.

Duties during the Planning Period:

1. Become familiar with the production concept (and script, if possible).
2. Familiarize yourself with the shop facility and tools. Know where materials and stock items are kept.
3. Sign-in and sign-out at all work sessions on the Backstage Lab attendance sheet by reporting to the TA in charge of the lab. It is necessary to keep track of hours spent on all projects for the purpose of refining future time estimations.
4. Review design and shop drawings with your Crew Head, discussing material choices and favored assembly methods.
5. Review the construction schedule and priorities with the Crew Head.

Duties during Construction, Assembly & Load-In Period:

1. Assist in the construction of all scenery, etc.
2. Alert the MC or Crew Head as to your material needs and any concerns regarding fabrication and personnel.
3. Label all units in accordance with the shop drawings.
4. Report all damaged or non-functional tools and equipment to the Shop Supervisor; provide a note with specific instructions/needs.
5. Participate as directed by the Lab TA in the daily cleanup of the scene studio and adjacent areas.
6. Clean all shop areas immediately following the completion of the scenery Load-in into the theatre.

Duties during the Technical Rehearsal & Performance Period:

1. Continue to be on call to make repairs, modifications, etc. as directed by Crew Heads.

Duties during the Clean-up Period:

1. Assume a role in the strike of the set, props, etc. and the salvage of all reusable units and materials. All areas must be cleaned and all equipment returned to its proper storage area.
2. Your job is not complete until all crews are done; ask the strike leader for a new assignment once yours is complete.

Line of Responsibility:

1. Your immediate supervisor is the MC or other scene studio crew head, followed by the TA in charge of the lab session.

JOB DESCRIPTION: SPECIAL PROJECTS

Students assigned to a **'Special Project'** takes responsibility for the planning, fabrication, assembly, finishing and installation of one or more specified elements of a production. Special projects are available in many areas: scenery, props, paint, soft goods, sculpture, costumes, millinery, etc.

Duties during the Construction and Assembly Period:

1. Meet with your designated supervisor, usually the Shop Supervisor) to determine the project parameters.
2. Determine a timetable and specified lab meetings in which the project will be fabricated.
3. Meet a least once a week with your project supervisor to determine your progress and any special needs.
4. Sign-in and sign-out at all work sessions on the Backstage Lab attendance sheet by reporting to the TA in charge of the lab. A Special Project is a goal-oriented assignment, but it is necessary to have your hours totaled for the purpose of refining future time estimations.

Duties during the Load-In Period:

1. Work a minimum of eight (8) hours during the production Load-in; coordinate your commitment with the load-in of your project(s). Develop your schedule prior to Load-in, in consultation with your project supervisor.

Duties during Clean up Period:

1. Assist in the strike in a position directed by your project supervisor. Your job is not complete until all crews are finished.

Line of Responsibility:

1. Your immediate supervisor is the Project supervisor as designated;, followed by the Lab TA or faculty/staff supervisor.

JOB DESCRIPTION: ASSISTANT TECHNICAL DIRECTOR

The job of the **Assistant Technical Director (ATD)** is to perform the duties below and to function as the Technical Director in the TD's absence.

Duties during the Preplanning Period:

1. Become familiar with the script and the production concept.
2. Assist the TD and Shop Supervisor in the organizational work required to prepare the shop for crews.
3. Verify levels of supplies, tool maintenance, condition of rigging systems and level of rigging supplies with the Shop Supervisor.
4. Locate and price out scenery materials as directed by the TD; prepare a list of alternatives, if requested.
5. Review proposed solutions to problems of construction and organization; play the role of devil's advocate to the TD.
6. Serve as Master Drafter for the preparation of shop drawings; coordinate a team of drafters, when necessary.
7. Assist the TD in determining the order of construction of units.
8. Prepare schedules mapping the time frame required in the construction and finishing steps of each unit; forms are available.

Duties during Construction, Assembly & Load-In Period:

1. Assist the TD and Master Carpenter (MC) in maintaining production QUALITY, SCHEDULE AND COST CONTROL.
2. Work one lab session per week as an assistant to the MC.
3. Order construction materials as directed by the TD.
4. Coordinate the security and maintenance of all materials, tools, hardware and props with the Shop Supervisor.
5. Make management decisions in the absence of the TD.
6. Assume a leadership role in the Load-in and Installation of the scenery and props.
7. Assist the TD in the coordination of the Load-In with other departments (costumes, lighting, paint, props, sound, and management).

Duties during the Technical Rehearsal & Performance Period:

1. Assist the TD as directed in the planning and execution of the choreography of scenery and props during performances.

2. Attend all technical rehearsals, take notes and assist the TD as directed.
3. Coordinate the execution of rehearsal and set/prop completion notes, as directed by the TD.

Duties during the Clean-up:

1. Assist the TD in planning the order of strike and the allocation of crew and work space.
2. Assume a leadership role during Strike.
3. Complete all production records (schedules, drawings, accounting and correspondence); collate items into an archival package (disks preferred) for University Theatre (UT) records.

Line of Responsibility:

1. Your immediate supervisor is the TD, followed by the faculty TD.

JOB DESCRIPTION: MASTER CARPENTER

The **Master Carpenter (MC)** supervises the construction of the scenery built by students enrolled in theatre Backstage Laboratory courses.

Duties during the Planning Period:

1. Become familiar with both the script and the production concept.
2. Familiarize yourself with the shop facility and tools. Know where materials and stock items are kept.
3. Review design and shop drawings with the Technical Director (TD) and Assistant Technical Director (ATD), discussing material choices and favored assembly methods.
4. Discuss the construction schedule with the TD and verify: time restrictions; the chosen order of construction; material selections; lab crews; crew experience.

Duties during Construction, Assembly & Load-In Period:

1. Supervise the construction of all scenery with the assistance of lab crews and special projects students.
2. Provide crews with information on the scenic requirements of the production and proper tool, material, assembly procedures; estimated time needed to complete the project; schedule updates.
3. Assist the Lab TA in directing lab students in daily cleanup, following each work session.
4. Coordinate your work daily with the work of the other MCs, if any.
5. Alert the TD and ATD as to your material needs and any concerns regarding construction and personnel.
6. Meet at least weekly with the TD and ATD (together) to keep informed of any changes in design, construction procedures or schedule. Review timetable daily.
7. Label all units in accordance with the shop drawings.
8. Perform a trial set-up of scenic units prior to load in, if possible.
9. Assign crews to the area of the shop in which they should work.
10. Report all damaged or non-functional tools and equipment to the Shop Supervisor; provide a note with specific instructions/needs.
11. Assist in the construction of difficult pieces, as directed by the TD.
12. Prepare the tool roadbox at least one day prior to Load-in, in consultation with the Shop Supervisor.
13. Clean all shop areas immediately following the completion of the scenery load-in into the theatre.

Duties during the Technical Rehearsal & Performance Period:

1. Continue to be on call to make repairs, modifications, etc. as directed by the TD.

Duties during the Clean-up Period:

1. Assist the TD and ATD in planning the order of strike and the allocation of crew and work space.
2. Assume a leadership role in the strike of the set and the salvage of all reusable units and materials. All areas must be cleaned and all equipment returned to its proper storage area.

Line of Responsibility:

1. Your immediate supervisor is the TD, followed by the faculty TD.

JOB DESCRIPTION: SCENIC ARTIST

The Scenic Artist (SA) supervises the application of all painted and textural finishes on all scenic and prop units; the SA is assisted by the paint crew.

Duties during the Planning Period:

1. Become familiar with both the script and the production concept.
2. Study the designs (rendering or model) and the paint elevations in consultation with the Designer.
3. Determine the methods of painting to be used in consultation with the Designer and Paint TA.
4. Conduct experiments with the painting techniques discussed; check the results with the Designer before beginning painting.
5. Estimate and order (through the Shop Supervisor) all needed paint materials and equipment two weeks prior to beginning. All purchases must be approved, in advance, by the Paint TA.
6. Prepare a schedule and sequence of tasks, in consultation with the Designer, Technical Director (TD) and Master Carpenter (MC). Determine the distribution of time and space needed.

Duties during the Construction Period:

1. Supervise the work of the paint crew. Before beginning the project, outline the work schedule and scenic requirements with the crew; train them in the painting technique(s) to be used.
2. Supervise or take responsibility for the preparation all stencils.
3. Prepare all flats that come out of storage for painting. Backpaint all units with a paint/flame proofing solution.
4. Prepare and label all paints PRIOR to crew work calls.
5. Direct crew members to not use spray equipment without the prior approval of the Designer, Shop Supervisor and TD.
6. Supervise the finishing coats and painting of all props.
7. Direct and participate in cleaning all equipment and the paint shop thoroughly following each work session. Return materials to their assigned place; save all paint that can be used again; cover all paint and glue containers *tightly*.
8. Coordinate the paint schedule with the scenery construction schedule in consultation with the TD and MC. Participate in weekly or regular meetings to monitor progress and adjust the schedule.

Duties during the Technical Rehearsal and Performance Period:

1. Assist in moving the scenery to the stage, as directed by the TD.
2. Perform painting touch-up or repainting tasks when the scenery is on stage.

Duties during the Clean-up Period:

1. Consolidate left-over paint for future use as a base coat.
2. Scrub the floors of all paint and put everything in order as soon as the paint area of the scene shop is cleared of scenery.
3. Direct the final cleanup of the paint shop and equipment during strike. When finished, assist other crews. One crew is not finished until everyone is finished.

Line of Responsibility:

1. Your immediate supervisor is the Scene Designer, followed by the Paint TA.

JOB DESCRIPTION: ASSISTANT SCENIC ARTIST

The **Assistant Scenic Artist (ASA)** is a lead painter working under the direction of the Scenic Artist (SA) and assists in the supervision of the paint crew.

Duties during the Construction Period:

1. Familiarize yourself with the script and the production concept.
2. Assist the SA in supervising the work of the paint crew. Help train the crew in the painting technique(s) to be used.
3. Assist the SA in the preparation and labeling of paints and stencils, equipment modification, flame proofing, finishing of props, or as otherwise directed by the SA.
4. Paint.
5. Supervise the crew in the clean-up of all equipment and the paint shop following each work session. Return materials to their assigned place; save all paint that can be used again; cover all paint and glue containers; clean brushes and other application tools.

Duties during the Technical Rehearsal and Performance Period:

1. Assist in moving the scenery to the stage, as directed by the TD.
2. Perform touch-up or repainting tasks as directed by the SA when the scenery is on stage.

Duties during the Clean-up Period:

1. Consolidate left-over paint for future use as a base coat paint.
2. Scrub the floors of all paint and put everything in order as soon as the paint area of the scene shop is cleared of scenery.
3. Direct the final cleanup of the paint shop and equipment during strike. When finished, assist other crews. One crew is not finished until everyone is finished.

Line of Responsibility:

1. Your immediate supervisor is the Scenic Artist, followed by the Paint TA.

JOB DESCRIPTION: MASTER FLYMAN

The Master Flyman (MF) is responsible for all scenic units flown during a performance. The MF supervises a crew responsible for moving existing linesets, the installation of new linesets and the coordination and installation of all flown scenic, lighting and audio units. The size of the fly crew is determined by the demands of the most complicated flying shift of the production.

Duties during the Planning Period: <u>NOTE</u>: All preparations must be made prior to Load-in.

1. Read the script and become familiar with the production concept.
2. Establish a list of the required tasks and a timetable to complete them at a meeting with the Technical Director (TD). At this time you will receive a list of everything to be flown drops, drapes, back walls, set walls, cycloramas, masking units, ceilings, electric pipes, etc. This meeting is to be held a minimum of two weeks prior to load-in.
3. Verify that the needed linesets as shown on the designer's GP are free or can be freed for use.
4. Mark up a scaled groundplan showing the scenery to be flown; verify that a lineset number has been assigned to each piece.
5. Determine the sequence in which units should be rigged and flown at a meeting with the TD, Deck Carpenter (DC) and Master Electrician (ME). Compile this information in writing; provide copies to the others.
6. Establish call times for members of the fly (rigging) crew at the meeting above; notify the crew 2 to 3 weeks in advance of the first call.

Duties during the Load-In Period:

1. Train all members of the rigging (fly) crew in the safe practice of running lines and installing equipment at the first session.
2. Direct the fly crew in preparing the grid and fly equipment for Load-in.

    NOTE: No overhead rigging work is to be done during times that the stage is occupied by others. If it is necessary to modify overhead rigging during a call involving others, the affected deck area shall be cleared of all personnel and cordoned with warning signs.

3. Hang all lighting equipment and flown scenic units prior to the load-in of deck pieces.
4. Label all linesets on the rail for ready identification.

5. CAUTION: Check to make certain that flown units are properly counterweighted before running operating lines full distance.

Duties during Technical, Dress Rehearsal and Performance Period:

1. Sign-in at the designated time: usually one hour prior to the start of rehearsal or opening the house (20 minutes to curtain).
2. Verify that the linesets you control are in balance and that none are fouled before the start of each rehearsal and performance. To do this bring each lineset into the performance position (in-trim) and return it to the storage position (out-trim). DIRECT YOUR CREW TO CHECK THAT THE TRIM MARKS ON THE LINESESTS THEY OPERATE ARE WHERE THEY OUGHT TO BE. THEY MUST NOT DELEGATE ANY PART OF THIS RESPONSIBILITY.
3. Follow the directions of the DC and Stage Manager (SM). The DC will give the MF a cue-sheet detailing the work of the fly crew. The SM will explain how cues are to be taken; wait for the SM to signal before lifting or lowering anything. In raising a flown piece, verify that furniture or properties are not fouling it; in lowering a piece, verify that no person or object is below it.

Duties during Clean-up Period:

1. Clear all pipes of flown units and masking, except units that are to be stored. This is to be done during strike under the direction of the TD. Restore all empty linesets to pipe weight.
2. Undo any special show rigging or modifications such as moved linesets, dead-hung units, etc. Remove spare or loose equipment from the grid; return it to the grid storage box.
3. Follow the directions of the TD during strike. Assist other departments, as directed. One crew is not finished until everyone is finished.

Line of Responsibility:

1. Your immediate supervisor is the Deck Carpenter, followed by the Rigging TA.

JOB DESCRIPTION: PROPERTY MASTER

The **Prop Master (PM)** is responsible for the planning and execution of all props, borrowed, rented or built. The PM has supervisory responsibility over both construction and running crews.

Duties during the Planning Period:

1. Become familiar with the script, production concept and the prop requirements.
2. Make a complete list of required props; classify them into groups: set props, trim props, hand props, food props, etc. Coordinate this list with lists made by the Stage Manager (SM), Director (and possibly the Prop TA).
3. Check whether there is anything suitable in prop storage before purchasing any props, or materials for making props. When in doubt, consult the Prop TA, Technical Director (TD) or Designer.
4. Establish deadlines for obtaining and building properties in consultation with the Prop TA. The Prop TA has forms.
5. Make a list of expendable props like cigarettes and food. **Make every effort to keep these expenditures to a minimum.**
6. Make a detailed budget for the purchase of props. Check this budget with the Prop TA. Obtain the approval of the Prop TA prior to any spending. Items not included in the approved budget may not be purchased without the explicit permission of the Prop TA.

Duties during the Construction Period:

1. Assist the Prop TA, as directed, in securing essential props (or substitutes) needed for rehearsal. Rehearsal props become the responsibility of stage management during the rehearsal period.
2. Assign crew members specific construction or refinishing projects on a per lab basis. Provide your crew with a detailed description of each property, including dimensions, finish, and some visual aid regarding style and other details.
3. Check with the Shop Supervisor or Master Carpenter (MC) for use of shop space when necessary to construct props in the scene studio.
4. Arrange a time with the SM when you can attend rehearsal(s).
5. Make a "by scene" list of required props and the characters handling them, listing the placement and movement of the props ON and OFF stage. Verify the list with the SM.

6. When borrowing a property (have a loan list prepared in advance):
    a. Assume a professional attitude when borrowing items; assure the loaning party that the item will be well treated and secure; offer listed insurance coverage, if desired.
    b. Never borrow without the consent of the Prop TA. The Prop TA will accompany you, if necessary.
    c. Never borrow expensive antiques or items having sentimental value.
    d. Make any necessary transportation arrangements through the Shop Supervisor; PMs having a driver's license are expected to obtain authorization to drive university vehicles. See the Prop TA for information.
7. Give requests for program acknowledgments to the Business Office immediately upon receipt or pledge; provide complete and specific information. Inform the loaning party of the nature of the program credit to assure they will be satisfied. Confer with the Business Manager for specifics.

Duties during the Tech Rehearsal and Performance Period:

1. Attend all tech and dress rehearsals. Check in with the Prop Crew Head to assure that all needs are being met and that props function as required.
2. Receive and forward Director notes following rehearsals. Follow up the next day to assure that notes have been completed. In the event that no lab crew is available, plan to complete the notes yourself.
3. Review the storage and handling of props by the running crew, in consultation with the Prop Crew Head (PCH).
4. Check with the SM and PCH to assure that the props remain their quality during the run of performances; be in close communication with the PCH to answer questions and provide direction as needed.

Duties during the Clean-up Period:

1. Direct the props crew in the safe removal and return of all props during strike. Coordinate the strike activities with the Prop TA and PCH so that all props can be removed quickly and safely prior to any dismantling of the set (except as necessary to access prop items).
2. Return all props to their storage spaces; store in the assigned location.
3. Empty and wash all bottles, glasses, dishes, ash trays, etc. before they are returned to the prop room or to their owners.
4. Throw out any perishable leftover food. Clean out the prop room refrigerator as part of strike.

5. Return all borrowed or rented props as soon as possible and no later than 72 hours after the final performance. Be sure that the loan agreement release form is signed by the owner and the signed form is returned to the Prop TA.
6. After all the props have been put away, join the rest of the strike with your crew. One crew is not finished until everyone is finished.

Line of Responsibility:

1. Your immediate supervisor is the Prop TA, followed by the faculty TD.

Appendix IV

Scenery Standards Handbook

Table of content

I. STANDARD WOOD FLAT CONSTRUCTION

A. Frame

1. FRAMING MEMBERS TO BE 1X3 OR 1X4 #2 PINE ON FACE, JOINED WITH ¼" PLYWOOD GUSSETS, WOOD GLUE AND PNUEMATIC STAPLES.
2. LOCATE TOGGLES 4' –0" O.C., BEGINNING FROM BOTTOM OF UNIT. ADD ADDITIONAL TOGGLES AS REQUIRED FOR SHOW.
3. USE LIGHT WEIGHT MATERIALS SUCH AS PINE OR POPLAR FOR FRAME.

B. Braces

1. BRACE ALL FLATS 4' –0" OR WIDER AT TOP AND BOTTOM.
2. ATTACH AT A 45 DEGREE ANGLE.
3. RUN TO CENTERLINE OF RAIL.
4. ATTACH BOTH BRACES TO SAME STILE.
5. AVOID LARGE PIECES OF ¾" PLY OR OSB WHEN CREATING PROFILES.
6. REDUCE WEIGHT BY CUTTING HOLES IN SOLID PIECES, LEAVING A PERIMETER OF 2 ½" OF MATERIAL.

C. Squarness

1. CHECK FLAT FOR DIMENSIONS AND SQUARENESS BEFORE ATTACHING GUSSETS.
2. USE THE 3/4/5 RULE TO CHECK FOR SQUARE OF LARGER FLATS.
   a) NOTE: See Appendix B for flat construction procedure.

CORNER BLOCK

ANGLE BRACE

STRAP

TOGGLE

1X4 TYP

RIGHT AND LEFT STILE

HALF STRAP

TOP AND BOTTOM RAIL

D. Gussets

1. TYPES AND SIZES
   a) Standard material is ¼" AC ply.
   b) Keystones should measure $2\frac{3}{8}$" x 8".
   c) Corner Blocks: 10" leg.
   d) See Appendix A for cutting procedure.
   e) Do not glue unless flat is a stock unit.
2. ATTACH WITH $\frac{7}{8}$" WIDE-CROWN STAPLES WITH 5/8" LEG.
3. USE STAPLE PATTERS SHOWN, WITH STAPLES PERPENDICULAR TO GUSSET GRAIN.

189

4. OBSERVE $\frac{7}{8}$ " KEEPBACK ON ALL GUSSETS FOR SOFT-COVERED FLATS; 1 $\frac{1}{8}$ " IF HARD-COVERED.

E. Stiffening

1. USE 1 X 4 PINE - AVOID WARPED OR TWISTED LUMBER.
2. ATTACH WITH L-BRACKETS OR BACK-FLAP HINGES, USING PAN-HEAD SCREWS (NOT FLAT-HEAD). ALTERNATE HARDWARE FROM ONE SIDE OF STIFFENER TO THE OTHER, TO KEEP IT PERPENDICULAR TO THE FLAT.
3. JOIN STIFFENER TO EACH FRAMING MEMBER CROSSED.
4. VERTICAL STIFFENERS:
   a) Run full height of flat, attaching to both rails, but maintain a 1" keepback from the top and bottom edges.
   b) One stiffener required for up to 4' wide flat, 2 for 6' flats. For wider flats, use vertical stiffeners with horizontal stiffeners in-between.
   c) When using one stiffener, locate it approximately at the centerline of the flat; when using two, locate approximately 1' from each side.
5. HORIZONTAL STIFFENERS:
   a) First two within 1' of top and bottom of flat. Use additional ones as needed to maintain 8-10' spacing.
   b) Attach to both vertical stiffeners and to flat frame.

F. Covering

1. STANDARD COVER IS #140 UNBLEACHED NATURAL-COLOR MUSLIN, 81" WIDE.
2. FOR WIDER FLATS, SEW PIECES TOGETHER, USING A 1" ALLOWANCE FLAT SEAM.
3. GLUE MUSLIN TO THE PERIMETER FRAME MEMBERS ONLY (INCLUDED ARE WINDOW, DOOR AND SIMILAR OPENINGS) WITH TEN PARTS WHITE GLUE TO ONE PART WATER.
4. USING A SHARP UTILITY (MATT) KNIFE, TRIM OFF THE EXCESS FABRIC BY CUTTING THE MUSLIN $\frac{1}{8}$ " BACK FROM EDGE (CUT SLIGHTLY INTO LUMBER).
   a) NOTE: See Appendix C for covering procedure.

FANCY BRACKET

VERTICAL STIFFENER

STAGE BRACE

G. An alternative covering method

1. WRAP THE MATERIAL AROUND THE FRAME, STAPLING IT TO THE BACK SURFACE.
2. USE THIS METHOD ONLY WHEN THE FLAT WILL NOT BE MOVED (DRAGGED) DURING THE RUN OF A SHOW SINCE THE BOTTOM EDGE WILL FRAY.
3. NO TRIMMING IS REQUIRED, BUT PREPARATION IS IDENTICAL TO SECTION H BELOW.

H. Sizing and Flame-proofing

1. SIZE FRONT SURFACE WITH A STARCH SOLUTION (SEE PECKTAL), NOT REQUIRED

WHEN USING LATEX PAINTS.

2. FLAMEPROOF REAR SIDE OF FLAT USING "STANDARD" SHOP FLAMEPROOFING COMPOUND, COVERING BOTH FABRIC AND LUMBER. MIX FLAME RETARDANT INTO BACKPAINT. NOTE: SEE SECTION VI FOR FLAME RETARDANT INFORMATION.

3. SIZE AND FLAMEPROOF WITH A TWO-PERSON CREW USING THE AIRLESS SPRAY GUN AND BRUSHING THE SOLUTION INTO THE SURFACE. ALLOW TIME FOR COMPLETE DRYING BETWEEN COATS.

I. Storage

1. STORE UN-STIFFENED FLATS PROPERLY TO AVOID WARPAGE: UNITS GO FACE-TO-FACE AND BACK-TO-BACK WITH THE LONGEST EDGE ON THE DECK.

2. KEEP THE STACK AS VERTICAL AS POSSIBLE.

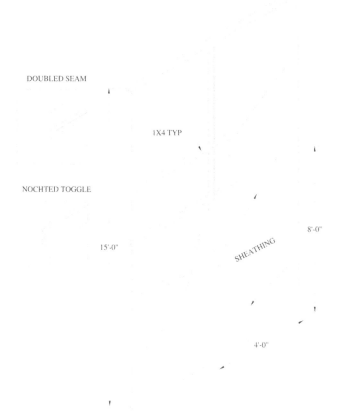

DOUBLED SEAM

1X4 TYP

NOCHTED TOGGLE

SHEATHING

8'-0"

15'-0"

4'-0"

II. ALTERNATIVE FLAT CONSTRUCTION

A. Hollywood or TV Style Flats

1. THE FRAME IS TYPICALLY 1 X 3 OR 1 X 4 ON EDGE, JOINED WITH EITHER 8D COATED NAILS OR 2" DRYWALL SCREWS.
2. THE COVER IS TYPICALLY A THIN PANEL MATERIAL SUCH AS LAUAN OR MASONITE.
3. FASTEN THE COVER USING:

    a) For ¼" cover, use ⅜" wide/narrow staples, flush with surface.

    b) For ⅛" fabric covered material, use glue and 4d box nails or ½" "hand" staples driven with the air tacker.

    c) For ⅛" material without a fabric cover, use glue and ⅝" narrow staples. Staples must not go completely through cover material.

    d) Support panel joints by:

    (1) For vertical seams, center the joint on a doubles framing member (sketch #1).

    (2) For horizontal seams, use a 1 x 3, face up, notched into and flush with the vertical frame members (sketch #2).

    (3) Use the covering material to square the flat corners. Attach the cover first to one side, and then flush the frame to the adjacent side of the panel. Repeat for remaining pieces. Works best with the flat laid on the floor or a framing table (saw horses are flimsy).

    GUSSET
    FILET WELDED

    (a) Preferred method is same as for standard wood flat. NOTE: See Section I, D and Appendix C.

    ALL JOINTS
    FILET WELDED

    (b) When production needs dictate, glue entire surface. NOTE: See Appendix D.

B. Metal Flats

1. DRILL ALL HOLES REQUIRED FOR JOINERY, BRACES, ETC. BEFORE WELDING.
2. USE 1 X 1 TUBE STEEL OR ALUMINUM, WELDED ACCORDING TO DRAWINGS. AVOID FACE WELDS, BUT IF NECESSARY, GRIND THE WELD FLUSH.

    1 X 1 TUBE
    STEEL

3. PREFERRED ADHESIVE FOR COVERING IS 3M NF-30 CONTACT CEMENT; SECOND CHOICE IS 3M SPRAY 77, IF ADEQUATE VENTILATION EXISTS. GLUE ONE END, THEN THE OPPOSITE END, THEN ONE SIDE, AND THEN THE OTHER.

III. STANDARD FRAMED WOOD PLATFORM CONSTRUCTION

A. Frames

1. USE 2 X 4 SPF (SPRUCE/PINE/FIR) FOR MOST STOCK AND/OR SHOW USES.
2. AT CORNER JOINTS, SHORT FRAME MEMBERS SHOULD OVERLAP LONG PIECE (DWG).
3. 1 X 6 OR 1 X 4 PINE IS AN ACCEPTABLE FRAME TO REDUCE WEIGHT, BUT
   a) Reinforce all joints with nail blocks or steel brackets.
   b) Nail block length is equal to the depth of the platform frame and oriented with the end-grain flush to the underside of the deck.
4. FASTENERS
   a) Join 2 x 4 with 12d common nails, or 3" DWS (or square-drive).
   b) Join 1 x 6 or 1 x 4 frames with 8d coated nails.
   c) Use 3 fasteners per joint; blunt nail tips to avoid splits.
   d) Do not use glue, so pieces can be replaced when damaged.

B. Deck

1. STANDARD MATERIAL IS SQUARE-EDGE ¾" OSB.
2. FASTENERS: USE EITHER
   a) 8d coated nails 6" o.c. along perimeter and 9" o.c. to interior framing or
   b) 2" DWS (drywall screws) 9" o.c. along perimeter and 12" o.c. interior. Square drive screws use the DWS pattern.
3. DO NOT GLUE DECK TO FRAME FOR STOCK UNITS.
4. GLUE DECK OF SHOW UNITS ONLY IF ABSOLUTELY NECESSARY.

C. Legs

1. MAXIMUM LEG SPACING IS 4' FOR 2 X 4 AND 1 X 6 FRAMED PLATFORMS. FOR 1 X 4 FRAMED UNITS, SPACING LIMIT IS REDUCED TO 2'.
2. TYPICAL LEG IS 2 X 4, BUT 1 X 3 OR 1 X 4 IS ACCEPTABLE IF PROPERLY BRACED. ALSO ALLOWED ARE 1 X 3 AND 1 X 4 "L" LEGS, AND 2 X 4 COMPRESSION LEGS. USE A 4 X 4, OR A DOUBLED 2 X 4 WHEN MINIMAL OR NO BRACING IS ALLOWED.

3/4" DECKING (PLY OR OSB)

2X4 FRAME

3 NAILS PER END OF JOIST

4' ENDS SHOULD CAP 8' SIDES

LAYOUT JOISTS 1'-0" ON CENTER, TYP.
FRAME LAYOUT SAME AS 2X4 FRAME.
NAILING PATTERN SAME AS 2X4 FRAME.
DECK WITH 3/4" PLY OR OSB.
FRAME MEASURES 4X8.

1X6 FRAME

2X4 LEGS

3. FASTENERS

a) For 2 x 4 framed platforms, attach legs with 2 countersunk ⅜" dia. machine (hex) bolts, with washers on both ends. Bolts should be on a diagonal pattern. Countersink with 1 ⅛" paddle bit first, then drill a ⁷⁄₁₆" hole for bolt shank.

b) For 1 x 6 or 1 x 4 frame, use 3, ¼" FHSB; do not use countersunk hex bolts.

c) 1 x 3 or 1 x 4 legs up to 16" tall may be either screwed (1 ¼" DWS) or stapled (1 ½" wide) into the frame using 3-4 fasteners per leg.

d) Avoid using carriage bolts if possible, but always use torque washers whenever using a carriage bolt.

e) Screw "L" legs to frame; attach small thickness piece to the piece with greater thickness.

f) Compression leg requires plywood gusset at least 10" long except when platform is less than 10" tall.

D. Stud Wall Legging System

1. USE 2 X 4 STUDS WITH SINGLE 2 X 4 TOP AND BOTTOM PLATES.
2. LOADING REQUIREMENTS GENERALLY DICTATE STUDS PLACED ON 2' –0" CENTERS. DO NOT EXCEED 3' –0" BETWEEN STUDS.
3. STUDS AND PLATES ARE JOINED WITH MINIMUM 2, 12D COMMON OR AIR NAILS PER JOINT.
4. FOR RIGIDITY, USE ½" OR ¾" PLY GUSSETS AT THE CORNERS AND APPROXIMATELY EVERY 10', SCREWED TO THE STUD AND PLATE ON THE FACE OF THE STUD WALL. USE 2" DRYWALL OR SQUARE DRIVE SCREWS.
5. DIAGONAL BRACING IS NORMALLY REQUIRED FOR BOTH SINGLE WALL BRACING OR BRACING A SERIES OF FRAMES. USE 1 X 3 OR 1 X 4.
6. TO JOIN A PLATFORM TO A STUD WALL, LAG (¼" X 3") OR SCREW (3" DWS) THE TOP PLATE OF STUD WALL INTO THE UNDERSIDE OF THE PLATFORM FRAME.
7. TO FASTEN THE BOTTOM PLATE TO FLOOR, USE 10D DOUBLE-HEAD NAILS OR 3" DWS.

E. Bracing

1. USE 1 X 3 OR 2 X 4 FOR BRACING AND RIBBONS DEPENDING ON FACING REQUIREMENTS. 1 X 3 PROVIDES ADEQUATE STRENGTH.
2. RIBBONS RUN AROUND THE PLATFORM LEGS AT APPROXIMATELY 2" ABOVE THE BOTTOM OF THE LEG. ALSO JOIN MIDDLE LEGS WITH RIBBONS. IDEALLY EACH LEG IS BRACED IN TWO DIRECTIONS.

3. NO BRACING IS REQUIRED FOR PLATFORMS UP TO 18" IN HEIGHT. RIBBON ALL LEGS GREATER THAN 18" HIGH; WHEN OVER 30", ADD CROSS BRACING.
4. ATTACH BRACING WITH PROPER SIZED DOUBLE-HEAD NAILS OR 2-3" DWS TO PERMIT EASY DISASSEMBLY. FASTENERS MUST NOT

INTERFERE WITH FACING. DO NOT STAPLE.

5. WHEN SEVERAL PLATFORMS ARE CONNECTED, RIBBONS AND BRACING MAY SPAN SEVERAL PLATFORMS, EACH PLATFORM NEED NOT BE DONE INDIVIDUALLY.

6. ATTACHING EACH LEG TO THE STAGE FLOOR REDUCES THE NEED FOR RIBBONS, DEPENDING ON THE LOADING CHARACTERISTICS OF THE SHOW.

7. WHEN PLATFORMING EXTENDS WALL TO WALL (I.E. THE HEMSLEY), RIBBONS ARE NOT REQUIRED.

F. Joining Platforms

1. USE $\frac{1}{8}$" ETHAFOAM SHEET BETWEEN WOOD PLATFORMS TO PREVENT SQUEAKS. LIGHTLY STAPLE THE ETHAFOAM TO ONE PLATFORM. WOOD/METAL JOINTS ALSO NEED ETHAFOAM, BUT JOINTS BETWEEN TWO METAL PLATFORMS.

2. CLAMPING PLATFORMS

   a) Use c-clamps or $\frac{3}{8}$" hex bolts; spacing is the same.

   b) Use 2 for a 4' joint, three per 8'. Tape clamp handles so they don't rattle as people walk on the stage. Fold over the end of the tape to provide a "handle" with which to take it off.

   c) The surface of adjoining platforms must be flush. Adjust leg height or use shims under legs to accomplish this.

G. Facing

1. USE ¼" AC PLY, MASONITE OR LUAN SECURED TO THE PLATFORM FRAME AT THE TOP AND TO NAILING STRIPS ALONG THE FLOOR (OR RIBBONS, IF USED). CORNER AND BUTT JOINTS BETWEEN ADJOINING PIECES OF FACING MUST BE SUPPORTED BEHIND WITH A NAILING BLOCK.

2. FACING SHOULD BE FLUSH WITH THE FLOOR AND +/- $\frac{1}{16}$" BELOW THE TOP SURFACE. THIS WILL ALLOW FOR IRREGULARITIES IN THE STAGE.

3. TO PREVENT BREAKAGE OF THE FACING WHEN PEOPLE STEP OFF THE PLATFORM, EITHER:

   a) Chamfer the top of the facing material (15-45 degrees), or

   b) Install facing flush and square to top of platform, then put surface layer of masonite (or other material) over facing.

   c) Use edge (or nosing) molding at the edge of the stage.

H. Railings

1. STANDARD HEIGHT IS 3-0" FOR ALL HORIZONTAL SURFACES; 32" ON STAIRS (MEASURED AT FRONT OF STEP).

2. USE 1" SQUARE STEEL TUBE, 2 X 3 OR 2 X 4, UNLESS SPECIFIED OTHERWISE BY DESIGN DRAWINGS.

3. RAILINGS MUST BE SOLID, WELL BRACED, AND SMOOTH. GRIND OR SAND AWAY ANY SPLINTERS OR BURRS. NOTE: SEE SECTION V,F FOR SUGGESTED RAILING.

I. Soundproofing

1. TWO EFFECTIVE METHODS ARE:

   a) Use a sheet of ½" sound insulation board between the frame and the deck. Increase deck fastener length: nail size to 10d; screw size to 3" DWS.

   b) Top the platform with a 2nd deck of $\frac{5}{8}$" or ¾" particleboard or MDF (Medium Density Fiberboard). The extra weight is effective.

2. AVOID USING FIBERGLASS AND OTHER IRRITATING AND FLAMMABLE MATERIALS.

3. USE A STRIP OF $\frac{1}{8}$" ETHAFOAM BETWEEN PLATFORMS TO INHIBIT SQUEAKING.

IV. ALTERNATIVE PLATFORM CONSTRUCTION

A. Metal-framed Platforms

1. FRAME SHALL BE 1" X 2" 16 GA. TUBE STEEL (2" DIMENSION VERTICAL) OR 1/8" X 2" X 2" ANGLE IRON (OR EQUIVALENT).
2. STOCK UNITS ARE TO MATCH SPECIFICATIONS OF "4010" PLATFORMS REGARDING JOINERY, LEG SOCKETS, ROTOLOCKS, WOOD EDGING AND DECK ATTACHMENT AND CORNER PROTECTION.
3. SHOW UNITS MUST HAVE AT LEAST TWO FACES OF EACH PIECE OF STEEL WELDED.
4. FRAMING SPACING MUST NOT EXCEED A 2' X 4' MODULE TO PROPERLY SUPPORT A ¾" THICK DECK.
5. DECK SHOULD BE ATTACHED WITH PLY-METAL TEK SCREWS, 9" OC FOR THE PERIMETER, 12" O.C. INTERIOR.
6. FOR 1" X 1" TUBE STEEL LEGS, MINIMUM WALL THICKNESS IS 16 GA.
7. 1" X 1" LEGS MUST USE STOCK PLATFORM FEET, WHICH TYPICALLY ARE ANCHORED INTO THE DECK BELOW WITH AT LEAST ONE SCREW PER LEG.
8. ALL STANDARDS FOR BRACING IN SECTION III. E., APPLY TO METAL PLATFORMS.

3/4" CDX PLY

FILLET WELD, TYP
GRIND SMOOTH

1X2 TUBE STEEL

1X2 HARDWOOD
SURROUNDS STEEL

B. Triscuit Platform Construction

1. Stress skin construction that typically uses $\frac{5}{8}$ " CDX ply skins top and bottom with $\frac{3}{4}$ x 2" (on face) frame sandwiched in-between for an overall 2 $\frac{3}{8}$ " height.
2. Standard framing pattern and dimensions are shown in figure.
3. Show platforms can be of varying combinations of materials and dimensions provided the 2 $\frac{3}{8}$ " height is maintained, and the skins are supported on 12" centers.
4. Glue all contacting surfaces generously, using a brush or applicator; fasten with 1 ½" wide staples 6" o.c., and allow to dry for 48 hours while fully weighted.
5. Stack units while drying. Place 6, 5-gallon pails on stop of the stack, each pail filled ¾ full with sand.

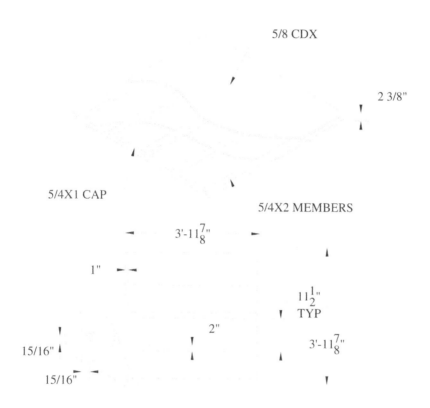

5/8 CDX

2 3/8"

5/4X1 CAP

5/4X2 MEMBERS

$3'\text{-}11\frac{7}{8}$"

1"

$11\frac{1}{2}$"
TYP

2"

$3'\text{-}11\frac{7}{8}$"

15/16"

15/16"

V. STAIR CONSTRUCTION

Unless specified otherwise by design dwgs, construct as follows:

A. Stringers

1. 24" O.C. MAXIMUM SPACING UNLESS RISE IS STRUCTURAL. SEE SECTION V.D.
2. USE ¾": AC PLY (OSB IS NOT ACCEPTABLE) WITH 1 X 2 NAILING BLOCKS ON THE INSIDE FACE (AVOID 1 X 12 AND 2 X 12). GLUE ALL SURFACES. STAPLE STRIPES WITH 1 ¼" NARROW STAPLES. SEE FIGURE ON RIGHT.
3. FOR 2-3 STEP UNITS, STRINGERS SHOULD BE CUT FROM SOLID PIECE OF PLY (I.E. STRINGER ALSO FORMS LEG) PICTURED BELOW.
4. UNITS HAVING FOUR OR MORE STEPS SHOULD BE CUT FROM A 1'-0" PLYWOOD STRIP UNLESS THE TREAD/RISER COMBINATION REQUIRES A WIDER STRINGER.

NAILING BLOCK

3/4 PLY

2X12 STRINGER

B. Treads

1. USE SINGLE OR DOUBLE THICKNESS OF ¾" PLYWOOD OR OSB.
2. NAIL INTO BLOCKS WITH 6D-8D COATED NAILS OR 2"-3" DWS. GLUE ALL SURFACES.

C. Legs/Bracing

1. USE 1 X 4 OR 2 X 4 LEGS BOLTED IN A DIAGONAL PATTER, SECTION III.C.3.
2. LEGS HIGHER THAN 1'6" MUST BE RIBBONED TO EACH OTHER AND TO THE LOWER END OF THE STRINGER. LEGS HIGHER THAN 3'0" SHOULD HAVE DIAGONAL BRACES PLUS THE RIBBON.
3. FASTEN BRACING/RIBBONS WITH DWS OR DOUBLEHEAD NAILS.

D. Riser Facings

1. USE ¼" AC PLYWOOD FOR RISER. THESE SPECIFICATIONS APPLY TO BOTH INDEPENDENT AND

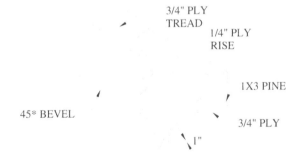

3/4" PLY
TREAD
1/4" PLY
RISE

1X3 PINE

45* BEVEL

3/4" PLY

1"

DEPENDENT STAIRS.

2. IF RISER IS 1X OR ½"- ¾" PLYWOOD, STRINGER SPACING CAN BE EXPANDED TO 3'0".

3. FACING SPECIFICATIONS IN THE SECTION ON PLATFORMING FACING APPLY HERE AS WELL.

4. OBSERVE STRINGER CUTOUTS AS SHOWN IN BOTH ILLUSTRATIONS ABOVE, PARTICULARLY WITH REGARD TO HOW 1 X 3 IS LET INTO STRINGER.

E. Railings for escape stairs

1. RAILING HEIGHT IS 32", MEASURED AT FRONT OF STEP.

2. USE 2 X 3, 2 X 4 OR 1" SQUARE STEEL TUBE FOR BOTH POSTS AND RAILING.

3. THE POST IS ATTACHED TO THE STRINGER WITH TWO HEX BOLTS WITH WASHERS BOTH ENDS OR OTHER EQUALLY SECURE METHOD.

4. THE RAILING IS ATTACHED TO THE POST AS SHOWN ABOVE RIGHT, USING 2, 3" DWS SUNK ⅛" BELOW THE SURFACE, ITS TOP SURFACE CONTINUOUS, ROUNDED AND SANDED SMOOTH.

VI. FLAME-RETARDING PROCEDURES

A. Cellulose-based material (wood, paper, muslin, etc.)

1. USE STANDARD COMPOUND, SPARTAN 742, USING THIS FORMULA: DILUTE 1 PART SOLUTION TO 3 PARTS WATER AND/OR PAINT.
2. MIX FLAME-RETARDANT INTO BACK PAINTS. TREAT BOTH FABRIC AND WOOD WITH SOLUTION. THIS INCLUDES PLATFORMS AND LEGGING SYSTEMS.

B. None-cellulose materials

1. RAW STYROFOAM AND BEADBOARD SHOULD BE TREATED WITH A MIXTURE OF FLEX GLUE AND POTTERS CLAY, MIXED APPROXIMATELY TWO PARTS GLUE TO ONE PART CLAY. APPLY IN THIN COATS TO AVOID CRACKING. 2-3 COATS ARE REQUIRED. USE GLUE RATHER THAN WATER TO THIN SOLUTION.
2. STYROFOAM AND BEADBOARD COVERED WITH CHEESECLOTH DO NOT NEED GLUE/CLAY MIXTURE. USE FLAM-RETARDANT IN PAINT.

C. Synthetic fabrics

1. TREAT WITH FLAMORT CP. DILUTE NO MORE THAN 1:1 WITH WATER.

VII. DROP AND SCRIM CONSTRUCTION

A. Top edge

1. 3 ½" JUTE WEBBING, SEWN TO REAR OF HEMMED FABRIC. #3 GROMMETS AT CORNERS AND 12" OC. CL OF GROMMETS 1" FROM TOP OF DROP, OR
2. DOUBLE 1 X 3 OR 1 X 4 BATTEN, STRAIGHT LUMBER! STAPLE FABRIC TO FIRST BATTEN, SCREW 2ND TO 1ST WITH 1 ¼" DWS. DRILL $\frac{7}{8}$" DIAM. HOLES EVERY 8-10' FOR PICKS. LOCATE HOLES IN THE MIDDLE OF THE BATTEN.

B. Sides

1. 1" HEM IF NO SIDE GROMMETS; 2 ½" WITH EXTRA MUSLIN ADDED IF GROMMETED.

C. Seams

1. ARE FLAT SEAMS, 1" SEAM ALLOWANCE, WITH EQUAL THREAD TENSION BOTH SIDES.

D. Bottom

1. HAS SEVERAL ALTERNATIVES:

   a) Pipe pocket without skirt. Used when bottom of drop doesn't show. Must accommodate minimum 1" ID pipe. Pocket requires 6" of material. (G4.1)

   b) Pipe pocket with skirt. Pocket requires 7 ½" of material. (G4.2)

   c) Chain pocket or skirt, with ties or grommets every foot. (G4.3) Useful for curved drops.

   d) Double batten. (G1.2) Used when drop must be anchored to floor.

VIII. Miscellaneous Construction and Material Notes

A. Nailing

1. Base nail selection on:
   a) Type(s) of wood being joined.
   b) Lumber dimensions.
   c) If it must be removed easily.
   d) Length: Nail to be 3 times the thickness of the thinnest member being joined, i.e. nailing ¾" ply to a 2 x 4 requires an 8d nail.
2. Choose an angle between 10-15 degrees off perpendicular for maximum holding power when nailing into end grain (I.E.: platform framing).
3. Avoid toenailing unless it promotes strength and is readily accomplished. If necessary, the nail should be at no greater angle than 30 degrees with respect to the work. Do not toenail set pieces and platforms together or to the stage floor.

B. Joining plastic foam to foam or other materials

1. Use a mastic panel adhesive. Dab mastic on 12-16" centers; do not spread it over the entire surface. For fast tack, apply mastic, join surfaces and press tight. Then remove the top surface, allowing both surfaces to air dry for 5-10 minutes, before rejoining.
2. Use contact adhesive (3M Fastbond NF-30). Apply adhesive to both surfaces and allow both to dry before assembling, usually 20-30 minutes. Use wood dowels, wax paper, visqueen, or equal to prevent surfaces from coming in contact during alignment. Eliminate air pockets.

C. Joining no-foam materials

1. Use construction mastic when one or both materials are non-porous.
2. Use white or yellow glue if both are porous.
3. Choose flex or rigid white glue based on the flexibility of the materials; I.E. use flex glue on soft goods, rigid glue on wood, etc.

D. Joining wood to metal

1. Use "Tek" screws without pilot hole for in steel up to 16 gauge.
2. If steel is thicker, pre-drill pilot hole. The screw should be long enough to allow drill tip to pass through entire thickness of steel (one wall in the case of tube steel).

E. Caster Plates

1. Using the following materials:
   a) 2 x 6 fir on face, joined by ¾" ply or OSB gussets (12" leg min.) placed on underside of plate.
   b) Attach casters to gusset using at least 2, $\frac{5}{16}$" – $\frac{3}{8}$" x 2" lag screws.

F. Foot irons

1. Use ¼" or $\frac{5}{16}$" lag screws for fixed unit. Floor depth is 1 ½".
2. If unit must move repeatedly, use threaded inserts (bolts or stage screws).

G. Recycling

1. Do not glue materials for show vs. stock scenery together unless loading requirements makes it necessary.

H. Material preparation for paint

1. Polystyrene sheets (vacuform) and Ethafoam (rod or sheet). Use:
   a) Full strength flexglue; NF-30 contact adhesive; or a 1:2 wash coat of white shellac
   b) (1 part shellac to 2 parts alcohol).

2. BEAD BOARD (WHITE FOAM) AND STYROFOAM (BLUE OR PINK FOAM)
   a) Flexglue, glue/clay mixture and/or cheesecloth; or Fastbond Contact Adhesive. See Section VI. regarding fire retardants.
3. CARDBOARD CORES – COVER WITH MUSLIN OR CHEESECLOTH AND FLEXGLUE.
4. STEEL
   a) First clean with denatured alcohol, Simple Green or equivalent.
   b) Prime with 1:2 wash coat of white shellac or manufactured metal primer.
5. PLYWOOD OR OSB
   a) Cover with 2 coats of 1:2 white shellac wash coat or
   b) One coat of full strength pigmented shellac (i.e.: BIN)

All stock platforming will require resurfacing and facing, the cost of which must be included in all estimates.
Current shop material price lists are available from the shop supervisor. Use these and current Fish Building Supply catalog as resource guides. Consult Dennis or Chuck for additional information.
During strikes remove all hardware and fasteners, including stock scenery and lumber to be re-used. Do not remove nails and staples from material that is to be discarded. Hinges, doorknobs and latches should be removed from doors, before storing.

I. Knot Knowledge
   1. BOWLINE, CLOVE HITCH, HALF HITCH, SHEETBEND, SQUARE, GASKET (FOR SECURING A COIL OF ROPE), PRUSSIC (FOR SECURING AN OUT-OF-WEIGHT PURCHASE LINE)

J. Stock lumber dimensions
   1. 1 x 2: ¾" x 1 ½"   2 x 2: 1 ½" x 1 ½"
   2. 1 x 3: ¾" x 2 ½" 2 x 3: 1 ½" x 2 ½"
   3. 1 x 4: ¾" x 3 ½"   2 x 4: 1 ½" x 3 ½"
   4. 1 x 6: ¾" x 5 ½" 2 x 6: 1 ½" x 5 ½"
   5. 1 x 8: ¾" x 7 ¼" 2 x 8: 1 ½" x 7 ¼"
   6. 1 x 10: ¾" x 9 ¼" 2 x 10: 1 ½" x 9 ¼"
   7. 1 x 12: ¾" x 11 ¼" 2 x 12: 1 ½" x 11 ¼"
      a) All widths from the lumberyard may vary up to ⅛" from these measurements.
      b) 1 x 2, 2 x 2, 1 x 3 and 2 x 3 should be ripped from wider stock in our studio rather than ordered from the yard, in order to get consistent measurements. Avoid using twisted, warped, or cupped lumber. It is nearly impossible to take these defects out of the material in any standard form of scenery construction.

IX. APPENDIX TO STANDARD STUDIO PROCEDURES

A. Cutting keystones and cornerblocks

1. RIP KEYSTONES 2 ⅜" WIDE FROM ¼" ACX PLY ON PANEL SAW (2 PEOPLE), THEN CUT TO 8" LONG ON RADIAL ARM SAW, STACKING STRIPS 4 HIGH. USE MARK ON SAW FENCE RATHER THAN STOP-BLOCK TO PREVENT BINDING.
2. FOR CORNERBLOCKS, RIP 7" WIDE X 8' LONG STRIPS FROM ¼" ACX PLY. SET RADIAL ARM SAW ON 45 DEGREE CUT. STACK PIECES 2 HIGH. CUT FIRST SIDE AS SHOWN AT RIGHT. FLIP PIECES OVER, ALIGN FIRST CUT WITH BLADE CUT-LINE ON TABLE, AND MAKE SECOND CUT. FLIP STACK AND REPEAT, CONTINUING UNTIL STRIP IS USED.

B. Building a wood flat

1. START WITH SNAP LINE ON FLOOR OR FRAMING TABLE. USE 6D DUPLEX NAILS TO NAIL FIRST BOARD TO FLOOR ALONG THIS LINE (USUALLY LONGEST EDGE OF FLAT). THIS ASSURES EDGE OF FLAT WILL BE STRAIGHT. PUT NAILS WITHIN THE ⅞" KEEP BACK ZONE.
2. SQUARE ADJACENT SIDES TO THE FIRST PIECE, USING FRAMING SQUARE FIRST AND THEN 3-4-5 (OR MULTIPLE) TRIANGLE. NAIL TO FLOOR AS ABOVE, AND CHECK FOR STRAIGHT EDGE WITH SNAP LINE. PULL BOWED EDGES TO LINE AND NAIL.
3. ADD 4TH EDGE, CHECK FOR STRAIGHT LINE WITH SNAP LINE.
4. CHECK OVERALL SQUARENESS OF FLAT BY MEASURING DIAGONALS. DIAGONALS MUST BE THE SAME FOR FLAT TO BE SQUARE (TOLERANCE IS ⅛" - 3/16"). ADJUST AS NECESSARY TO MAKE THEM EQUAL.
5. LOCATE AND NAIL TO FLOOR ALL TOGGLES, WINDOW/DOOR FRAMING AND BRACES.
6. VERIFY THAT DIMENSIONS ARE CORRECT BEFORE STAPLING FRAME TOGETHER. ENTIRE FLAT SHOULD BE NAILED TO FLOOR BEFORE ANY PIECES ARE STAPLED.
7. WHEN BUILDING SEVERAL FLATS, USE ANGLE IRON, SCREWED TO THE FLOOR, TO MAKE A LARGE FRAMING SQUARE.
8. NOTE: FOR STAPLING SPECIFICATIONS, SEE SECTION I.

C. Covering a wood flat

1. WORK IN A STANDING POSITION WHENEVER POSSIBLE
2. LAY FLAT (FACE UP) ON TABLE OR SAW HORSES, CONNECTED WITH LONG BOARDS (SEE SKETCH).
3. BE CAREFUL TO ALLOW ENOUGH SAG – FLATS 4' OR WIDER SHOULD HAVE MUSLIN SAGGING APPROXIMATELY ¾" BETWEEN TOGGLES. NARROWER FLATS SHOULD BE PROPORTIONALLY MORE TAUT.
4. CUT MUSLIN COVER 2-3" LARGER IN ALL DIRECTIONS.
5. AFTER POSITIONING MUSLIN, STRETCH USING STAPLES DRIVEN HALFWAY IN FOR EASY REMOVAL. STAPLES GO APPROXIMATELY 18" O.C. AND ARE ON INSIDE FACE OF STILES AND RAILS. SEE DRAWING.
6. STRETCH MUSLIN USING FOLLOWING PATTER (SEE SKETCH): STEPS 1-4 ARE SINGLE STAPLES, 5-8 INDICATE DIRECTION TO WORK TOWARD CORNERS TO AVOID WRINKLES IN CORNER. PULL FABRIC ON BIAS (DIAGONAL).
7. GLUE FLAPS DOWN USING SOLUTION OF UNDILUTED WHITE GLUE. IF DIFFICULT TO SPREAD, DILUTE TO NO MORE 10 PARTS GLUE TO 1 PART WATER. SOLUTION SHOULD FEEL TACKY AND NOT RUNNY. USE LIBERAL AMOUNTS OF GLUE, SPREAD QUICKLY.
8. SMOOTH OUT WRINKLES AND REMOVE STAPLES.
9. POUNCE GLUED EDGES WITH WHITING BAG (NOT REQUIRED FOR FLATS PAINTED WITH LATEX PAINT).
10. ALLOW THE GLUE TO DRY OVERNIGHT BEFORE TRIMMING.

D. Covering a hard surface with fabric

1. PROCEED AS WITH REGULAR WOOD FLAT, SECTION APPENDIX C.
2. GLUE FABRIC TO ENTIRE SURFACE. TECHNIQUE IS:
3. PREPARE GLUE MIXTURE 10:1, GLUE: WATER; GET OLD ROLLER, ROLLER PAN AND GLUE BRUSH.
4. LAY FABRIC ON SURFACE AND FOLD BACK 1ST 2'.
5. ROLL GLUE ON WOOD, BRUSHING EXTRA ON EDGES.
6. FOLD FABRIC BACK ONTO GLUE-APPLIED AREA, BEING CAREFUL TO SMOOTH OUT ALL WRINKLES.
7. FROM OTHER END OF UNIT, ROLL FABRIC UP ONTO GLUED AREA.
8. SPREAD GLUE AS ABOVE, FOR 1-2'.
9. ROLL MATERIAL ONTO THIS AREA, BEING CAREFUL TO SMOOTH OUT ALL WRINKLES. REPEAT IN 2' INCREMENTS UNTIL FLAT IS COVERED.

Scenic Studio Safety Agreement

To be granted the privilege of using the scenic studio facilities of the Department of Theatre, you are required to be familiar with, and to observe, the safety regulations governing their use. Those regulations are posted in the studio and provided with your course syllabi. Violations of any safe working practices may cause the loss of privilege or disciplinary actions.

I _____ (print name) hereby acknowledge that I have completed an orientation program for the purpose of acquainting me with the proper and safe operation of the tools and equipment of the scenic studio and agree to abide by the safety rules of the studio, department, and university.

(Signature) _____ (Date) _____

Please complete the form below to provide us with information that could be helpful in the case of an accident or medical emergency. Please print.

Full Name _____ Date of birth _____

Local Address _____ ZIP _____

Phone (H) _____ (M) _____ Blood Type (if known) _____

Name of person to contact in the event of an emergency

Name _____ Phone _____

Address _____ Relationship _____

Please answer the following questions:

1. Do you wear contact lenses?   Yes_____ NO_____
2. Do you have back problems?   Yes_____ NO_____
3. Do you take any prescribed medication?   Yes_____ NO_____
   a. Name of Physician_____ Phone_____
   b. Medical Clinic (or association) _____
4. Do you have a history of any of the following?
   a. Diabetes   Yes_____ NO_____
   b. Epilepsy   Yes_____ NO_____
   c. Asthma   Yes_____ NO_____
   d. Allergies   Yes_____ NO_____
      i. Please specify _____
   e. Any other medical information that might be valuable in an emergency:
   _____
   _____

Labor Estimation Guidelines

Note: All jobs are considered single persons projects.

NA = Not Applicable

Line Item	Category	Task	Hours Required		
			Experienced	Very-Experienced	Multi-Unit Factor
1	FLATAGE	Cut, assemble, cover –			
		: simple 4'x12' flat	3	2.5	0.8
2		: irregular 4'x12' flat	4	3	0.8
3		: curvilinear 4'x12' flat	4.5	3.5	0.8
4		: profile 4'x12' flat	6	4.5	NA
5		: cutout 4'x12' flat	4.5	3.5	NA
6		Hinge & Dutchman 2, 4'x12' flats	1.5	1	NA
7		Attach rigging hardware & cables for 4'x12' flat (rough trimmed, ready to fly)	2	1.5	0.9
8	SOFT GOODS	Sew up 20'x40' muslin drop (pipe pocket, side hem); add 2 hours for grommets	6	4-5	NA

(Continued)

Line Item	Category	Task	Hours Required		Multi-Unit Factor
			Experienced	Very-Experienced	
9		Cut drop & adhere netting (add to line 8)	15	10–15	NA
10		Sew 20'x40' canvas ground cloth (seam all edges)	12	9–10	NA
11	CEILINGS	Roll ceiling 18'x30'	12	10	NA
12		Book ceiling 18'x30'	18	15	NA
13	PLATFORMS	Build –			
		: rectangular 4x8 unit	2–3	2	.7
14		: Non-rectangular 4x8 unit	4	3	.7
15		: Curvilinear 4x8 unit	6	4–5	NA
16		: Parallel 4x8 unit	7–8	6	.6
17		: ramped 4x8 unit	5	4	.7
18		Leg 4x8 unit –			
		: under 4'-0" high	2	1.5	.8
19		: over 4'-0" high	1	2	.9
20		Cross Brace/ribbon legs (4x8)	1	.5	.8
21		Caster 4x8 wagon (6 casters)	2	1.5	.9
22	STAIRS	Build –			
		: 3' wide 3-step unit	4	3	.7
23		: 3' wide 11-step unit	8	5–6	.7
24		: Curvilinear stairs (double lines 22 & 23)			NA

Line Item	Category	Task	Hours Required		Multi-Unit Factor
			Experienced	Very-Experienced	
25	RAILINGS	Escape unit	4	3	NA
26		Finished unit, eg. Balustrades	10-15	10	NA
27	DOORS	Build -			
		: Simple door (2 sided)	3	2.5	.8
28		: Complex door	10-15	10	NA
29		: Door jamb/trim	2.5-6	2-6	NA
30		Hang - Door	2-3	2	NA
31	WINDOWS	Build -			
		:Window (non-functional)	2.5	2-4	.8
32		:Window (functional)	5-12	4-8	.8
33	MOLDINGS	Build -			
		: Simple cornice (10' piece)	2	1.5	.8
34		: Elaborate cornice (10' pc)	4	3	.8
35	MOLDS	Build -			
		: Vacuum-form mold	3-20	3-20	NA
36		:Vacuum-form an object	.5	.25	.8
37	PROPS	Build -			
		: Simple table	6	4.5	.8
38		: Simple armchair	12-20	10-15	NA
39	FINISHING	Base 4'x12' flat	.5-.75	.5	NA
40		Paint wallpaper pattern 4x12 flat, 1 color	2.5	2	NA

(Continued)

USITT Guideline for a Standard Technical Information Package

INTRODUCTION

In 1988 the USITT Technical Production Commission began what was originally called "The Tech Rider Project." The purpose of this project was to produce a standard form for theatres to utilize in the exchange of technical information about their facilities. The proposed form was to be as inclusive as possible, providing detailed information about a theatre, including: staging, rigging, lighting, sound, wardrobe, props, management, and contact information necessary for any production considering use of a facility. At the same time, the form was to be flexible enough to be adapted for venues both large and small.

While recognizing that many theatre facilities have already compiled this information, the desired standard format allows direct comparisons to be made between facilities without the need to search through lengthy, dissimilar documents. The outline, now known as the "Standard Technical Information Package," provides a concise, standardized form for use by both theatres and producers for the efficient exchange of technical information. The resulting "Package" does not replace the need for personal communication but addresses all of the major areas of information and provides a starting point for any questions which may arise.

FORMAT GUIDELINES

1. All measurements should be listed in both feet and meters (1 FT=0.3048M, 1M=3.28FT).
2. Each underlined heading within the outline should form a separate page (e.g. **CARPENTRY** on one page, **LIGHTING** on a separate page.)
3. All notes should be listed under the proper headings. If you wish to reiterate these notes, put them at the end of the form, and before the attachments.
4. Line sets, floor plans, circuit charts, maps, etc. may be put under the proper headings or at the end of the form as an attachment.
5. Any other information not included in this outline which is specific to your theatre should be put under its proper heading. As each theatre is different, there will be some differences in each technical form.
6. All equipment listed must be available and in working order or noted as being inoperable and/or needing repair.
7. Seek prior approval before listing contact information for any individuals or departments.
8. Keep information succinct and to the point. Clarity is essential.
9. Use an original from which to make copies so forms are always crisp and clear.

Sample

USITT STANDARD TECHNICAL INFORMATION PACKAGE OUTLINE

COVER PAGE

Name of Theatre: mailing and street address (including Zip+4), phone, fax, electronic mail

TABLE OF CONTENTS

Optional: (but encouraged)

GENERAL INFORMATION

Address: mailing and street address

Technical Services: staff names, phone numbers, fax numbers, electronic mail

Programming: names, phone numbers (of both Programmer and Front-of-House Manager), fax numbers

Box Office: names, phone numbers (optional)

Area Hotels: names, phone numbers, address, distance from theatre (list three or four)

Taxi Services: names, phone numbers

Restaurants: names, phone numbers, addresses, cuisine, distance from theatre, (list three or four)

Handicapped Access: quantity and location(s) of handicapped seating and facilities

Emergency numbers: (note if "911" is used to dial emergency services)
  Fire: phone number, address
  Police: phone number, address
  Ambulance: phone number, address
  Hospital Emergency Room: phone number, address
  Urgent Care Clinic: phone number, address
  Chiropractic Clinic: phone number, address
  Dental Clinic: phone number, address

Parking: where to park trucks, busses and cars, list any problems

Laundry: name, phone number, address

Travel Directions: from north, south, east, and west

Time Zone:

MANAGEMENT

Production Room: location, note availability of phone lines, computer lines, output devices, fax machine, copier, modem

Green Room: size, location, relationship to stage and dressing rooms

Stage Manager's Console: location, audio monitor, video monitor, production communication

Rehearsal Room(s): size, location of each

Crews: type of crews (union, student, volunteer, etc.); availability; if union, name and phone number of business agent

Handicapped Access: location, description

Policies: house open time, alcohol use, smoking areas, other…

LOAD-IN AREA

Dimensions: width and height of dock, number of trucks that can be accommodated, description and size of access to stage, note if special loaders are required

Map: include here, or as an attachment, if attached, note here, i.e. "See Attachment"

CARPENTRY

Seating: number of seats with orchestra pit and without orchestra pit; note if chart is provided, i.e. "See Attachments"

Stage Dimensions:

Proscenium: width and height, stage depth, apron depth

Wing space: stage right, stage left, list any obstructions

Grid height: from deck to top of grid surface

Orchestra pit: width, depth, elevator type and operation (this entry may be repeated under **PROPS**)

Stage height: relative to auditorium floor

Stage Floor: material, color, condition, available traps; note any fasteners that cannot be used in this floor

House Draperies (Goods):

House Curtain: color, type, location, manual or powered

Legs: quantity, color, size, flat or sewn-in fullness

Borders: quantity, color, size, flat or sewn-in fullness

Full Stage: color, size, flat or sewn-in fullness

Scrims: quantity, color, size

Cyclorama: color, size, fabric, seamed or seamless

Line Set Data:

Line Plot: provide as an attachment and note that fact here, i.e. "See attachments"; list all immovable pieces such as shell ceilings, and other dedicated storage pipes; leave space in margins for notes

Working height of battens: high trim, low trim

Battens: quantity, length, pipe diameter, on-center distance and number of lift lines

Type: single purchase, double purchase, winch, motor assist, hydraulic, rope; note number of each

Arbor capacity: maximum load (in pounds) per pipe

Available weight: amount and location

Winch capacity: maximum working load

Loading gallery: location, access

Pin rail: location, height

Support Areas:

Crossover: dimensions and location

Access: from front of house, dressing rooms, green room, etc.

Shop Area: location, accessibility, type, equipment

Storage: describe area(s), list dimensions, availability, accessibility

Notes: list anything unique about the stage, shop, rail, line sets, etc. that may affect load-ins and stage use

LIGHTING

Power: voltage, phase, amperage (e.g. 120/208V; 3 phase, 400A/leg); list all available power sources and locations; note anything unusual such as no separate ground, non-standard connectors, type of tie-in, need for a licensed electrician, etc.

Dimmers: quantity, type, capacity (kW per dimmer), quantity of spare and replacement dimmers

Control Board: manufacturer, model, software release, e.g. V6B, location

Houselights: control location; note if board operator cannot control

Circuits: number, capacity (amperes), type (moveable or fixed)

Circuit Chart: here, or as an attachment with note, i.e. "See attachment"

Front of House Transfer: required connection, quantity and capacity of dimmers/circuits involved

Front of House Positions: length of throw and angle for box booms, beams, balcony rail, any other house locations

Equipment Inventory:

Front of House Instruments: quantity, type, e.g. 6x12 ERS, manufacturer, wattage, color frame size, and connector type; note any irised instruments, instruments which cannot be moved

Stage Instruments: quantity, kind, brand, wattage, gel frame size, and type of connectors; list irised instruments, for strips and cyc lighting list number of circuits or lamps; note if rental equipment is necessary or available

Followspot(s): number, brand, lamp, color cut size, standard location

Hardware: top hats, barn doors, pattern holders, booms , ladders, etc., quantity and size of each item; note if boom circuits must run across stage floor or if boom circuits are not easily accessed

Cable: quantity, length, gauge, kind of connectors, quantity of two-fers, available adapters, i.e. type and quantity

Film, Video, And Projection Equipment: type, quantity, lens sizes, etc. (this entry may be repeated under **PROPS)**

Notes: list anything unique about lighting areas, power, equipment, etc.; list additional amenities such as video monitors, cue lights, telephones, and running lights

Lighting

Power: 120/208V, 3 phase, 400A/leg, Posi-lock connector stage left proscenium wall

Dimmers: 188 Colortran, 2.4k W dimmer, 6 spare and replacement dimmers available

Control Board: Colortran, Compact Elite, located in control booth at rear of house

Houselights: Control locations both stage right and in lighting control booth

Circuits: 188 - 2.4kw circuits, 4 on-stage electrics, 6 - 4 circuit drop boxes

Circuit Chart: See Attachment G

Front of House Transfer: None available

Front of House Positions: 1st beam, 38' throw (11.58m) at 45 degrees
2nd beam, 44' throw (13.4m) at 40 degrees
2 - Overheads, 18' throw (5.4m) at 60 degrees
Box booms, 30' throw (9.1m) at 30 degrees

Equipment Inventory:

Front of House Instruments:
25 Colortran 20 ERS, 1kw, 3 pin twist lock pin-in
16 Strand Century 6x16 ERS, 1kw, 3 pin twist lock pin-in
Color cut size is 7 1/2" throughout

Stage Instruments:
10 Colortran 40 ERS, 750w, 3 pin twist lock pin-in
10Colortran 30 ERS, 750w, 3 pin twist lock pin-in
18 Strand Century 6x12 ERS, 750w, 3 pin twist lock pin-in
30 Altman 6x12 ERS, 750w, 3 pin twist lock pin-in
8 - 8' four circuit strips, 300w, 3 pin twist lock pin-in
12 - 6" Fresnels, 750w, 3 pin twist lock pin-in
Color cut size is 7 1/2" throughout

Followspots: 2 Colortran Color Arc 2000, Xenon, 10" color cut, located at center booth rear of auditorium

Hardware: 24 Top hats, 12 - 6" barn doors, 30 pattern holders, 8 - 21' booms (6.4m), 4 - 8 instrument ladders

Cable: 1200 feet in 10's, 20's, 30's and 40's (365m), 12 gauge - SJO, 3 pin twist lock pin-in, 36 two-fers, no adapters available

Film, Video, And Projection Equipment: 4 Kodak Ektagraphic 3A projectors

Notes: Cue lights, telephones, and running lights available

SOUND

Power: voltage, phase, amperage (e.g. 120V 1 phase, 15, 20A circuits); list all available power sources and locations; note anything unusual such as no separate ground, non-standard connectors, type of tie-in, need for a licensed electrician, etc.

Wiring: quantity and location of all inputs and outputs; note any special requirements for cable runs

Control Locations: booth location; house mix position(s) including size, specific location, and removable seats; power and line signal; note if position is under a balcony; length of "snake" required to reach sound locations

Hearing Assist System: type, quantity of patron receivers

Monitor/Paging System: areas covered (e.g. dressing rooms, green rooms), program input and capabilities

Production Communications: manufacturer and model, number of channels, number of headsets, location of stations

Equipment Inventory:

Mixing Consoles: quantity, manufacturer, model, number of inputs/outputs for each console

Fixed Speakers: quantity, manufacturer, model, wattage of LF and HF power, description, location

Portable Speakers: quantity, manufacturer, model, wattage of LF and HF power, description, dimensions

Microphones: quantity, manufacturer, model

Playback: quantity, manufacturer, model, speed, and type, e.g. reel to reel, CD, cassette

Signal Processors: quantity, manufacturer, model, description of each item

Amplifiers: quantity, manufacturer, model, output power, location if fixed

Cable: quantity, length, connectors types, snakes, direct boxes; available adapters, i.e. type and quantity

Notes: list anything unique about sound areas, power equipment, etc.

PROPS

Orchestra Pit: width, length, adjustable or not; if an elevator, list standard heights and operation requirements (this may be repeated in **CARPENTRY**)

Music:

Chairs: quantity, manufacturer, model, color

Stands: quantity, manufacturer, model, color; note if a conductor's stand is available

Stand lights: quantity, power, availability of stringers and dimming

Conductor Podium: quantity, style, height, access

Orchestra Shell: quantity, manufacturer, model, size, color

Platforms: quantity, size, manufacturer, model

Dance Floor: quantity, size, color, manufacturer; note if there is a problem with tape

Lecterns: quantity, style, color

Notes: list anything unique about prop areas

WARDROBE

Dressing Rooms: quantity, type, capacity, and location in relationship to stage and green room; list standard equipment, e.g. showers, sinks, tables, mirrors, make-up lighting, clothes racks (type and size)

Wardrobe Area: location, description, accessibility to stage and dressing rooms

Irons: quantity

Ironing boards: quantity

Steamers: quantity

Washers/dryers: quantity, location, coin operated

Racks and hangers: quantity, type, size (height, width, depth)

Quick Change Booths: quantity, size (height, width, depth), mirror, possible locations

Notes: list anything unique about wardrobe areas, equipment etc.

STANDARD ATTACHMENTS

Map detailing theatre location: indicate "North" on map

Plan of the theatre: 1/4" scale or larger

Centerline section of the theatre: 1/4" scale or larger

Line plot of the theatre: complete list, include all storage lines

Photographs of stage and audience seating

Seating chart

Circuit chart

Policy handbooks

ACKNOWLEDGMENTS

This project was originally chaired by Alan Bailey. Most recently, Happy Robey has served as project chair and under her able leadership this document was completed. Many other USITT members have contributed to the development of these guidelines and we are grateful for their assistance. A draft version of this document was published in 1993 in an issue of *Sightlines* with a request for review and comment. The final version of the guidelines was adopted by the Board of Directors of USITT at their regular meeting in November 1995.

Submitted for adoption and publication by Mark Shanda and John Darling, Co-Commissioners, Technical Production Commission.

Production Crew Evaluation Form

INTRODUCTION

Crew work is an integral part to the success of any theatrical production and is intended to provide the student with hands-on experience that will give each participant the confidence in the proper application of textbook instruction in the work place and to contribute to the art of theatre.

The following categories of personal behavior and performance within the crew experience are to be carefully examined and evaluated by the appropriate supervisor for each crew role.

Score:_____ ***Effort and Results***—Speed, efficiency, organization, skill and commitment

Failing (0)—Sloppy, disruptive, undisciplined, ineffective, tries little, achieves little
Poor (1–2)—Work habits occasionally get in the way of progress; work needs to be redone
Average (3–5)—Moderate effort and energy to achieving acceptable results; neither fast nor slow
Good (6–8)—Usually organized, productive and often does solid work with notable speed and efficiency
Excellent (9–10)—Organized, committed, and imaginative student, fully engaged with any task assigned, seeks out extra tasks with consistently positive results

Score:_____ ***Initiative and Leadership***—Recognizes the importance of the task at hand, takes assertive role in devising effect and efficient solutions

Failing (0)—Negative attitudes, seemed to work against group goals
Poor (1–2)—Little or no drive or organizational ability, unreliable and discouraging output
Average (3–5)—Moderate effort in applying pressure to get assigned tasks done, has partial understanding of their role and impact on the entire production
Good (6–8)—Marked ability to perceive goals, gets good work from others and sets an example of merit, strong ability
Excellent (9–10)—Superior understanding of everyone's role, motivating superior personal and group commitment and drive

Score:_____ ***Learning***—Seeks new skills, collaboration, and methods for problem solving

Failing (0)—Learns nothing and obstructs others from learning
Poor (1–2)—Occasionally tries, but learns little

Average (3–5)—Absorbs some new material, particularly if it comes easily, but demonstrates low interest in more complex topics

Good (6–8)—Exhibits an alert interest resulting in good learning and imaginative application

Excellent (9–10)—Seeks out and becomes proficient at most new material; shows superior growth

Score:_____ *Dedication and Responsibility*—Cares enough to ensure that group effort has positive result on production

Failing (0)—Couldn't care less, needs constant supervision

Poor (1–2)—Seldom shows interest, cannot be left unsupervised for long periods of time

Average (3–5)—Moderate interest in end results, can sometimes work without supervision

Good (6–8)—Highly responsible, conscientious, strives to improve

Excellent (9–10)—Brings every effort towards achieving maximum project impact with little supervision

Score:_____ *Attendance*—If you aren't present, you can't accomplish the goals of the practicum.

Unsatisfactory (–2 pts)—for each excused absence, double (–4 pts) for unexcused

Satisfactory (10 pts.)—Attends all assigned hours, makes up any absences

Bonus (1–10 pts)—Credit given for additional work done beyond minimum

Final Score = Total ____/5 A = 9–10, B = 6–8, C= 3–5, D = 1–2, F = 0

Student Name: _____ Supervisor: _____ Final Grade:_____

Index

Note: Page numbers with *f* indicate figures.